THE EMERGENCE OF PERSONHOOD

The Emergence of Personhood

A Quantum Leap?

Edited by

Malcolm Jeeves

WILLIAM B. EERDMANS PUBLISHING COMPANY

GRAND RAPIDS, MICHIGAN / CAMBRIDGE, U.K.

Published 2015 by
Wm. B. Eerdmans Publishing Co.
2140 Oak Industrial Drive N.E., Grand Rapids, Michigan 49505 /
P.O. Box 163, Cambridge CB3 9PU U.K.

Printed in the United States of America

20 19 18 17 16 15   7 6 5 4 3 2 1

Library of Congress Cataloging-in-Publication Data

The emergence of personhood: a quantum leap? / edited by Malcolm Jeeves.
      pages   cm
   Includes bibliographical references.
   ISBN 978-0-8028-7192-3 (pbk.: alk. paper)
   1. Philosophical anthropology.   2. Human beings.
   3. Theological anthropology — Christianity.
   I. Jeeves, Malcolm A., 1926- editor.

   BD450.E44   2015
   126 — dc23

                              2015029839

www.eerdmans.com

Contents

CONTENTS

vi

Foreword

In more than fifty years as a priest, briefly in English parishes and for decades engaged in the long, hard, and eventually successful effort to overturn the apartheid policies of a ruling minority in my own country of South Africa, I have pondered the question of who we are — the wonder of human uniqueness, the worth of every one of us as children of God, and our ability to determine, despite our own weaknesses and the oppression of others, who we will be. A book that sheds light on these issues of overriding importance is a volume to treasure. All the gold ever mined in the Transvaal, the land of my birth, cannot compare to the value of the knowledge we mine — discover and create — as we pursue the great story of our emergence as distinctly human persons.

I met Malcolm Jeeves, the editor of this book, in London in the spring of 2013, when I was honored by receiving the Templeton Prize. At King's College London, where I had studied theology in the early 1960s, the eminent neuropsychologist and several other contributors to the volume held a public conversation about what may lie at the very heart of our humanity. I said to them then that you cannot be human in isolation. The African belief of *ubuntu* affirms that only through others do people achieve humanity. Paul teaches over and over that "we are members of one another" (Rom. 12:5; 1 Cor. 12:27; Eph. 4:25). And so we are.

I learned much, however, in listening to the authors of the essays collected in this book. It seems that research on the behavior of humans and of nonhuman primates, research in which they and their colleagues have been engaged for a score of years, has provided tantalizing clues to the why and how questions about the emergence of our capacities to reason, reflect, and imagine the future. Even after the long flight from Cape Town to London, my ears pricked up when I heard them ask how our moral sense might have come about. In developing codes of behavior, what was the role of language? The neuroscientists speculated about the relationship of core human properties to complex patterns of interactivity within the brain, and I was intrigued by the notion that my subjective sense of self might be a product of evolution. It seemed to me that the East African–born paleoarchaeologist Ian Tattersall must be right that it is the "unique cognitive condition" of men and women that sets human beings apart qualitatively from other creatures. The dispersal out of Africa of our species is a fascinating tale, and I found the ideas expressed about when ritual practices and, eventually, institutionalized religion developed arresting, even — or perhaps especially — to a priest, as were accounts of what cognitive science could add to the picture. It was good to hear another fellow of King's College London, theologian Anthony Thiselton, caution against singling out distinct capacities as characteristic of *imago Dei,* then go on to focus on relationality, which struck a chord with me. As did theologian Alan Torrance's argument that the very concept of a person requires a theistic vision. Indeed, as he says, God has chosen human beings for a relationship with him that has all kinds of implications for our relationships with others.

Over the course of my lifetime, the human capacity for evil, and our capacity for love, has been illustrated in South Africa as boldly as anywhere in the world. Here is an example of the remarkable things I was privileged to be part of, when people of all races left one speechless with their magnanimity, their capacity to forgive, their generosity of spirit. One of our black liberation groups, the Pan African Congress (PAC), argued that the armed struggle against apartheid was still continuing in 1992 while negotiations were going on for the ending of apartheid. The PAC launched a hand-grenade attack on a wine-tasting event at the Kingwilliamstown all-white golf club in the Eastern Cape. The casualties were high. Several people were killed and others badly injured, including Mrs. Beth Savage, who had to have open-heart surgery and spent several months in intensive care. After being discharged, she was still quite disabled; her children helped to bathe her and feed her. She described all of this in her testimony at our Truth and Reconciliation Commission public hearing. She left most of us quite speechless as she went on to describe what had happened to her as an experience that had enriched her life. Quite unbelievable! She then bowled us over completely when she said she wanted to meet the perpetrator, the person who had thrown the hand grenade. She hoped he would forgive *her!* People can be amazing, and Beth Savage was one such.

Who are we? The question must be answered by each generation. But the research and reflections of scientists and scholars represented in this collection of essays offer contemporary readers some answers, as well as pointing to lingering questions of immense importance to us all.

DESMOND TUTU
Archbishop Emeritus of
Cape Town, South Africa

Introduction: The Agenda

Malcolm Jeeves

> *The distinction between men and animals is in one sense only a difference in degree. But the extent of the degree makes all the difference.*
> A. N. WHITEHEAD (1938, 37-38)

> *[I]n the current historical moment, broad swathes of the American and European public — as well as the American and European academies — are engaging in heated debate concerning what it means to be human. Many ask the question: What lies at the core of humanity?*
> AGUSTIN FUENTES (2013, 106)

With so many increasingly well-documented similarities — genetic, cognitive, neural, behavioral, social, and cultural — between us and our evolutionary forebears, a self-evident and significant gulf still remains between us and them. Why is that, and how did it come about?

To date, no one has reported on a remote group of chimpanzees or other nonhuman primates boasting schools, hospitals, libraries, symphony orchestras, medical research establishments, and so on. And yet our brains and theirs are in many ways so similar. How did this clear discontinuity between us and our nonhuman primate cousins come about? Was it a gradual process or were there — at some points along the way — discontinuities, that is, quantum leaps? If so, how did these come about and when? And what is their significance?

To begin to answer some of these questions, we need the help of scholars from a range of disciplines, which allows us to probe into the origins of our mysterious human nature — each bringing distinctive but highly relevant specialist skills, each contributing well-informed current insights into answering continuing puzzles about our human nature. How did we come to be the way we are?

In inviting the participants in this book, I knew that their underlying worldviews would vary widely. Some are humanists, some atheists, some theists — yet all are acknowledged as leading scholars in their specialized fields. All are open-minded, and certainly none would be empty-minded. They would bring a genuine *multiplicity of voices* to speak to common themes. Referring to "multiple voices" brings to mind the writings of Mikhail Bakhtin, the theorist of so-called polyphonic discourses. Bakhtin was aware of the limitations of "monologic discourse," arguing that reality was often too complex to be stated simply as a packaged truth. For Bakhtin, *dialogic,* or *polyphonic,* discourse is owned by a collective, intersubjective, mutually responsible community (1984, 6-7; cf. 67-69). We like to think that those who have contributed to this book are such a community.

While Bakhtin nowhere explicitly defines *polyphonic discourse,* he argues for its ability to address issues too complex for *monologic discourse.* He notes, for example, that Einstein's paradigm outstripped Newton's, not because Newton was wrong, but because Einstein could address issues that seemed to be stark contradictions in Newton's paradigm. While some kind of unity is necessary to make sense of life, he preferred the term "concordance" to "unity," the latter implying a finished system. However, it is important to note that he also emphasized that the polyphonic approach has nothing in common with relativism.

Perhaps we may extend Bakhtin's insights by saying that, while the contributors to this book were certainly not "all singing from the same hymn sheet" (indeed, singing from any hymn sheet at all might have been a new experience for some!), they were all demonstrating how — to borrow the metaphor of an orchestra — the sounds of the instruments on which they are acknowledged to be highly skilled performers blended together to produce a recognizable set of variations on a recurring theme or set of themes. My hope has been that, by sharing our insights into how we came to be the unique animals that we are, we could begin to put together a coherent answer to our primary question: How and when did human personhood emerge?

I believe that there is a harmony, if not a unison, in what follows. Of course, we must be careful here, because the problem with any picture or metaphor is that it can be overused or misused outside of its intended context. Properly used, however, metaphors may make valid cognitive truth claims. What, then, were the recurring themes produced by this small orchestra? And what were some of the distinctive notes that readers should be alert to as they read the contributions to this volume? Are there also pointers to some of the unanswered questions for our successors to work on?

In his recent essay on this subject, Agustin Fuentes argues for the need for "more effective transdisciplinary conversations." In developing his argument, he selects a set of sub-areas of disciplines that represent, he believes, the central locus for investigation. (Surprisingly, his list omits neuroscience.) He argues that "core factors in a transdisciplinary approach include team-based collaborations, rigor, openness and tolerance." All of these, I believe, were present in the meetings of those who participated in this book. Fuentes quotes with approval the statement by the historian A. J. McMichael that "transdisciplinarity is more than the mixing and interbreeding of disciplines. Transdisciplinary transports us: we then ask different questions, see further, and we perceive the complex world and its problems with new insights" (Fuentes 2013, 106, 109). Fuentes believes that this kind of approach is necessary if we are to better understand human nature. I agree, and what follows is my attempt to begin to do this.

The title of this volume, *The Emergence of Personhood: A Quantum Leap?* was aimed at ensuring that the major focus of all our thinking would be on the understanding of distinctively human personhood. This, I hoped, would lead to a deeper understanding of the nature of human uniqueness and of how it came about. Had I been interested in providing an answer focused elsewhere to the question of what a person is, I would have looked to different contributors. For example, sociologist Christian Smith has already gone down that road in writing his comprehensive, penetrating, and insightful discussion under the title *What Is a Person?* It is worth pausing to note, however, the answer that Smith gives to his own question:

> By *person* I mean a conscious, reflexive, embodied, self-transcending center of subjective experience, durable identity, moral commitment, and social communication who — as the efficient cause of his or her own responsible actions and interactions — exercises complex capacities for agency and intersubjectivity in order to develop and sustain his or her own incommunicable self in loving relationships with other personal selves and with the nonpersonal world. (2010, 61)

Smith is alert to an obvious reaction to such a definition when he comments that "this is an unwieldy concept," and that it refers to a normal person who develops normally (2010, 61). He recognizes the need to qualify his definition in the real world. For example, what about people who suffer from brain development disorders and who cannot manifest all the qualities listed by Smith: Are they not persons? What about those who in later life see their normal functioning severely affected by diseases, such as Alzheimer's or dementia: Are they progressively ceasing to be persons? On this, as on so many issues, it remains the case that, as theologian Austin Farrer put it many years ago, "Reality is a nuisance to those who want to make it up as they go along" (1964, 12). It is a view later echoed by scientists Paul Gross and Norman Levitt, who note that "reality is the overseer at one's shoulder, ready to rap one's knuckles or to spring the trap into which one has been led by overconfidence, or by too-complacent reliance on surmise. Science succeeds precisely because it has accepted a bargain in which even the boldest imagination stands hostage to reality. Reality is the unrelenting angel with whom scientists have to wrestle" (Gross and Levitt 1994, 234).

While this book focuses primarily on the evidence from sciences relevant to answering deep questions about human uniqueness, it also recognizes that there are other sources of knowledge relevant to answering questions about what makes us uniquely human. Hence it also asks what theologians have to say and how their stories relate to the scientists' stories.

As the Whitehead quote at the head of this chapter indicates, questions about what makes us different are not new. We might speculate about what Whitehead would have written today, three-quarters of a century after his 1938 book. Since then, so much has happened in so many areas of science that one cannot but speculate that his views concerning the degree of difference between humans and animals might well have changed significantly. This year we celebrate the sixtieth anniversary of one of the great discoveries of the twentieth century, the cracking of the genetic code by James Watson and Francis Crick, which has had knock-on effects that would surely have caused Whitehead to pause and rethink his position.

Today a great deal is made of the genetic closeness we bear to our nearest nonhuman relatives, and in this sense alone the extent of the difference between animals and humans has become seemingly very small. Or again, the dramatic advances in neuroscience and neuropsychology have demonstrated quite remarkable similarities between the architecture of our own brains and those of chimpanzees and other apes. Not just the general outline of our cerebral architecture, but the details: so that, for example, the areas that we now know are primarily concerned in the processing of face perception in the superior temporal sulcus are the same areas in apes and in humans. But even here, with the striking demonstrated similarities between ourselves and apes from many studies of our cerebral architecture, there remain reminders that there is a striking difference in, for example, our capacity for language. What would Whitehead have thought of the amazing advances in evolutionary psychology where capabilities previously thought to be uniquely human have now been researched in detail in nonhuman primates with the discovery of remarkable overlaps between our abilities and those of apes? Or in the fields of anthropology and archaeology, where the very possibility of the postulated interbreeding between our forebears and the Neanderthals has raised fresh questions about our uniqueness?

One suspects that Whitehead, along with us, would have been very puzzled about how, with so many similarities along so many dimensions between ourselves and our nearest animal relatives, there yet remains what seems like a great gulf fixed. Why, with such similar cognitive and social abilities, do humans remain so different?

In what follows, acknowledged leaders in relevant areas of science offer their views of human uniqueness and personhood. As they do, I encourage the reader to note how, in similar and in different ways, they invoke some form of *emergence* in telling the stories from their particular perspective. But, it may be asked, are they all using *emergence* in the same sense? That is an important question because, as we learned more than half a century ago in discussions about how properly to relate knowledge gained from the scientific enterprise to knowledge from other domains of learning, such as the theological, the concept of complementarity, initially very helpful, was soon — as the late Professor Donald MacKay put it — in danger of being "overworked by the Athenians on the one hand and abused by the Laodiceans on the other" (1953, 153).

The principle of complementarity in physics quickly became widely used as an analogy when seeking to relate theological and scientific statements about the same set of events. At that time, MacKay wrote about the need for "a good deal of consecrated hard work on the part of Christians to develop a more coherent and more Biblical picture of the relationship between knowledge from two perspectives." This surely applies today to the widespread use — and at times, abuse — of the concept of emergence. Readers should be alert to this. Later in the book, Tim O'Connor attempts to apply a bit of semantic hygiene to the various ways in which the concept of emergence has been used by the contributors to the earlier chapters.

The title of this collection of essays is, in one sense, what psychologists call a "projection test": present an ambiguous picture or statement, and see what different people read into it. In another sense, it is an attempt to discover the variety of possible answers to an important and yet unanswered question. The projection test part is in the attempt to discover how scientists and theologians use the word "personhood." Different people understand different things by what it means to be a person (evident in Smith's *What Is a Person?*). Is there any overlap, or are we looking at separate language domains? One key unanswered question is whether it is necessary, as some people have contended for a long time, to claim that there is, between our nearest biological relatives and ourselves, a "quantum leap," and, if there is, how we may discover what this quantum leap was and when it occurred. My hope is that, in probing these issues, we shall come a little nearer to discovering what it is that makes us uniquely human.

Faced by the diversity of disciplines represented in the ensuing pages, readers might find it all too easy to, as it were, lose the plot. Here are some pointers to help the reader keep the main issues in mind and see how, from their divergent standpoints, the contributors fill out the overall picture.

The reader will soon discover that all the authors accept the explanatory powers of what is usually referred to as the neo-Darwinian version of the theory of evolution. Yet all are equally aware that, like any scientific theory, it remains open to fine-tuning in the light of new evidence. Opening Section One, evolutionary psychologist Richard Byrne focuses on the potential importance of the evolution of the capacity for language, something that Francisco Ayala later identifies as one of the key factors required for the development of moral codes. Byrne asks this question: "Do any substantive differences remain that distinguish us from animals, in a way that can properly justify separate treatment in terms of personhood and morality?" For him, the Holy Grail has always been to understand the evolutionary basis of language.

Ian Tattersall, while endorsing the general evolutionary story of emergence, nonetheless makes a strong claim that "the acquisition of our unique cognitive style did not involve a strong process of *long-term burnishing* that a traditionally *gradualist* view of evolution would suggest." And then readers are immediately alerted to the creative tension present in these essays as Colin Renfrew makes clear the essence of his views in the title of his chapter, "Personhood: Toward a Gradualist Approach." He asks key questions, such as, "Where along the narrative line does one situate the emergence — or no doubt in reality the multiple emergences — of personhood? Where and how did those qualities that we recognize as those of sentient persons emerge, of people imbued with the qualities that we recognize as inherently human?" Renfrew believes that, in looking ahead, the notion of a "quantum leap" is not necessary.

Roy Baumeister, a social psychologist, picks up a theme introduced by Francisco Ayala, namely, the concept of culture. A key quote from Baumeister's chapter alerts readers to his argument: "Human selfhood and identity, and indeed human personhood per se, can be understood as adaptations (or side effects of adaptations) that make culture possible." Baumeister's contribution is further exemplified in statements such as "the human person is a unique being," "culture is a biological strategy," "human personhood emerges from our collective and individually competing efforts to participate in culture." For him, "the emergence of self and identity is seen as a suggested guide to understand the emergence of personhood per se."

Starting out Section Two, Francisco Ayala, one of today's leading evolutionary biologists, alerts the reader to be aware of an important distinction between biological evolution and cultural evolution. His central thesis is that the capacity for ethics is an outcome of biological evolution, and that moral norms in populations are products of cultural evolution. Neuropsychologists Warren Brown and Lynn Paul argue that the properties of personhood are rooted in physical processes and seem to be emergent in our evolutionary trajectory. They underscore "embodiedness" as a key feature of who and what we are. This theme of embodiedness is then taken up by neurologist Adam Zeman. The reader should note that, just as Richard Byrne has referred to the "*mystery* of aspects of our humanness," so Zeman refers to "*mysterious* elements of our being, namely uniqueness and inwardness." There is a disarming intellectual honesty here that is devoid of the arrogance sometimes present in scientific claims: that is, when we face puzzles, we acknowledge them, accept the limits of our current knowledge, and emphasize the need for more sustained further research. Brown/Paul and Zeman underscore the fact that, as Zeman puts it, "all the minds we know are vested in matter; all the matter we encounter is represented in our minds." Readers should note that just as Zeman talks about aspects of our *mysterious* being, he also talks about the power of our *uniqueness*.

It is at this point that we need the critical thinking of philosopher Tim O'Connor to scrutinize the varied uses of *emergence* in the scientists' contributions to this volume. What do they have in common? How do they differ? O'Connor's analysis is later extended by Alan Torrance in his account of the concept of emergence as it is used by some theologians.

The first chapter in Section Three is by Justin Barrett, a specialist in the field of the cognitive science of religion, and his student Matthew Jarvinen. They see the cognitive science of religion as "the scientific study of religious thoughts and actions that draws on the cognitive sciences and evolutionary psychology." For Barrett and Jarvinen, the cognitive equipment that gives rise to religious expression is presumed to have evolved under selection pressures unrelated to religion or religious entities. Their chapter represents an important link between what has gone before and what follows, as they refer early in this chapter to the *imago Dei*, a key concept for theologians. Barrett and Jarvinen say that they begin with two assumptions: (1) humans are *imago Dei* — we did not earn it and we cannot lose it; (2) only humans among animals are *imago Dei*.

The idea of the *imago Dei* is the focus of the chapter by theologian and hermeneutics scholar Anthony Thiselton. He applies the main brushstrokes of the picture of humankind from a theological approach. After a detailed exposition of what is meant by claims that "humans are made in the image and likeness of God," an exposition that covers contributions over the past two millennia and before, as well as more recent trends, Thiselton looks at three key aspects of what it means to be made in the image of God: relationality, representation, and vocation (or attainment). He does this in the light of some of the contributions from the scientists in earlier chapters, repeatedly and very helpfully cross-referencing the contributions of the scientists, thus foreshadowing the final overview chapter.

Systematic theologian Alan Torrance focuses squarely on questions about the essential nature of a person. He argues that, just as the empirical sciences have demonstrated their impressive explanatory powers, so, he believes, there is a similar explanatory power in Christian theism. Both are crucial; both are limited in scope. That is their nature. He then offers a way in which these two accounts should be interpreted from the perspective of Christian thought. The reader will note that once again the concept of emergence has been invoked by some leading theologians, for example, as Torrance points out, the contemporary Orthodox thinker John Zizioulas.

Torrance argues that starting from an approach of Christian theism enables us to come to a more open-minded understanding of personhood. He also argues that his approach points us away from any kind of desperate search for a quantum leap in the scientific emergence of personhood.

In the afterword, I stand back and try to identify key features of the picture that has emerged, or, to return to our metaphor, try to detect what the principal and pervasive themes are produced by our small orchestra of accomplished performers. Where is there harmony? Where is there discord? What are the next questions to be tackled in order to resolve any seemingly continuing discordant notes?

REFERENCES

Bakhtin, Mikhail. 1984. *Problems of Dostoevsky's poetics.* Ed. and trans. Caryl Emerson. Minneapolis and London: University of Minnesota Press.

Farrer, Austin. 1964. *Saving belief.* London: Hodder and Stoughton.

Fuentes, Agustin. 2013. Evolutionary perspectives and transdisciplinary intersections: A roadmap to generative areas of overlap in discussing human nature. *Theology and Science* 11, no. 2.

Gross, Paul R., and Norman Levitt. 1994. *Higher superstition.* Baltimore: Johns Hopkins University Press.

MacKay, Donald M. 1953. *The Christian graduate.* London: InterVarsity Press.

Smith, Christian. 2010. *What is a person? Rethinking humanity, social life and the moral good from the person up.* Chicago: University Chicago Press.

Whitehead, A. N. 1938. *Modes of thought.* New York: Macmillan.

Section One

The Dividing Line: What Sets Humans Apart from Our Closest Relatives?

Richard W. Byrne

It shouldn't be too difficult to answer the question posed in the title, should it? After all, humans make sense of the world by categorizing. In many cases, our perceptual systems pick out natural categories, "carving nature at the joints": everyday categories of birds, clouds, and seashells need little re-finement by scientists simply because they are based on real constellations of co-varying features. But we impose other categories on a world in a way that suits our purposes but does not correspond exactly to objective reality: "living things" (are fingernail trimmings living?), "foreigners" (and whose ancestry does not include the results of past immigration?), and — the case in point — "human." Of course, our species, *Homo sapiens,* is at least as valid as most others: we do not and probably cannot interbreed with any other species; members of the human species can readily be identified by many clear and objective features. But even aside from this zoological sense of human — as just another unique species — people categorize humans as different from the category "animal," or more precisely from "other animals." Moral codes of most societies, and the laws to back them, routinely make this distinction as fundamental and self-evident. But is it so obvious?

Psychology has investigated human categorization at many levels, and

I am indebted to the John Templeton Foundation and Malcolm Jeeves for the chance to have attended the stimulating meeting from which this book derives and to Mary Ann Meyers and Paul Wason for the excellent organization of the meeting. Many interactions at the meeting went to sharpen my ideas for the chapter, but I particularly wish to thank Roy Baumeister and Ian Tattersall for helpful comments on an early draft.

one of the strongest generalizations is that we always exaggerate the differences between members of contrasting categories, even if — objectively — we are well aware that the dividing line is narrow or arbitrary. Two patches of gray of different densities appear to have a sharper dividing line than physics measures (the Mach band phenomenon, a result of lateral effects in the retina); when synthetic speech is used to make a complete spectrum of intermediates between two phonemes, we are unable to perceive those intermediates as such, categorizing every instance as "definitely" one or the other (the "categorical perception" of speech sounds); and the in-group/out-group phenomenon is infamously involved in prejudice and genocide, while both groups appear as remarkably similar people to impartial outsiders. When it comes to the human/animal distinction, none of us are impartial outsiders, so we need to use some trick to attain psychological distance to help clarify our views. I propose a thought-experiment as a way of seeing with new eyes some of the discoveries that we are perhaps so used to pigeonholing in familiar ways that we may not easily notice their implications.

Seeing Our Closest Relatives through New Eyes

The thought-experiment is a simple one. Imagine that the chimpanzee *(Pan troglodytes)* and the bonobo *(Pan paniscus)* were *not* discovered in the nineteenth and twentieth centuries, respectively, as they in fact were. On the other hand, imagine that all our knowledge of the other nonhuman great apes remains just as it is now. In this imagined world, our closest animal relatives are the two species of gorilla (the eastern *Gorilla beringei* and the western *Gorilla gorilla*). Molecular comparisons show that their DNA sequences (and the structures of all the other large molecules downstream of DNA transcription) are closer to the human sequence than to any other species, and calibration with more distantly related species for which there is some fossil evidence points to a divergence date: the time when the "last common ancestor" we share with a nonhuman walked the earth — about eight million years ago (mya). Gorillas have many humanlike qualities that accord with this evolutionary closeness. They live in extended family groups, in which one male or several related males (often brothers, or father and son) are closely affiliated with several females, and remain so over periods of years. A gorilla juvenile is dependent on the mother for food until it is three or four years old, and even then the young gorilla remains dependent on the mother for protection and (it is believed by those who study them) for the chance to absorb a great deal of knowledge from her for several more years. At puberty, a young female may choose to leave the group she has been associated with to be with a male of her choice, who will protect her from the risk of predators — and do his best to keep her away from other males! Young males have a tougher life if they decide to leave the protected world of their patrilocal society: they will have to make their way in the world on their own, until such time as they can persuade one or more females to join them and form their own family group. Many choose to stay in their natal family group, helping their male relatives defend the group and their females, deferring to their male elders — but maybe managing to have sex with some of the younger females who succumb to their youthful charms.

Gorilla social life within the group is regulated mostly by gestural communication, because their vocal system is a simple one compared to human speech. They have the ability to use their natural manual gestures in a goal-directed, intentional way to convey a wide range of meanings. Their diet appears simple at first sight, since it is wholly vegetarian and based on commonly occurring herbs and fruits. However, studies of the eastern species have revealed that they are able to learn and apply "clever" behavioral routines to the preparation of their plant food: to avoid painful stings, damaging spines, or simply hard and inedible casings. These skilled routines are specific to local areas — indeed, to specific plants, which have very limited ranges — and young gorillas acquire them by imitation of the behavioral "gist" of what they see their mothers do. Multistage processes are built up out of the gorilla's rich, innate repertoire of manual actions; the learned behavior of an infant is accommodated to the quite different strengths and sizes of their hands, and to any manual disabilities they have, as young gorillas are often injured by snares set by humans. Perhaps most impressively of all, gorillas in captivity have shown the capacity to comprehend that their mirror image is of themselves, something that most animals cannot grasp. It is thought that the difficulty that precludes mirror self-recognition for most species of animal is a lack of any mental representation of the individual itself (Byrne and Bates 2010; Gallup 1982); so this result shows that gorillas have some sense of self, though it is likely to be less elaborated and explicit than our own.

Moving further from the human lineage, the next closest relatives (i.e., in technical terms, from the human/gorilla clade) are the two closely related species of orangutan, living in Borneo and Sumatra respectively. Unlike gorillas, these species spend most of their lives solitarily, though it is puzzling that in captivity they seem just as social as gorillas. Some researchers have hypothesized that the wild population has only adopted solitary ranging because of the low-quality forests in which they are forced to range (as a result of competition with humans); others suggest that orangutans are cognitively social even though they do not meet their fellow "group" members very often. In captivity, orangutan gestural communication has been found to be just as intentional and goal-directed as that of gorillas. Less is known of their manual skills under natural conditions, though orangutans have a particular reputation for skilled physical problem-solving in captivity — indeed, for using their manual skills to escape! Much more an arboreal species than are the gorillas, orangutans show considerable imagination in planning routes through the 3-D maze of lianas and branches they inhabit: routes that take into account future deformations that their weight will cause when they move. This planning has been suggested to require the ability to view the self as an engineering problem, "de-centering" from the usual egocentric perspective (Povinelli and Cant 1995). In turn, this nonegocentric perspective is hypothesized to have led to the ability to understand the self as seen in a mirror, which orangutans — like gorillas — have been shown to possess. Thus, though molecular comparisons show that the common ancestor of the human/gorilla clade and the orangutans lived much longer ago, about 14 mya, their cognitive abilities are perhaps not very different: in both cases, the "cognitive gap" between them and us is quite a wide one.

Distinguishing the human from the animal — and thus justifying a quite different set of moral attitudes and legal requirements even for the most closely related nonhuman animals than for ourselves — does not in this imagined world present too much trouble. The definition of humanity encapsulated in "man the tool-maker," a phrase attributed to Benjamin Franklin, works pretty well. Then there is the perennial favorite of anthropologists, "man the hunter." Of course, many obligate carnivores also hunt, but the point is that, in the case of humans, the activity is not a matter of species-typical behaviors under genetic guidance, but a result of human behavioral flexibility and collaboration. Psychologists would point out that the underlying mental characteristic of these and other human specialties is that humans plan ahead. Animals can react appropriately to a huge range of perceptible circumstances, either when innately specified as "releasers" of behavior, or to the learned "stimuli" that behaviorist psychologists study in the laboratory. But only humans think ahead, working through in their minds what they are aiming to do in the future — to discover potential pitfalls to avoid or needs to preempt — so that they are well prepared in anticipation. Sociologists, more cynically, might point out that these self-congratulatory human traits are all very well, but *Homo sapiens* is also the only species that makes war — perhaps as a result of those same antici-patory planning abilities. One way or another, we are not much like our closest (known) relatives.

But now imagine that, in 2015, the chimpanzee is discovered in some "lost world" of central Africa, where individuals are still unafraid of man and thus can readily be studied. A raft of new projects is begun by excited scientists who are keen to chart its behavior. As the results begin to come in, it appears that this new animal, though apelike in appearance, is in some ways disconcertingly human in behavior. Not only do chimpanzees use ges-tures for intentional communication, as has been also shown in gorillas and orangutans, but they use tools — as humans do. Different communities of chimpanzees use different repertoires of tools: more than twenty-five differ-ent tool types have been found in some populations, whereas in others, few or none are recorded. The physical properties of these tools are elegantly matched to the different purposes to which they are put. Most chimpanzee tool use is seen in feeding, but other functions for tools — as weapons, for body cleaning, for comfort, and so on — are also noted. Nothing like this has been found before, in any other species except humans. Moreover, chimpan-zees do not just use "found objects" as tools, as has been seen occasionally in many species of animal. They *make* many tools, modifying stems and twigs by removing side-branches, sharpening tips, and so forth. And it is clear, from the way their modifications stop at a specific point, that they have an approximate *design* in mind in each case, a schematic anticipation of the tool — a plan in mind. Most extraordinary of all, at one site chimpanzees regularly make and use more than one tool in series for a single task; in all, eleven different types of multiple-tool use have been recorded in chim-panzees of the Goualougo Triangle, Republic of Congo (Sanz and Morgan 2007; Sanz and Morgan 2009). In each case they need two different kinds of tools, applied one after the other to achieve successive steps toward the goal. I will describe just one such process. A much-favored species of termite makes its nests 50 centimeters below the forest floor, and its entry tunnels are too small to trace back by excavation. Therefore, the first tool needed is a probe: to locate a nest and make an access route to it. For this, Goualougo chimpanzees use a sturdy, straight, and rigid rod, about 1 meter long. Side branches and leaves may need to be stripped off a suitable branch, which must be shaped to a sharp tip with the chimpanzees' incisors. This probe is inserted deep into the ground, sometimes needing a grip with feet as well as hands to force it in, then extracted and sniffed. When the scent reveals a nest has been penetrated, the chimpanzee can go on to the next step. For this, a quite different tool is needed: a slender, flexible, but tough probe at least 50 centimeters long, with one end deliberately frayed by pulling over the teeth to make a brush-tip. The chimpanzee now probes with this shorter, flexible tool, into the hole that has previously been made to the underground nest — "fishing" for the termites. Because soldier termites attack the foreign object they detect in their nest, they can be gently withdrawn on the fishing probe and eaten.

When the materials for their tools are not available at the site of use, chimpanzees have the forethought to make them in advance and carry them for later use. Chimpanzees can sometimes be seen making insect fishing tools hundreds of meters from any possible termite nests, then setting off with several functional tools held in the lips, to arrive at a termite nest some minutes later already equipped with tools. Remarkably, chimpanzees can plan further ahead than the next action in sequence. In some of the Goualougo two-tool tasks, it is sometimes the tool used second in the sequence that they bring with them, rather than the one used first (Byrne et al., 2013). Why? Because the chimpanzee has remembered that serviceable examples of the first type are often lying around locally and has correctly anticipated that no manufacture may be needed. Although orangutans were already known to show some degree of anticipatory planning (e.g., in their choice of routes through the canopy that showed they could predict future branch deformations under their weight), the chimpanzee's advance tool preparations took planning to a new level of sophistication. In order to (correctly) anticipate both the likely lack of a need to make a puncturing rod, yet the essential need for a brush-tipped fishing probe, the mental representation of the task in prospect — its mental program, or plan — must be rehearsed or inspected "off line." Of course, humans can do this, too: such as, when standing in the supermarket, we mentally run through the ingredients we will need to cook supper (Byrne 1981). A commonplace activity, this nevertheless gives evidence of a planning ability that has often been claimed to be *uniquely* human.

Discovering similarities between chimpanzees and humans does not always prove to be flattering to the ape: chimpanzees are not "nice" animals — in several ways. They are recorded to have killed and eaten many species of large mammals and birds. Usually they do the killing with bare hands, though at one site chimpanzees regularly use a spearlike tool to thrust into tree cavities, with the aim of skewering a nocturnal galago (a small, inoffensive primate) that might be sleeping there. In most cases, zoologists who study a species' gut anatomy can predict its diet; but in this case chimpanzee anatomy implies they should be vegetarian, like gorillas, since they have a very large colon compared to the small intestine. (Humans have the reverse, clearly showing our more recent adaptation to a diet of tender meat or cooked food.) The adaptability shown by chimpanzees — where a primate adapted to a vegetarian diet is able to exploit such a wide range of foods — is most unusual. In many cases, chimpanzee mammal- and bird-killing is opportunistic: they simply react quickly to circumstances. But at some sites hunting is clearly deliberate, as groups of (mostly) males set off together and pass up opportunities to feed in other ways until they have killed, usually a monkey. From the monkey's point of view, the hunting is done cooperatively, by a team: some chimpanzees block exits from a tree, while others rush the monkey and yet others wait patiently below in case it falls. It is hard to be sure that the chimpanzees plan it this way, but they certainly share the kill once made, allowing only those who have taken part in the hunt to tear off large hunks of meat to consume, after which latecomers will be lucky to get scraps via prolonged begging.

More alarming still was the discovery that chimpanzee communities carry out a sort of warfare. Groups of males set off silently and purposefully, like a commando unit, to raid neighboring communities. If they can, these raiders kill males and coerce females to return with them. The killings are brutal and may take many minutes, with a group of males all joining in: beating, biting, and pummeling the unfortunate victim, usually leaving it dying rather than quite dead. This violence is not an isolated or pathological phenomenon. Warfare is known in many chimpanzee communities, though it is usually sporadic, with periods of "guarded peace" between communities. The adult males of some groups have been entirely wiped out by intercommunity violence, with the consequence that the females — with nobody left to protect them — have had to join a new community, usually that of the aggressors. This option has the predictable consequence that some of their young infants will be killed, since regular suckling acts as a contraceptive and thus reduces the females' value to their new community. (Infanticide in such circumstances is not unique to chimpanzees, but also found in gorillas and even more regularly in some other species, such as hanuman langurs.) Civilized humans have undoubtedly brought war to a far more sophisticated pitch of mechanized mass destruction, but anthropologists who study "primitive" tribes free of such horror would readily recognize the chimpanzee behavior as war. Males of the Yanomami community, for instance, regularly make commando-style raids into neighboring Amazon communities, often killing the isolated or undefended males they encounter, and aiming to kidnap young females, who are forced to return with them and join their community. Even the more unpleasant facets of this species show disturbing similarities to our own.

The "discovery" of this species would set the cat among the pigeons. No longer will snappy catch phrases like "man the hunter" or "man the tool-maker" be so useful in distinguishing the human from the animal. No longer can we even claim to be unique by waging war. And for psychologists, most alarming of all, the mental capacity to plan for the future seems unusually developed in this new species — harder to ignore than the relatively sparse evidence of planning that was available before. In the light of all these similarities to mankind, it takes little effort to imagine the intense interest in the results of the first molecular analysis of chimpanzee genes. Consider the response when the answer comes back: that the chimpanzee DNA sequence is *closer* to the human than it is to any other nonhuman animal, even the gorilla. That is, for these violent, tool-making African apes, their closest living relatives are the hairless but clothed people who have come to study them rather than the black and hairy gorillas they sometimes encounter in the forest.

I suggest that, had these events turned out as imagined, the moral status of these apes as persons would be seriously in question. Taxonomically, the obvious genus in which to put the new species is *Homo,* unless a case could be made that the differences are so great that a new genus must be defined; if so, the range of similarities between it and *Homo* are so striking that joining both in a new subfamily might seem appropriate. In the light of all this, how should we treat these creatures? The previous two hundred years of shameful abuse of people, merely because it was possible and could be retrospectively "justified" by their very different appearance and their behavior toward the pale-skinned European conquerors, would surely act as a brake on any immediate dismissal of chimpanzees as "mere animals." (The toolkit of some chimpanzee communities is actually larger than those of some human cultures, such as the Tasmanian aborigines, though that statistic hides the fact that they constructed shelters and wore clothes.) So, if the simplistic dictums are set aside, and they should be, do any substantial differences remain that distinguish us from animals — even from those troublesome chimpanzees — in a way that can properly justify our separate treatment in terms of personhood and morality?

Searching for a More Robust Dividing Line

With the aim of casting a wide net and thus allowing my own biases to appear less prominent in this chapter, I have carried out a search for books about humans whose titles followed the famous formulation of Desmond Morris's bestseller *The Naked Ape*. A wholly unsystematic search revealed seventeen readily available titles of this format, but some of these are actually about other species of ape than ourselves *(forgotten, lost, aquatic, intimate, neglected)*. Others are based on purely morphological differences, and though the differences are valid, they do not seem useful for considering which apes are persons of moral aspect *(naked, upright, scented, well-dressed)*. Given the evidence I have reviewed already, some of the remaining titles are not going to help with detecting a qualitative difference, since their whole point is to emphasize continuity *(hunting* and, my own contribution, *thinking)*. This preliminary sorting leaves three categories of (implied) theory: teaching *(educated, learned)*, technology *(artificial)*, and language (*talking, lopsided* — since, though focused on behavioral laterality, the real interest is in the laterality of language). Each category points to a psychological trait that is thought to differ between humans and nonhuman great apes. I will treat them in order, paying particular attention to aspects that may have led to the origins of modern human cognition.

Teaching

Social learning can bring benefits to any animal capable of learning at all. By learning within a group, the individual potentially profits from what it sees (or otherwise perceives) others do. Its attention may thereby be drawn to rewarding places to explore, or useful things with which to interact. This is technically called "stimulus enhancement" (Spence 1937) or "local enhancement" (Thorpe 1956). In addition, its choice of what action from its repertoire to use in the circumstances may be affected by the behavior it notices among others. This is called "response facilitation" (Byrne 1994, 1998), a special case of *priming*. Moreover, the actions of others may reveal useful things about the environment, such as whether an unfamiliar nut is breakable or edible: *affordance learning* (Tomasello et al. 1993). By these various means, an individual growing up in a supportive social milieu gains many benefits from social learning, and might be described as "educated" by the experience.

But there is something special about human education, that is, deliberately targeted teaching, or pedagogy (Csibra and Gergely 2006). Because human pedagogy requires an intention to educate, and this is hard to detect in animals, most studies of teaching in animals have relied on a functional definition of teaching: behavior performed only in the presence of a naïve individual, which gives no benefit or incurs a cost to the teacher and results in learning benefits to the naïve individual. Teaching that fits these criteria has been identified in meerkats (a small, social mongoose), pied babblers (a social, dry-country bird), and a species of ant (Thornton and Raihani 2008); conversely, no evidence from any of the large-brained species that in other ways seem humanlike — great apes, cetaceans, elephants — has made the cut, perhaps because of the difficulty of experimenting on these species. There is a growing suspicion that the baby may have been thrown out with the bathwater (Byrne and Rapaport 2011): that is, by not requiring intentionality as part of the definition, anthropologists may have picked up exclusively *un*intentional teaching, evolved mechanisms that have no relationship to human pedagogy. If the criteria are relaxed slightly, there are intriguing data from those large-brained species waiting in the wings. Killer whales that hunt seals on beaches, and therefore need to learn how to get free of the sand after an attack, have been seen to force a slow-learning youngster onto a beach deliberately (a highly risky maneuver), then help it get free, apparently to demonstrate the right technique. Experienced female elephants know that the safest male to be with when in estrus is a huge musth bull. When a member of their family first comes into estrus and (understandably) shies away from musth bulls and thereby ends up being harassed by young bulls, the older female has been observed to simulate estrus herself and approach the musth bull, apparently to show the younger female what to do (Bates et al. 2010; the fact that evidence from elephants is relevant to this question illustrates the fact that it is important to study not only the species closest to humans, but also distantly related animals that have converged on similar abilities: see Plate 1).

In some areas, chimpanzees crack nuts on a stone anvil with a cobblestone, and juveniles are often slow to learn: mothers regularly allow access to their own well-chosen rocks and stores of nuts, and occasionally have been shown to deliberately demonstrate the correct grip on an awkward cobble (Boesch 1991). Although none of these cases will convince determined learning theorists of the behaviorist school (Byrne and Bates 2006), there is clear experimental evidence that chimpanzees, at least, do understand the difference between knowledge and ignorance, so pedagogy should not be beyond them. Given that, it would be unwise to build a strong argument that no nonhuman animal, even a chimpanzee, can teach in a humanlike way: that is, based on understanding the gaps in knowledge of specific individuals and working in a goal-directed way to remedy these knowledge gaps. The jury is still out.

Technology

While there is no doubt that chimpanzees are accomplished tool-users and tool-makers, the term "technology" conveys more. No tool made by a wild chimpanzee involves construction, the putting together of more than one component to make a whole. All chimpanzee tool-making is based on detachment. Moreover, the early tools of hominins (i.e., extinct species that are more closely related to modern humans than to chimpanzees), though similarly based on detachment, involve the planned detachment of flakes of rock from a core by percussion: knapping. This also is something that no wild chimpanzee has ever done. Do these differences matter enough to form an important component of a "dividing line"?

In the case of construction, tool-making by addition rather than subtraction, the distinction may be a rather artificial consequence of the popular definition of a "tool" in animal studies as a "detached object." The stone dropped on an egg by an Egyptian vulture, therefore, counts as a tool; the rock on which a thrush breaks a snail does not. In fact, chimpanzees and other great apes do construct things by putting components together to make a whole: every day they make nests in which they sleep at night, and they do not reuse old nests. A terrestrial-living gorilla may construct a rudimentary circle of leaves to avoid damp and mud; some orangutans even build roofs for their much more elaborate arboreal structures. They weave branches into a structure that is more compliant at the center for comfort, and they choose particularly rigid and strong branches to produce a robust structure, demonstrating considerable technical knowledge (van Casteren et al. 2012). Unlike chimpanzees, early hominins made tools by carefully directed percussion blows to a stone core, that is, knapping. The case for knapping as uniquely human is a more powerful one, because — though undoubtedly the flaked stone tools of early hominins represent only the easily preserved sector of a toolkit that surely included many tools made of branches, vines, and other plant material, as in the case of chimpanzees — it does seem impossible for a living great ape to knap in the way almost universal in hominins, perhaps because of an inability to coordinate both power and accuracy when hitting (Byrne 2004). It may be that evolutionary reorganization of the hand was essential for our ancestors to be able to knap (Marzke 1997); however, the advantages of flaked stone show up most in the cutting of tough hide, and it may be that even the earliest knapped stone results from a long, prior development (Roche et al. 1999).

If so, then the dividing line might be argued to be the human capacity to develop a technological culture of cumulatively increasing richness: this view has been strongly argued (Tomasello 1999), and is sometimes taken as self-evident and case-proven (Pagel 2012). There is no question, of course, that this is how modern civilization develops. As Newton famously said, "If I have seen further it is by standing on the shoulders of giants." But ruling out the possibility of cumulative culture in chimpanzees is tricky, as with any case of proving the negative. It is easy to assert that the elaborate tool-using skills of chimpanzees do not change over the years. But why should they, when they work well? Just the same might be said of the manufacturing techniques of any tribal human group, if studied by anthropologists for no longer than chimpanzees have been studied (just over fifty years). One recent experiment gave children and chimpanzees a puzzle-box task that gave better and better rewards to those who developed more and more elaborate skills at opening boxes. Chimpanzees did not; children did (Dean et al. 2012). However, children are brought up in an environment that constantly replicates the challenge of puzzle-boxes, so this may not be a fair test. How would children fare at termite fishing, and should we expect them to develop a better method than chimpanzees have settled on?

Language

If a hard-and-fast cognitive dividing line is ever to be found, my own vote is for human language. But then, as Mandy Rice-Davies memorably put it, "He would say that, wouldn't he?" As a cognitive psychologist, using the natural behavior of nonhuman animals to discover precursors of human mental abilities, for me the Holy Grail has always been the evolutionary basis of language. Indeed, it is generally accepted in psychology that to study "the development of linguistic competence, reasoning, and the ability to objectify the world around us" is tantamount to asking about "the emergence of our capacities for reflection, rationality, and deliberation, including ethical decision-making and planning for the future" (both quotes from the invitation letter to contribute to this volume). That is, if we understood the origins of language, the rest would fall into place. Nor is this view in any way unique to psychology: "Language is regarded, at least in most intellectual traditions, as the quintessential human attribute, at once evidence and source of most that is considered transcendent in us, distinguishing ours from the merely mechanical nature of the beast" (Wallman 1990, 5). Nevertheless, human language did not emerge de novo: it was built on cognitive foundations we share with the living great apes.

During the twentieth century there was a series of efforts to tackle this mystery directly by attempting to teach language to our closest relative, the chimpanzee. Given the almost universal acceptance of modern evolutionary theory, and of the critical importance of language evolution in particular, one might expect the results to have become a cornerstone of scholarship in the humanities. They have not. Reactions have varied, but Thomas Sebeok's (which he expressed at a 1980 press conference) is only unusual for its candor: "In my opinion, the alleged language experiments with apes divide into three groups: one, outright fraud; two, self-deception; three, those conducted by Terrace." Terrace himself concluded that none of the apes acquired any trace of language. The reactions of linguists, philosophers, and other human scientists have been almost universally negative. Indeed, methinks they do protest too much. Might it be that some of the results of this work brought intellectual discomfort — especially to scholars unduly wedded to a comfortable separation between man and beast?

The early studies certainly did not bring such discomfort, since they were utter failures. Two projects brought infant chimpanzees into the researchers' own homes, where the researchers treated them exactly as they treated their own children (Hayes and Hayes 1951; Kellogg and Kellogg 1933). The young apes showed their intelligence in many ways, except linguistically. We now know that chimpanzees lack fine motor control of their voices and cannot imitate any novel sounds: indeed, most animals cannot learn new sounds, an ability that seems limited to birds, cetaceans, and humans (Janik and Slater 2000). Therefore, chimpanzees' inability to learn human speech sounds is unsurprising. Subsequent projects used the gestural system of American Sign Language (ASL) (Gardner and Gardner 1969), a magnetic board for stick-on tokens (Premack and Premack 1972), and a computer-controlled display of "lexigrams" (Rumbaugh 1977).

All these projects were to some extent successful: chimpanzees learned and used ASL gestures, and they responded appropriately to questions posed via visual symbols. However, doubt remained as to whether any of the subjects really appreciated that they were *communicating,* in the sense of exchanging ideas with another mind, rather than simply solving artificial puzzles in order to gain reward or comfort. Even the ASL-using apes mainly used the signs to express immediate needs or follow instructions, and their utterances were repetitive and redundant, lacking any clear sign of syntax (Terrace 1979). Controversy over their findings terminated most projects by withering their funding. But one continued, and it explored more realistic conditions. More than one ape was trained in the lexigram system, and "conversations" were held in real-world surroundings rather than in front of a machine keyboard (Savage-Rumbaugh 1986). Notable successes included chimpanzees' use of taught or novel symbols to refer to out-of-sight objects, and spontaneous turn-taking in communicative exchanges; but their syntax remained minimal (e.g., weak word-order effects), and usage was still largely a matter of comprehension of commands and generation of requests.

However, with one subject, Kanzi, all this changed (Savage-Rumbaugh et al. 1993b). Like human children, Kanzi picked up his knowledge of language without being taught: in addition to symbolic lexigrams, he recognized spoken English words, making reliable distinctions on the basis of single phoneme differences; he followed conversations, comprehending meaning at normal speech rates; and he related his lexigram symbols to the equivalent spoken words. Most remarkably, Kanzi understood syntactical rules: use of "it" to refer back in a conversation; expressions such as "now" or "later" for time shifts; and the relative pronoun "that," as in "the oranges that are in the refrigerator" versus "the oranges that I am holding" (Savage-Rumbaugh et al. 1993a). The abilities were tested by careful experimentation under blind-scoring conditions, and these data were hard to ignore.

This history illustrates two points. The first is that language, and the crucial cognitive powers it conveys, may exist in the absence of speech. The idea that humans evolved through a phase in which their language was gestural, not spoken, has a long history (Hewes 1973), particularly encouraged by the intricate relationship between the neural substrates for human language and manual skills, as shown by similar damage causing both apraxias and aphasias (Corballis 2010). Supporting that conjecture is recent evidence that a community of deaf children has spontaneously developed a shared sign language with the central properties of language (Senghas et al. 2004). Perhaps, then, the origins of language should be sought in the manual skills of our ape relatives, rather than their (much studied) vocalizations. The second point is that Kanzi is not, in fact, a chimpanzee *(Pan troglodytes)* but a bonobo *(Pan paniscus)*.

These are sibling species, separated only by about 1 mya of independent evolution, and not recognized as distinct until 1928. Their behavioral ecology, however, is very different. In bonobos, alliances of females are able to dominate the larger males; overt aggression is rarer, and social interactions are more tolerant and cooperative; and bonobo nonreproductive sexual behavior is extremely varied. Although bonobos are at least as skillful as chimpanzees doing practical tasks in captivity, scientists have not noted tool use in wild bonobos; nor has intercommunity violence been described, and even hunting is rare. The contrast to the competitive, male-dominated chimpanzee societies, with their prevalence of tool-making and violence, could not be more marked. Intriguingly, long ago Robert Yerkes described one of his captive chimpanzees, Prince Chim, as unlike any other he'd studied: "Doubtless there are geniuses even among the anthropoid apes. Prince Chim seems to have been an intellectual genius" (Yerkes 1925, 255). After the bonobo was recognized as a species, there was a belated realization that Prince Chim was a bonobo. Although both species are equally related to us, several lines of evidence suggest that chimpanzees have diverged more markedly, so the bonobo may more closely resemble the shared common ancestor with humans. Therefore, the natural gestural communication of the bonobo deserves special attention; that is how my hypothesis of a linguistic dividing line can most easily be tested.

Gestural "Language" in a Great Ape?

Because of the traditional anthropological focus on material culture, research on great ape manual skills has been dominated by tool-use and tool-making. If the focus is shifted away from the object and toward the cognitive ability, however, all great apes are seen to differ strikingly from monkeys in their manual skills, in ways that are reminiscent of our own everyday abilities. The origin of these special skills is most likely in feeding ecology: ape manual skills allow them to forage on high-quality foods that monkeys cannot reach or cannot process efficiently. Paleontology shows that the monkeys evolved more recently than the apes, and most early ape lineages became extinct soon after the arrival of monkeys. With smaller body size and more efficient long-distance locomotion, monkeys are potentially devastating competitors for apes: and they now share almost all the same habitats. It has been suggested that the development of enhanced manual skill ability in the early ancestors of the surviving apes, including ourselves, was partly driven by this competition — and the only reason any apes survived at all (Byrne 1997).

Unlike monkeys, great apes can build up motor actions into novel, organized, multistage routines in which the two hands take different roles in the service of a single aim, and in which modules of action can be repeated, omitted, or substituted according to environmental demands (Byrne and Byrne 1993; Byrne 2001, 2004; Corp and Byrne 2002; Russon 1998). We use these capacities every time we make a salad or a stew, put up a shelf, or mend a car engine, so it takes effort to realize that almost no other animal can do anything similar. These learning abilities allow the development of distinctive local traditions of food-procurement and food-processing in nonhuman great apes, which some suggest are simple "cultures" (Byrne et al. 2011; Whiten et al. 1999; but see Byrne et al. 2004; Laland and Janik 2006), and which evidently depend on some kind of imitation. The simplest account of great ape imitation is that it relies on behavior parsing: statistical extraction of the recurring elements and sequences of elements in natural behavior watched many times (Byrne 2003, 2006), combined with the ability to construct novel programs of action. Constructing sequences of motor action, in which order is critical for success, and in which modules can be combined hierarchically to build larger structures, shares many of the characteristics of linguistic syntax, at the level of a phrase-structure grammar; I have used the term "behavior parsing" advisedly. In contrast, no trace of syntax has been detected in the vocal behavior of great apes. Indeed, even in the much more extensively studied monkeys, evidence of syntax has been sparse: the prefixing of one call to another, modifying its meaning by adding a caveat of uncertainty, is the most convincing (Arnold and Zuberbuhler 2006, 2008). If language has a "mosaic" origin, the syntactical structuring "machine" so central to Chomsky-inspired linguistics is more convincingly derived from great apes' manual food-processing abilities than their vocalizations.

Remarkably, research on great ape gestural communication itself has been sparse. Indeed, almost all work on that subject comes from only two research groups: the team led by Tomasello and Call at Leipzig MPI, summarized in Call and Tomasello (2007); and our own group at St Andrews (Cartmill and Byrne 2007, 2010, 2011; Genty et al. 2009; Genty and Byrne 2010; Hobaiter and Byrne 2010, 2011a, 2011b, 2014; Tanner and Byrne 1993, 1996, 1999). Through these projects, there is now an emerging consensus about the operation of gestural communication in the apes, although much no doubt remains to be discovered.

As I noted earlier in the chapter, great apes use gestures in a strikingly "intentional" way (Bruner 1981). Gestures are directed to specific goals that require particular behavior from the audiences (Tomasello and Call 2007):

they monitor and check whether the audience is attending to them (Hobaiter and Byrne 2011b), and in the absence of the desired response, they persist and elaborate their gesturing (Cartmill and Byrne 2007; Leavens et al. 2005). Gestures are made with the signaler's attention clearly on a particular target individual: after gesturing, signalers typically wait for the target to respond; and if response is lacking or inappropriate, signalers try again, repeating the gesture or using other means to achieve their purpose. Researchers are even able to insist that every datum, each instance of gesture analyzed, has some definite indication of intentional use: doing so typically reduces the corpus by less than 50 percent (Genty et al. 2009). In contrast, primate vocalizations generally appear to lack evidence of intentionality (Seyfarth et al. 2005). The choice of gesture is also appropriately adjusted to the attentional state of the audience: for instance, among chimpanzees, the signalers are significantly more likely to use a silent gesture to a target who is looking at them, and if the target is looking away, they are more likely to use a contact gesture (Hobaiter and Byrne 2011b) or to relocate into the target's visual field before gesturing (Liebal et al. 2004). Thus, apes do understand the physical basis of gestural communication. Most impressively of all, there is evidence that apes perceive the degree to which the audience has understood their gestures — that is, they monitor the mental states of other individuals (Cartmill and Byrne 2007). Orangutans were given a choice between a preferred and a nonpreferred food, out of reach, but with a familiar keeper at hand. Naturally, they gestured enthusiastically toward the preferred food. The keeper, working as a confederate of the experimenters, gave either the preferred food ("full understanding"), half of the preferred food ("partial understanding"), or the nonpreferred food ("misunderstanding"). In the latter two cases, the orangutans continued to communicate. When the keeper had apparently misunderstood them entirely, orangutans switched the kinds of gesture they were using, whereas with partial understanding, they kept to the same gestures but increased the rate of gesturing. These reactions match our own behavior in a game of "charades," when our mimes are wholly or partly misunderstood.

Despite these clear parallels with how language is used, great ape gestural repertoires are not learned by imitating others (Genty et al. 2009; Tomasello et al. 1989), nor even learned over successive interactions with them (Genty et al. 2009; Hobaiter and Byrne 2011b): despite earlier claims, neither cultural learning nor ontogenetic ritualization is required as explanation. The natural gestural repertoires of apes are species-typical, products of their biology, just as the displays of other animals are. Indeed, many of their gestures are shared with *other* ape species: no fewer than thirty-one gestures are shared between chimpanzee, gorilla, and orangutan (Hobaiter and Byrne 2011b). These facts were not recognized at first because the very large size of the repertoire gave the impression, in relatively short-term studies, that each individual had a different repertoire, with widespread idiosyncrasy. Comparing across many sites (Genty et al. 2009) and longer-term studies of wild communities (Hobaiter and Byrne 2011b) showed that the idiosyncrasy was illusory. As they develop, young apes first explore the extensive possibilities of their species' repertoire, often using whole series of gestures to be sure of a result, even though their gesture series often proves to be less efficient than a single gesture (Hobaiter and Byrne 2011a); then they begin to reduce their repertoires as they discover which gestures are most efficient to use. Therefore, adults show the smallest active repertoires, and different individuals may settle on different sets of preferred gestures (Hobaiter and Byrne 2011a). But this does not mean they have "forgotten" the fuller range of species-typical gestures. The phenomenon of "gestural imitation" (Byrne and Tanner 2006; Call 2001; Custance et al. 1994) can best be explained as a result of priming particular actions in the very extensive latent gestural repertoire of adult great apes. Typically, subjects are trained to copy a demonstrated gesture; then more novel, arbitrary actions are presented, and the apes copy them, though their copies are often imperfect. In one study, the ape (a gorilla) was part of a long-term project, and her repertoire over eleven years had been recorded: searching this huge database showed that the "copies of novel actions" were in fact reiterations of gestures she had made herself spontaneously in the past (Byrne and Tanner 2006). This explained not only the ability apparently to imitate, but also why the "imitations" were often imperfect: they were not copies of arbitrary action, but closest matches from an existing passive repertoire.

In contrast to human language, the semantics of ape gestures seems to be very limited (Cartmill and Byrne 2010): many gestures are used interchangeably for the same purpose, and only a few dimensions of meaning are separately encoded in gesture. Captive studies undoubtedly accentuate this paradox, since needs and wants of zoo animals are highly constrained; but even in the wild, chimpanzee gestures are used for only nineteen clearly different purposes (Hobaiter and Byrne, 2014). These include signals to: co-ordinate actions (climb on me, climb on you, follow me, move away, travel with me); beg (acquire object) or manipulate another's attention (attend to specific location); coordinate friendly actions (contact, initiate grooming, play start); respond to sexual attention (to female, to male); and terminate ongoing activity (stop that). This limited set of needs explains why, despite strong evidence that apes can imitate arbitrary novel actions (Hobaiter and Byrne 2010), they seldom use imitation to acquire new gestures culturally. Nonhuman great apes are already equipped by nature with numerous gestural synonyms for their purposes, and they develop their repertoires by pruning rather than addition. It does not explain how these species benefit from the potential to use so many gestures (e.g., sixty-six in wild chimpanzees: Hobaiter and Byrne 2011b); nor why apes are so limited in their appreciation of the benefits of a more diverse semantic system, in contrast to the developing child.

For now, these mysteries remain. And gestural communication remains unstudied in the wild bonobo, the species shown by captive discoveries to have the greatest potential of showing humanlike communication. Bonobos live entirely in the Democratic Republic of Congo (DRC), which has not been the easiest place in the world in which to conduct research over recent decades. When bonobo research finally gets going in DRC, will they prove to challenge the linguistic dividing line for which I have argued?

Conclusion

Many of the "obvious differences" between humans and all other animals are misapprehensions: like us, chimpanzees can make tools to a plan; they use a series of different tools toward a single aim; they recognize themselves in a mirror; they show forethought in planning; they hunt mammals; and they deliberately kill members of neighbor communities in "commando-style" raids. Nor do genetic insights help: the chimpanzee is more closely related to us than it is to any other animal. This chapter argues that linguistic communication is the only robust "dividing line," and even that was undoubtedly built on cognitive foundations we share with other species. These include the social cognition to represent the contents of other minds, for instance, that a child lacks some specific knowledge and hence would benefit from instruction; the physical cognition to put causal knowledge to use when constructing tools and structures; and the facility to communicate intentionally, shown in the goal-directed and purposive gestural communication of all great apes. Discovering what cognitive barriers hold back our closest relatives — especially the unusual and little-studied bonobo — from acquiring a simple language is the greatest challenge to comparative and evolutionary psychology.

REFERENCES

Arnold, K., and K. Zuberbuhler. 2006. Semantic combinations in primate calls. *Nature* 441: 303.

————. 2008. Meaningful call combinations in a non-human primate. *Current Biology* 18: R202-3.

Bates, L. A., et al. 2010. Why do African elephants *(Loxodonta africana)* simulate oestrus? An analysis of longitudinal data. *PLoS ONE* 5, no. 3.

Boesch, C. 1991. Teaching among wild chimpanzees. *Animal Behaviour* 41: 530-32.

Bruner, J. 1981. Intention in the structure of action and interaction. In *Advances in infancy research,* ed. L. Lipsett, 41-56. Norwood, NJ: Ablex.

Byrne, R. W. 1981. Mental cookery: An illustration of fact-retrieval from plans. *Quarterly Journal of Experimental Psychology* 33A: 31-37.

————. 1994. The evolution of intelligence. In *Behaviour and evolution,* ed. P. J. B. Slater and T. R. Halliday, 223-65. Cambridge: Cambridge University Press.

————. 1997. The technical intelligence hypothesis: An additional evolutionary stimulus to intelligence? In *Machiavellian intelligence II: Extensions and evaluations,* ed. A. Whiten and R. W. Byrne, 289-311. Cambridge: Cambridge University Press.

————. 1998. Imitation: The contributions of priming and program-level copying. In *Intersubjective communication and emotion in early ontogeny: Studies in emotion and social interaction,* ed. S. Braten, 228-44. Cambridge: Cambridge University Press.

————. 2001. Clever hands: The food processing skills of mountain gorillas. In *Mountain gorillas: Three decades of research at Karisoke,* ed. M. M. Robbins, P. Sicotte, and K. J. Stewart, 293-313. Cambridge: Cambridge University Press.

————. 2003. Imitation as behaviour parsing. *Philosophical Transactions of the Royal Society of London B* 358: 529-36.

————. 2004. The manual skills and cognition that lie behind hominid tool use. In *Evolutionary origins of great ape intelligence,* ed. A. E. Russon and D. R. Begun, 31-44. Cambridge: Cambridge University Press.

————. 2006. Parsing behavior: A mundane origin for an extraordinary ability? In *The roots of human sociality,* ed. S. Levinson and N. Enfield, 478-505. Oxford: Berg.

Byrne, R. W., and J. M. E. Byrne. 1993. Complex leaf-gathering skills of mountain gorillas *(Gorilla g. beringei):* Variability and standardization. *American Journal of Primatology* 31: 241-61.

Byrne, R. W., and L. A. Bates. 2006. Why are animals cognitive? *Current Biology* 16: R445-R48.

Byrne, R. W., and J. E. Tanner. 2006. Gestural imitation by a gorilla: Evidence and nature of the phenomenon. *International Journal of Psychology and Psychological Therapy* 6: 215-31.

Byrne, R. W., and L. A. Bates. 2010. Primate social cognition: Uniquely primate, uniquely social, or just unique? *Neuron* 65: 815-30.

Byrne, R. W., and L. G. Rapaport. 2011. What are we learning from teaching? *Animal Behaviour* 82, no. 5: 1207-11.

Byrne, R. W., C. Hobaiter, and M. Klailova. 2011. Local traditions in gorilla manual skill: Evidence for observational learning of behavioural organization. *Animal Cognition* DOI 10.1007/s10071-011-0403-8.

Byrne, R. W., C. M. Sanz, and D. B. Morgan. 2013. Chimpanzees plan their tool use. In *Tool use in animals: Cognition and ecology,* ed. C. M. Sanz, C. Boesch, and J. Call, 48-63. Cambridge: Cambridge University Press.

Byrne, R. W., et al. 2004. Understanding culture across species. *Trends in Cognitive Sciences* 8: 341-46.

Call, J. 2001. Body imitation in an enculturated orangutan *(Pongo pygmaeus).* *Cybernetics and Systems* 32: 97-119.

Call, J., and M. Tomasello. 2007. *The gestural communication of apes and monkeys.* Hillsdale, NJ: Lawrence Erlbaum Associates.

Cartmill, E. A., and R. W. Byrne. 2007. Orangutans modify their gestural signalling according to their audience's comprehension. *Current Biology* 17: 1345-48.

———. 2010. Semantics of primate gestures: Intentional meanings of orangutan gestures. *Animal Cognition* 13: 793-804.

———. 2011. Addressing the problems of intentionality and granularity in non-human primate gesture. In *Integrating gestures: The interdisciplinary nature of gesture,* ed. S. Gale and M. Ishino. Amsterdam: John Benjamin.

Corballis, M. C. 2010. The gestural origins of language. *Wiley Interdisciplinary Reviews: Cognitive Science* 1: 2-7.

Corp, N., and R. W. Byrne. 2002. The ontogeny of manual skill in wild chimpanzees: Evidence from feeding on the fruit of *Saba florida. Behaviour* 139: 137-68.

Csibra, G., and G. Gergely. 2006. Social learning and social cognition: The case for pedagogy. In *Processes of change in brain and cognitive development: Attention and performance XXI,* ed. M. H. Johnson and Y. Munakata, 249-74. Oxford: Oxford University Press.

Custance, D. M., A. Whiten, and K. A. Bard. 1994. The development of gestural imitation and self-recognition in chimpanzees *(Pan troglodytes)* and children. In *Current Primatology,* vol. 2, *Social Development, Learning and Behaviour,* ed. J. J. Roeder et al., 381-87. Strasbourg: Université Louis Pasteur.

Dean, L. G., et al. 2012. Identification of the social and cognitive processes underlying human cumulative culture. *Science* 335, no. 6072: 1114-18.

Gallup, G. G., Jr. 1982. Self-awareness and the emergence of mind in primates. *American Journal of Primatology* 2: 237-48.

Gardner, R. A., and T. Gardner. 1969. Teaching sign language to a chimpanzee. *Science* 165: 664-72.

Genty, E., and R. W. Byrne. 2010. Why do gorillas make sequences of gestures? *Animal Cognition* 13: 287-301.

Genty, E., et al. 2009. Gestural communication of the gorilla *(Gorilla gorilla):* Repertoire, intentionality and possible origins. *Animal Cognition* 12: 527-46.

Hayes, K. J., and C. Hayes. 1951. The intellectual development of a home-raised chimpanzee. *Proceedings of the American Philosophical Society* 95: 105-9.

Hewes, G. W. 1973. Primate communication and the gestural origins of language. *Current Anthropology* 14: 5-24.

Hobaiter, C., and R. W. Byrne. 2010. Able-bodied wild chimpanzees imitate a motor procedure used by a disabled individual to overcome handicap. *Public Library of Science One* 5, no. 8: e11959.

———. 2011a. Serial gesturing by wild chimpanzees: Its nature and function for communication. *Animal Cognition* DOI 10.1007/s10071-011-0416-3.

———. 2011b. The gestural repertoire of the wild chimpanzee. *Animal Cognition* DOI 10.1007/s10071-011-0409-2.

———. 2014. The meanings of chimpanzee gestures. *Current Biology* 24: 1596-1600.

Janik, V. M., and P. J. B. Slater. 2000. The different roles of social learning in vocal communication. *Animal Behaviour* 60: 1-11.

Kellogg, W. N., and L. A. Kellogg. 1933. *The ape and the child.* New York: McGraw-Hill.

Laland, K. N., and V. Janik. 2006. The animal cultures debate. *Trends in Evolution and Ecology* 21: 542-47.

Leavens, D. A., J. L. Russell, and W. D. Hopkins. 2005. Intentionality as measured in the persistence and elaboration of communication by chimpanzees *(Pan troglodytes). Child Development* 76, no. 1: 291-306.

Liebal, K., et al. 2004. To move or not to move: How apes adjust to the attentional state of others. *Interaction Studies* 5: 199-219.

Marzke, M. W. 1997. Precision grips, hand morphology, and tools. *American Journal of Physical Anthropology* 102: 91-110.

Pagel, M. 2012. Adapted to culture. *Nature* 482: 297-99.

Povinelli, D. J., and J. G. H. Cant. 1995. Arboreal clambering and the evolution of self-conception. *Quarterly Journal of Biology* 70: 393-421.

Premack, A. J., and D. Premack. 1972. Teaching language to an ape. *Scientific American* 227: 92-99.

Roche, H., et al. 1999. Early hominid stone production and technical skill 2.34 myr ago in West Turkana, Kenya. *Nature* 399: 57-60.

Rumbaugh, D. 1977. *Language learning by a chimpanzee.* New York: Academic Press.

Russon, A. E. 1998. The nature and evolution of intelligence in orangutans *(Pongo pygmaeus). Primates* 39, no. 4: 485-503.

Sanz, C., J. Call, and D. B. Morgan. 2009. Design complexity in termite-fishing tools of chimpanzees *(Pan troglodytes). Biology Letters* 5, no. 3: 293-96.

Sanz, C. M., and D. B. Morgan. 2007. Chimpanzee tool technology in the Goualougo Triangle, Republic of Congo. *Journal of Human Evolution* 52, no. 4: 420-33.

Savage-Rumbaugh, E. S. 1986. *Ape language: From conditional response to symbol.* New York: Columbia University Press.

Savage-Rumbaugh, E. S., et al. 1993a. Language comprehension in ape and child. *Monographs of the Society for Research in Child Development* 58, nos. 3-4: 1-222.

———. 1993b. Language comprehension in ape and child. *Monographs of the Society for Research in Child Development* 58: 1-252.

Senghas, A., S. Kita, and A. Ozyurek. 2004. Children creating core properties of language: Evidence from an emerging sign language in Nicaragua. *Science* 305: 1779-82.

Seyfarth, Robert M., Dorothy L. Cheney, and Thore J. Bergman. 2005. Primate social cognition and the origins of language. *Trends in Cognitive Sciences* 9, no. 6: 264-66.

Smet, A. F., and R. W. Byrne. 2013. African elephants can use human pointing cues to find hidden food. *Current Biology* DOI 10.1016/j.cub.2013.08.037.

Spence, K. W. 1937. Experimental studies of learning and higher mental processes in infra-human primates. *Psychological Bulletin* 34: 806-50.

Tanner, J. E., and R. W. Byrne. 1993. Concealing facial evidence of mood: Evidence for perspective-taking in a captive gorilla? *Primates* 34: 451-56.

———. 1996. Representation of action through iconic gesture in a captive lowland gorilla. *Current Anthropology* 37: 162-73.

———. 1999. The development of spontaneous gestural communication in a group of zoo-living lowland gorillas. In *The mentalities of gorillas and orangutans: Comparative perspectives,* ed. S. T. Parker, R. W. Mitchell, and H. L. Miles, 211-39. Cambridge: Cambridge University Press.

Terrace, H. S. 1979. *Nim.* New York: Knopf.

Thornton, A., and N. Raihani. 2008. The evolution of teaching. *Animal Behaviour* 75, no. 6: 1823-36.

Thorpe, W. H. 1956. *Learning and instinct in animals.* London: Methuen.

Tomasello, M. 1999. *The cultural origins of human cognition.* Cambridge, MA: Harvard University Press.

Tomasello, M., and J. Call. 2007. Intentional communication in nonhuman primates. In *The gestural communication of apes and monkeys,* ed. J. Call and M. Tomasello, 1-15. Mahwah, NJ: Lawrence Erlbaum Associates.

Tomasello, M., D. Gust, and T. A. Frost. 1989. A longitudinal investigation of gestural communication in young chimpanzees. *Primates* 30: 35-50.

Tomasello, M., E. S. Savage-Rumbaugh, and A. C. Kruger. 1993. Imitative learning of actions on objects by children, chimpanzees, and enculturated chimpanzees. *Child Development* 64: 1688-1705.

van Casteren, A., et al. 2012. Nest-building orangutans demonstrate engineering know-how to produce safe, comfortable beds. *Proceedings of the National Academy of Science U.S.A.*

Wallman, J. 1990. *Aping language.* Cambridge: Cambridge University Press.

Whiten, A., et al. 1999. Cultures in chimpanzees. *Nature* 399: 682-85.

Yerkes, R. M. 1925. *Almost human.* New York: Century Company.

Human Evolution: Personhood and Emergence

Ian Tattersall

Introduction

All organisms, even colonial algae, are in some way individuated; but "personhood" — as we recognize it among human beings today — implies an active sense of self. That is, it implies the ability of each individual not only to view himself or herself as simultaneously engaged with, and entirely distinct from, the surrounding environment, but also to acknowledge an identity similar to that of other members of the same species. Such cognitively complex organisms as elephants and dolphins, and even some birds, are able to recognize themselves in mirrors (e.g., Plotnick et al. 2006; Reiss and Marino 2001). But, not least because whether or not these fellow vertebrates possess an internalized and objectified sense of self has to be judged (by us) from very indirect proxy indicators, their possession of this quality must remain highly debatable (by us).

Closer to home, however, it seems very unlikely that even our closest living primate relatives possess our particular form of self-awareness. Richard Byrne (in this volume and in other works referred to in chapter 1) has very eloquently presented the case for considering the great apes, and

I thank the John Templeton Foundation, and particularly Mary Ann Meyers and Paul Wason, for the opportunity to attend the splendid conference, ably chaired by Malcolm Jeeves, for which this contribution was originally prepared. I equally thank the other participants for stimulating discussion, and Dick Byrne and Colin Renfrew for astute comments on an early draft of this chapter.

particularly chimpanzees and bonobos, as creatures of considerable cognitive complexity; indeed, hardly a month seems to pass in which one or another of them is not reported to do something we had thought only we (humans) did. But for all their evident cognitive resemblances to us (no surprise, considering how much evolutionary history we have in common), there is no doubt that they do not mentally process information in exactly the way we do. Chimpanzees apparently do have a limited understanding of the psychological states of other individuals (Tomasello et al. 2003), but they do not have the complex theory of mind (broadly, the ability to predict the future intentions of others) that humans possess (Kaminski et al. 2008). One eminent group of comparative cognitive psychologists neatly expressed it this way: "There is no evidence anywhere that chimpanzees understand the beliefs of others" (Tomasello et al. 2003, 156). Similarly, while chimpanzees certainly recognize themselves in mirrors (Gallup 1970), we have no good reason to believe that they are "self-conscious" in the same way that human beings are. If it is permissible to generalize such observations to the domain of self-reflection, then modern human beings are, for all intents and purposes, unique in the living world in possessing something we can call personhood — as opposed to mere individuality.

Personhood in the sense that I am implying here most likely derives directly from the highly distinctive ability of members of *Homo sapiens* to think in a symbolic manner (see discussion and references in Tattersall 2012). We have the cognitive capacity to break down our internal and external worlds into a huge vocabulary of discrete symbols that we can shuffle, according to mental algorithms, to create novel combinations. Such rearrangements add up to our unique capacity to envision previously unimagined and unobserved possibilities, and to form new interpretations of the world around us. The resulting facility allows us to perceive our own personal universes not only as they are but as they might be; indeed, this capability of ours is so pervasive throughout our existences that we live for much of the time in individual worlds that are largely of our own construction. What is more, what we perceive as individuals looks different depending not only on where we are, but on who we are; and the resulting view may not only take in the material world that impresses itself on our senses, but may expand to embrace abstract, unseen worlds that lie beyond the boundaries of direct perception.

An additional correlate of our unique cognitive condition is that, with our symbolic sense added to the ancient cognitive substrate on which it is imposed, we experience our surroundings as a set of discrete stimuli, to each of which we can attach its own particular importance. As a result, our perceived individual personhood is at least as much a story we tell ourselves about ourselves as it is a sum of all those complex emotional responses that we undoubtedly share with chimpanzees and, to varying degrees, with other primates.

As far as we can tell, all of this makes modern human beings *qualitatively* different as cognitive entities from every other inhabitant of the planet. Readily as we perceive all the manifold similarities among us and our living primate relatives, we equally readily recognize that we are separated even from the closest of them by a significant (if, in the wider scheme of things, narrow) cognitive gulf. Yet our knowledge not only of our biological history but of our broader zoological context makes it clear that we are descended from remote ancestors that very broadly resembled chimpanzees and other great apes in the ways in which they perceived and interacted with the world around them. As the cognitive psychologist Daniel Povinelli once surmised, those ancestors would have been "intelligent, thinking creatures who deftly attend[ed] to and learn[ed] about the regularities that unfold[ed] in the world around them. But . . . they [did] not reason about unobservable things: they [had] no ideas about the 'mind,' no notion of 'causation'" (Povinelli 2004, 34). This proposition is intrinsically impossible to substantiate, but it seems reasonably corroborated by what we know both of our archaically proportioned early bipedal precursors and of our closest living relatives. And a reasonable extrapolation from it is that those ancestors also had no idea of "self" — certainly not in any sense that we would readily resonate to.

Of course, we are ourselves equally prisoners of our own cognitive style. Having crossed the symbolic barrier, we human beings find it more or less impossible to put ourselves in the cognitive place of any creature that does not process information about the world as we do. This not only renders it highly problematic for us to understand what is going on behind the eyes of our living ape relatives; it also calls into question whether we can use our modern human mindset as any kind of guide whatsoever to its counterpart in even the closest among our extinct hominin ancestors. Thus, while our rapidly enlarging fossil and archaeological records make it possible for us to examine our biological and behavioral histories in remarkable material detail (see review in Tattersall 2009), we are conceptually hugely limited in our ability to imagine the ways in which even our largest-brained extinct predecessors subjectively experienced the worlds they lived in. What is more, we glimpse their interior lives and perceptions only through a strictly limited series of proxy indicators. And those proxies are embedded only in the very small proportion of their behaviors that left durable material expressions behind.

Still, we already see enough in those tantalizing indicators to suggest that the acquisition of our unique cognitive style did not involve a process of long-term burnishing (Tattersall 2008). We did not achieve our current cognitive status through a continuous and insensibly modifying sequence of minor acquisitions, as a traditionally gradualist view of evolution would suggest: as far as we can tell, our ancestors did not get smarter in tiny increments over vast periods of time, as cleverer individuals out-reproduced dumber ones. Indeed, for most of the time, no detectable innovation seems to have been happening at all. In other words, the record suggests that, cognitively speaking, we are not simply an advanced extrapolation of what went before us. It is true that, on average, hominid brains were on a steady trajectory of size increase over the two million years or so leading up to the appearance of *Homo sapiens* (see Holloway et al. 2004). Indeed, at least three lineages within the genus *Homo* independently exhibited this trend. But the indications are pretty clear (albeit in a less-than-perfect record) that, while hominids were doubtless getting smarter in a general sense over this period, the shift to our unique symbolic mode was made in a single step. This unusual capacity of ours was apparently not acquired piecemeal, at least on the biological level.

Moreover, while large brain size may be an essential underpinning for our remarkable way of dealing with information, pure neural mass evidently does not equate directly with symbolic thought; witness, for example, the stark contrast between the archaeological records left behind by the large-brained but evidently nonsymbolic Neanderthals and the fully symbolic Cro-Magnons (modern *Homo sapiens*), who replaced them in Europe and western Asia. Instead, it is becoming increasingly clear that our characteristic cognitive style is the result of an emergent event, a phase change, if you will, in which the addition of some new factor — probably unremarkable in itself — gave rise to a brain with an entirely unprecedented information-processing potential.

The Human Fossil Record

Evidence for the conclusion just given comes from general patterns of both biological and cultural innovation that were established very early on in hominid history. In contrast to the neo-Darwinian expectation of linearity inherited from the almost century-old "New Evolutionary Synthesis" (see Mayr 1982), there have typically been multiple hominids in Africa — and later on throughout the Old World — at any one time (Tattersall 2000). We see this from the appearance of the very first "bipedal apes" (Figure 1): small-brained, short-legged, and diminutive creatures who remained at home in the trees even as they moved on two legs across the ground. Fossils of these creatures begin to show up in African sites that date to between seven and six million years ago (mya) (see Plate 2). This was a period that coincided with a phase of environmental change as forests began to fragment with decreasing rainfall and more pronounced seasonality of climate, though the fossils themselves tend to be found alongside indicators of forested or at least of mixed forest/woodland/bushland conditions. The consequent expansion of edge habitats and woodlands evidently spurred the pattern of experimentation with the hominid potential that was to characterize the family (or the subfamily — in this context it makes no practical difference) throughout the Pliocene and Pleistocene epochs. Given the strong subsequent tendency toward species multiplicity among the hominids, it is at least as plausible to attribute any evolutionary trends we might see within the family (such as increasing brain size) to the preferential success of entire (bigger-brained) species, as to the success of individuals within those species. This makes more sense than trying to force the data we have into a neo-Darwinian framework of steady within-lineage modification under the guiding hand of natural selection (especially at a time when climates and environments were supremely unstable). After all, it is of little evolutionary use to be the most splendidly adapted exemplar of your kind if your entire species is being outcompeted into extinction, or if your environment suddenly changes — as seems typically to have occurred.

Yet, for all the species diversity that the hominid family has typically shown, significant change in both the biological and cultural realms has tended to be both sporadic and rare. Perhaps as early as 3.4 mya, hominids had begun to use (probably naturally occurring) sharp stone flakes to de-flesh animal carcasses (McPherron et al. 2010). But it was not until almost a million years later that hominids deliberately began to make and use stone tools (see review in Klein 2009). And stone implements were not made to a consistent form until yet another million years had passed. Clearly, technological innovation did not feed on itself in those early days as it does now. And even though early hominids were clearly resourceful and adaptable, they evidently accommodated to sometimes dramatic environmental change by using old technologies in new ways, rather than by inventing new tools for new purposes (see Plates 3 and 4).

What is more, the periodic technological innovations that *are* seen con-

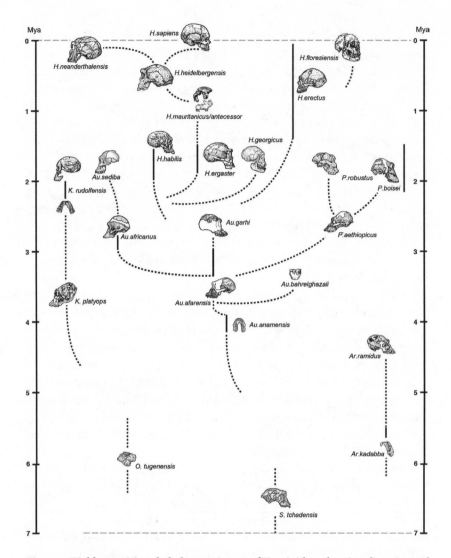

Figure 1. Highly provisional phylogenetic tree of Hominidae, showing diversity and longevity of taxa, and indicating some very speculative evolutionary relationships among them. Drawn by Jennifer Steffey; ©Ian Tattersall.

spicuously failed to coincide with the arrival of new kinds of hominid. The first stone tools were made by bipedal apes (Asfaw et al. 1999); and when a truly new kind of human (the earliest morphologically definable *Homo*, with a body build essentially like ours) did show up, at about 1.9 to 1.6 mya (Walker and Leakey 1993), it was not accompanied by a new kind of toolkit. Instead, the new hominids (belonging to the species *Homo ergaster*) made stone tools that were virtually indistinguishable from those their archaic precursors had already been making for the better part of a million years. Nor were these new creatures significantly foreshadowed morphologically in the fossil record. This suggests that the basically modern body form was achieved in a single event that also involved some reduction of the facial skeleton relative to the braincase into which it was hafted. Recent advances in molecular genetics (see review in DeSalle and Tattersall 2008) suggest that this event was plausibly due to a change in gene regulation with cascading developmental consequences throughout the body (see Plate 5).

Despite its insignificant initial impact on the lithic record, the appearance of the genus *Homo* (the radical new body form, which suggests on its own a radical shift in lifeways) does mark the beginning of a striking trend toward significantly increasing encephalization (Holloway et al. 2004). It is interesting to note, as I have mentioned, that we can trace the same trend occurring independently in at least three separate hominid lineages in different continents (Tattersall 2012): Africa (*Homo sapiens* and its antecedents); Europe (*Homo neanderthalensis* and its precursors); and Asia *(Homo erectus)*. This suggests that there is something specific to our genus (rather than to the modern human lineage within it) that has predisposed its members to (metabolically expensive) brain-size increase. It is possible that, in an apparently rare instance, the dynamic here may have been at least partially propelled by competition among groups of conspecifics that placed an ongoing selective premium on improved cognitive abilities. Whatever its exact nature, however, the novelty involved clearly underpinned modern human cognition without being its proximate cause, since only one of the lineages just mentioned achieved symbolic thought (see below). What is more, because of the sheer diversity of the (not very well-known) fossil species within the genus *Homo,* we cannot take average brain-size increases over time as prima facie evidence of a linear pattern of improvement. Instead, modern *Homo sapiens* appears simply as one more product of the hominid family's continuing experimentation with its underlying potential.

Perhaps most significantly, despite the odd possible straw in the wind, in the period prior to the emergence of *Homo sapiens,* there is nothing in the archaeological record that we can unequivocally interpret as a product of a symbolically reasoning mind. It has long been argued that such complex activities as shelter-building, or the manufacture of compound tools, can be taken as indicators of a modern mindset. But in reality, while many more recent technologies may indeed depend on chains of reasoning that can only be achieved through symbolic thought processes, Paleolithic industries prior to the emergence of *Homo sapiens* conspicuously lack technologies of this kind (Klein 2009). Even *Homo neanderthalensis,* a hominid just as encephalized as we are, showed evidence in its considerable technological and economic achievements only of what we may presume to have been a complex and sophisticated form of intuitive, nondeclarative intelligence, rather than a symbolic one (Tattersall 2012). And in the absence of the symbolic faculty, there is little reason to conclude that these relatives possessed a self-objectifying sense of self of the kind that modern humans display. It is worth repeating that, by the standards of other hominoids, and even of other hominids for which we have reasonably good records, the Neanderthals were clearly very sophisticated creatures in both technology and lifestyle. But while they may consequently have possessed an advanced form of self-awareness, it was almost certainly unlike ours.

The Origin of Modern Cognition

Significantly, even the earliest anatomically recognizable *Homo sapiens,* which show up in the African fossil record at under 200 thousand years ago (kya) (McDougall et al. 2005; White et al. 2005), left nothing that would lead us to suppose that they possessed the symbolic faculty. And it is not until under 100 kya that — also in Africa — we begin to pick up the earliest evidence firmly suggestive of the dawning of the symbolic spirit. This comes first in the form of marine snail shells pieced presumably for stringing into body ornaments (e.g., D'Errico et al. 2009), and thereafter in the form of overtly symbolic objects (Henshilwood et al. 2002, 2004). What's more, the full flowering of the modern sensibility is not documented in its complete richness before we have the extraordinary cave art of the European Upper Paleolithic, beginning around 40 kya (see Clottes 2008; Klein 2009; Pike et al. 2012). This late timing for the first appearance of overtly artistic activity in Europe is doubtless an artifact of an incomplete record; nonetheless, it helps us bracket the period during which the human symbolic spirit emerged. Little if any evidence exists for the workings of symbolic minds significantly before 100 kya; yet by ~40 kya such minds were magnificently expressing themselves (see Plates 6, 7, and 8).

As we have seen, a disconnection of the kind just described between anatomical and behavioral change is nothing new in the hominid record. Instead, it is something we might actually expect, given that the biological potential for any new behavior must obviously be in place before that behavior can be adopted. Most likely, the cerebral potential for symbolic thought was born exaptively in the major developmental reorganization that gave rise to *Homo sapiens* as a (highly) distinctive physical entity. It then lay fallow until the new cognitive style was finally expressed though the action of what was necessarily a cultural stimulus (see discussion in Tattersall 2012). Very likely, that stimulus was the invention of language, which we know can be spontaneously invented by humans possessing the biological wherewithal (e.g., Kegl et al. 1999).

Language is the most remarkable and undeniably ubiquitous of uniquely human behaviors, and, equally importantly, is virtually synonymous with symbolic thought. Not only do both language and our cognitive capacity depend on the creation of vocabularies of mental symbols, it is effectively impossible to imagine one in the absence of the other. And whether or not, as seems entirely possible, the greatest significance of language is as a portal to interior thought rather than as a medium of communication, it is also undeniably a communal, externalized attribute, and thus one likely to spread rapidly through a population already possessing the biological capacity to acquire it. This gives language a great advantage over such rival stimuli for cognitive modernity as multilevel theory of mind. For such qualities are internalized, and are thus presumably much less susceptible to cultural spread.

Just what biological attribute constituted the final biological keystone in the arc of symbolic cognition is not known, though speculations abound (see Lieberman 2007; Coolidge and Wynn 2009). But what *is* evident is that our unique way of processing information about the world was not gradually driven into existence over the eons by natural selection. We see no evidence in the archaeological record prior to the advent of *Homo sapiens* of the slow acquisition of the modern sensibility, element by element. That record is, of course, but a dim mirror of the full behavioral richness of any bygone hominids; nonetheless, it contains very little to support the gradualist picture. Renfrew (this volume) succinctly describes regular but incremental augmentation in the complexity of human society since the end of the last Ice Age. But it is significant that Renfrew's account of stepwise lifeway change in our species begins only with the achievement of behavioral modernity. What is more, the tempo of the change he depicts subsequent to the acquisition of symbolic thought processes is vastly accelerated compared to anything that went before.

Judged merely by the remarkable velocity of transformation in human life since the first African stirrings of symbolic behaviors (and particularly, as Renfrew points out, since the beginnings of sedentarism at the end of the last Ice Age), our modern cognitive style emerges as something considerably more than an incremental improvement on what preceded it. Evidently, our mode of reasoning is qualitatively unique. And the indications of an admittedly imperfect record are that the potential for this radically new cognitive mode, and for all of its behavioral sequelae, was acquired as a single package. What's more, that acquisition was very recent, having occurred *within* the tenure of our anatomically recognizable species, *Homo sapiens.*

This geometry of events places the origin of our symbolic cognition in the realm of emergence, whereby a fortuitous combination of elements gives rise to a whole new order of complexity. In our case, an addition or modification to a brain that had a long evolutionary history of accretion and modification over several hundred million years, produced a structure with an entirely new potential. That potential then had to be "discovered" by its possessor before it could be expressed. On one level, this process of discovery was more or less instantaneous, unleashing symbolic thought. But symbolic reasoning is so flexible a mental tool that the uses to which it can be put are legion; indeed, a mere glance at our neophilic technological and social proclivities today is enough to confirm that, after many tens of thousands of years, we are still in the process of energetically discovering what can be done with the potential we already have.

Two decades ago, Merlin Donald (1993) proposed that the process of assembling the modern human mind is still incomplete: that the history of human consciousness unfolded in a modular stepwise progression in which oral culture, then writing, then such modern contrivances as the Internet and social networking all acted — and continue to act — to fine-tune the human brain. To put this conclusion another way, as mediator between brain and culture, our cognitive system continues to refine itself and its supporting structures in an elaborate and ongoing feedback process. And there is certainly ample evidence that the human brain actively rewires itself — particularly but (significantly) not exclusively — during childhood development, as it is subjected to new stimuli. But while the human brain is without doubt an imperfect piece of engineering (see Marcus 2008), the prospects for its future biological enhancement seem dim in the light of current demographic trends (Tattersall 1995, 2012). Instead, the auguries are for continued rapid cultural change, as our species continues to actively explore the limits of the human cognitive potential.

The implications of this interpretation of modern human origins for the history of personhood are fairly evident. If I am correct in believing that personhood — at least in the sense in which we human beings individually experience it today — is necessarily based on the capacity for self-reflection, then human beings have possessed this quality only as long as their cognitive mode has allowed it. And the archaeological record seems to indicate that this means since a point, perhaps only about a hundred thousand years ago, that lay well within the tenure on earth of what we recognize anatomically as *Homo sapiens*. Renfrew (below in this volume) is generously disinclined to exclude the big-brained *Homo neanderthalensis* from personhood, based on the large brains and complex lifeways of members of this recently extinct species. And there is certainly an argument to be made for the inclusivity he advocates. The Neanderthals were without doubt cognitively and behaviorally complex creatures, with considerable technological achievements to their credit. But we also need to recognize that attributing personhood to them — or even to the very first anatomically modern humans, identical to us in appearance but not in behavior — probably involves broadening the definition of personhood to include a form of awareness of self that was probably distinctively unlike our own, and was certainly based on a different cognitive mode. Personhood is not something that we can arbitrarily attribute to another being; it is something that the other attributes to itself.

Conclusion

A history of the kind just briefly outlined makes it relatively easy, at least in principle, to explain the complexities and vagaries of human nature. This is because all of the products of those hundreds of millions of years of evolution — the fish brain, the reptile brain, the early mammal brain — are still there inside our skulls, merely overlain by a recently acquired veneer of reason that nonetheless changed all the rules. Our brains have *not* been exquisitely fashioned by evolution to an optimized state (which is, according to the evolutionary psychologists, only out of kilter with our prevailing self-manufactured circumstances because of extremely recent change). Instead, our brains are splendidly jury-rigged affairs, creative precisely because they have not been optimized to any particular function. Yes, we can indeed be supremely rational animals; but much of the time we are not, and we cannot always determine when we will be. This is why we are such demonstrably poor judges of risk, why the "human condition" is so hard to specify, and why even individuals are typically bundles of behavioral paradoxes.

In terms of human personhood, then, it seems hard to avoid the conclusion that the quest for the origin of the human sense of self-individuality is more or less synonymous with the search for the origin of the unique modern human symbolic cognitive mode. Even though they are biologically so clearly intimately connected to and integrated among the many millions of other species that make up the great tree of life, human beings really are *different* in a profound sense — and not just from their closest living relatives but also from their closest extinct ones. I have already pointed out that it is impossible for us to understand just how extinct hominids viewed and subjectively experienced the world; but that makes it all the more important that we should not fall prey to the temptation to view them as simply "less intelligent" versions of ourselves. We need to dignify them with their own identities, and to acknowledge that their ways of perceiving themselves and the world around them were almost certainly not ours. And that means also acknowledging that our own sense of identity, of personhood, is unique, and of astonishingly recent origin.

REFERENCES

Asfaw, B., T. White, O. Lovejoy, B. Latimer, S. Simpson, and G. Suwa. 1999. *Australopithecus garhi:* A new species of early hominid from Ethiopia. *Science* 284: 629-35.

Clottes, J. 2008. *Cave art.* London and New York: Phaidon.

Coolidge, F. L., and T. Wynn. 2009. *The rise of* Homo sapiens: *The evolution of modern thinking.* New York: Wiley-Blackwell.

DeSalle, R., and I. Tattersall. 2008. *Human origins: What bones and genomes tell us about ourselves.* College Station, TX: Texas A&M Press.

D'Errico, F., M. Vanhaeren, N. Barton, A. Bouzouggar, H. Mienis, D. Richter, J.-J. Hublin, S. P. McPherron, and P. Lozouet. 2009. Additional evidence on the use of personal ornaments in the Middle Paleolithic of North Africa. *Proceedings of the National Academy of Sciences USA* 106: 16051-56.

Donald, M. 1993. *Origins of the modern mind: Three stages in the evolution of culture and cognition.* Cambridge, MA: Harvard University Press.

Gallup, G. G. 1970. Chimpanzees: Self-recognition. *Science* 167: 86-87.

Henshilwood C., F. d'Errico, M. Vanhaeren, K. van Niekerk, and Z. Jacobs. 2004. Middle Stone Age shell beads from South Africa. *Science* 304: 404.

Henshilwood, C. S., F. d'Errico, R. Yates, Z. Jacobs, C. Tribolo, G. A. T. Duller, N. Mercier, and 4 others. 2002. Emergence of modern human behavior: Middle Stone Age engravings from South Africa. *Science* 295: 1278-80.

Holloway, R. L., D. C. Broadfield, and M. S. Yuan. 2004. *The human fossil record.* Vol. 4, *Brain endocasts: The paleoneurological evidence.* New York: John Wiley and Sons.

Kaminski, J., J. Call, and M. Tomasello. 2008. Chimpanzees know what others know, but not what they believe. *Cognition* 109: 224-34.

Kegl, J., A. Senghas, and M. Coppola. 1999. Creation through contact: Sign language emergence and sign language change in Nicaragua. In *Comparative grammatical change: The intersection of language acquisition, creole genesis, and diachronic syntax,* ed. M. deGraaf, 179-237. Cambridge, MA: MIT Press.

Klein, R. G. 2009. *The human career.* 3rd ed. Chicago: University of Chicago Press.

Lieberman, P. 2007. The evolution of human speech: Its anatomical and neural bases. *Current Anthropology* 48: 39-66.

Marcus, G. 2008. *Kluge: The haphazard evolution of the human mind.* New York: Houghton Mifflin.

Mayr, E. 1982. *The growth of biological thought.* Cambridge, MA: Harvard University Press.

McDougall, I., F. H. Brown, and J. G. Fleagle. 2005. Stratigraphic placement and age of modern humans from Kibish, Ethiopia. *Nature* 433: 733-36.

McPherron, S., Z. Alemseged, C. W. Marean, J. G. Wynne, D. Reed, D. Geraads, R. Bobe, and H. A. Béarat. 2010. Evidence for stone-tool-assisted consumption of animal tissues before 3.39 million years ago at Dikika, Ethiopia. *Nature* 466: 857-60.

Pike, A. W. G., D. L. Hoffmann, M. Garcia-Diez, P. B. Pettit, J. Alcolea, R. De Balbin, C. Gonzalez-Sainz, C. de las Heras, J. A. Lasheras, R. Montes, and J. Zilhao. 2012. U-series dating of Paleolithic art in 11 caves in Spain. *Science* 336: 1409-13.

Plotnick, J. M., F. B. M. de Waal, and D. Reiss. 2006. Self-recognition in an Asian elephant. *Proceedings of the National Academy of Sciences USA* 103: 17053-57.

Povinelli, D. J. 2004. Behind the ape's appearance: Escaping anthropocentrism in the study of other minds. *Daedalus* 133, no. 1: 29-41.

Reiss, D., and L. Marino. 2001. Mirror self-recognition in the bottlenose dolphin: A case of cognitive convergence. *Proceedings of the National Academy of Sciences USA* 98: 5937-42.

Tattersall, I. 1995. *The fossil trail: How we know what we think we know about human evolution.* New York: Oxford University Press.

———. 2000. Once we were not alone. *Scientific American* 282, no. 1: 56-62.

———. 2008. An evolutionary framework for the acquisition of symbolic cognition by *Homo sapiens. Comparative Cognition and Behavior Reviews* 3: 99-114.

———. 2009. *The fossil trail: How we know what we think we know about human evolution.* 2nd ed. New York: Oxford University Press.

———. 2012. *Masters of the planet: The search for our human origins.* New York: Palgrave Macmillan.

Tomasello, M., J. Call, and B. Hare. 2003. Chimpanzees understand psychological states — the question is which ones and to what extent. *TRENDS in Cognitive Sciences* 7: 153-56.

Walker, A., and R. E. F. Leakey, eds. 1993. *The Nariokotome* Homo erectus *skeleton.* Cambridge, MA: Harvard University Press

White, T. D., B. Asfaw, D. DeGusta, H. Gilbert, G. D. Richards, G. Suwa, and F. C. Howell. 2003. Pleistocene *Homo sapiens* from Middle Awash, Ethiopia. *Nature* 423: 742-47.

Personhood: Toward a Gradualist Approach

Colin Renfrew

The wonder of the newborn is enacted in each one of us at the moment of our birth, and in each new child who comes into the world. This tiny baby will soon see and cry and then smile, soon respond and demand, will soon grow and learn, walk and talk, act and react, and develop into a person to whom the full range of opportunities involved in being human is available. That is the wonderful phenomenon we see with the birth of each new human individual. This is the emergence of personhood in the ontogenetic sense.

So how, in the perspective of deep time, did this come about? Ten million years ago there were no humans on earth. There were multitudes of living species, including the great apes from which our hominin ancestors evolved. Over those ten million years, as paleontological research has established, a succession of ancestral species, including *Australopithecus* and *Homo erectus*, developed, culminating (from our perspective) in the emergence of our own species, *Homo sapiens*, apparently in Africa, more than 100,000 years ago. The out-of-Africa diaspora of *Homo sapiens* seems to have started about 60,000 years ago. These were hunter-gatherers, already equipped with quite an elaborate material culture. Some ten thousand years ago, transitions toward a new agricultural economy can be seen in the communities living in different parts of the world, accompanied by a move toward sedentarism. Out of these sedentary communities emerged the first literate societies and the first cities, five or six thousand years ago. This is the phylogenetic story of our species, concisely summarized.

So where, along this narrative line, does one situate the emergence —

or doubtless, in reality, the multiple emergences — of personhood? Where and how did those qualities emerge that we recognize as those of sentient persons, of people imbued with the qualities that we recognize as inherently human? Each of the contributors of chapters to this volume approaches this question from a different perspective. Mine is that of a prehistoric archaeologist seeking to understand the human story on the basis of the material remains that have come down to us from the human past. It is a story that is becoming clear in outline (Clark 1961; Childe 1936; Stringer 2011; Renfrew 2007; Malafouris, 2013).

Personhood in Other Species?

A first issue is one of species. In an everyday sense we may speak of "persons" as "people," and we might restrict the use of that term to members of our own species, *Homo sapiens*. But the wider implications of such definitions should not escape us. Eighteenth-century formulations of the rights of man were strong on statements of equality, countering the views of colonial administrators (today perceived as racist) who sometimes denied the status of personhood to the indigenous human inhabitants of some regions of the earth. Or they were content to assign to personhood degrees of ranking: "separate but equal," for instance, was for a time thought to be a justification for racial segregation. The inherited ranking implicit in the caste system of India raises comparable questions. And though I am myself a monarchist in the context of British politics, it is difficult to avoid recognizing some inconsistency with egalitarian principles in the concept of inherited rank. The ethical implications of a concept such as personhood cannot be avoided. The equanimity of Greek and Roman philosophers in a social system dependent on slavery is impressive.

So it is worth examining the logic by which we might deny the status of personhood to other animals, especially some mammals, that we may certainly recognize as individuals. Anyone who has kept a dog as a pet has enjoyed a relationship that can, for some dog owners, be an important one, one whose emotional strength is demonstrated by the owner's grief when the dog dies (and sometimes, conversely, by evidence of the dog's adverse reaction at the death of the owner). The philosopher John Searle has written of his dog Ludwig (named in honor of Wittgenstein) in affectionate terms, and was inclined to accord to him consciousness and awareness.

This opens for consideration the possibility of granting to Ludwig the status of "personhood." The Roman emperor Caligula allegedly planned to appoint his horse Incitatus to the rank of consul. The portrait by George Stubbs, painted in 1762, of the Marquess of Rockingham's racehorse Whistlejacket is one of the masterpieces of the National Gallery in London. The example of strong interspecies relationships, which in the human partner can evoke feelings or sentiments as strong as those felt for other persons, usefully highlights the problem of defining the inherent qualities of personhood. These aspects of personhood are not simply intellectual but clearly involve emotional responses and individual qualities.

That this is so may be exemplified by the notion of encountering an "alien" being from outer space. The possibility of contact with intelligent life elsewhere in the universe is taken seriously in some quarters, and of course has already been anticipated in fiction and in film. What would be the criteria for ascribing personhood to such a creature? The extraterrestrial being in the 1982 film *E.T.*, directed by Stephen Spielberg, was allegedly first created by the director as an imaginary friend after his parents' divorce in 1960. The personhood of E.T. was central to the film. That did not seem particularly paradoxical at the time, and this suggests that the concept should not automatically be restricted to our own species. Moreover, the respect increasingly accorded to chimpanzees and bonobos in the light of more systematic studies of their behavior in the wild (Goodall 1986) has led recently to moves to grant them some legal status. Whether or not it would be meaningful to regard such individuals as persons, it is widely felt that they should be respected as intelligent and sentient beings.

Ritual and Play

Various forms of play are seen among other animal species, including games of flight, pursuit, and retrieval (Burghardt 2005). These indeed form one further basis for the empathetic behavior that a human individual can share with "man's best friend." The "companionship" that can develop between a dog and its owner, based on daily walks together, often supplemented by games of fetch and carry, makes it easy for many people to regard a household pet as possessing many of the qualities of a person, and to name him or her accordingly. The speech act of naming, of bestowing a personal name, is a significant one, and it can be reinforced by the recognition and seeming acceptance of the name by the animal that answers to it.

Ritual behavior is another field of activity that, on closer inspection, may serve to blur somewhat the exclusively human character of personhood. Some behavioral patterns among animals and birds, repeated formulaically, are commonly termed "ritual," seen particularly when two individuals are engaged in mating behavior, termed "courtship." It would be difficult to formulate an effective definition for ritual behavior that would exclude such activities among other (i.e., nonhuman) species.

This point is particularly relevant when we consider our nearest hominin cousins, the Neanderthals. Indeed, their status as potential humans themselves seems to shift with anthropological fashion. Sometimes classified as *Homo neanderthalensis,* sometimes as *Homo sapiens neanderthalensis,* they were capable of breeding with *Homo sapiens,* recent DNA research suggests, thus fulfilling one of the prime criteria for conspecifics. The point was made very effectively on the cover of *Time* magazine of April 30, 2001 ("Meet your ancestor"), where a Neanderthal man of 35,000 years ago comes face to face with a man of today. There is evidence that they carried out rituals of burial for their dead (J. Renfrew 2009). It is difficult now to say what a "modern" human in the Europe of 40,000 years ago would make of a personal encounter with a Neanderthal, but the offspring from such a union would have been unlikely to question the "personhood" of either parent.

Music and song are observed among various species ("Thou wast not born for death, immortal bird"), and a propensity for music has been seen as a special feature of *The Singing Neanderthals* (Mithen 2005). A case can certainly be made for personhood in some non–*Homo sapiens* species, notably Neanderthalers.

Criteria for Personhood

It is inevitable perhaps that if one is seeking to define personhood, one should look first to the definition of what it is to be human. In a taxonomic sense, the question is already answered by the paleoanthropologist who chooses to include (or exclude) the Neanderthals from the species *Homo sapiens,* or to include *Homo erectus* within the genus *Homo.* But these are mere classifications, whose implications we cannot directly experience, since all other hominin species are today extinct.

So many things are wrapped up in our concept of humankind. In Act III, Scene I, of *The Merchant of Venice,* Shakespeare puts the issue this way, in words in the mouth of the merchant of Venice that can be applied to all of humankind:

[Have we not] hands, organs, dimensions, senses, affections, passions, fed with the same food, hurt with the same weapons, subject to the same diseases, heal'd by the same means, warm'd and cool'd by the same winter and summer. . . ? If you prick us, do we not bleed? If you tickle us, do we not laugh? If you poison us, do we not die? And if you wrong us, shall we not revenge? If we are like you in the rest, we will resemble you in that.

Shakespeare arouses our sympathy for the merchant by allowing us to empathize with him as a fellow human being. The feeling that "we are all in this together" is predominant: that the human condition is a shared condition. There is in this commonality of feeling a moral dimension, so that the mention of "wrong" does not strike a discordant note, but resonates with the other observations.

Personal Identity

To be a person seems to also carry with it the implication that one is a unique individual. The first component of personhood must be the recognition of the individual. This implies that there is in the life of a person a continuity of being, and furthermore that only one individual can be that person. (Identical twins may seem to present a paradox, but it is a paradox open to resolution because they can readily be distinguished by those who know them well.) We expect to be able to distinguish individuals one from another. But at the same time, such recognition of individuals is only a necessary condition for personhood, not a sufficient one. Some species of birds take a single mate for life and yet are separated from that mate for long periods, returning to reunite the following year. They can certainly recognize their partner and perhaps other individuals also, and clearly they organize their lives on that basis. But we would probably not be inclined to accord "personhood" to birds, however faithful in their personal relations.

It seems implicit also in the notion of personhood that there are indeed other persons, similar to us and to others in many ways, as Shakespeare described, yet different, too, in the distinguishing traits of the individual. All of this implies that personhood is not a solitary condition: it implies the existence of others. The human condition implies also that there are men, women, and children, and it may seem natural for us to view them all as persons. However, there is evidence to suggest that some past societies did not regard very young children as persons. On the other hand, some religious faiths would set the inception of personhood at conception rather than (as in most contemporary legal frameworks) at birth.

All in all, the criteria for personhood seem difficult to separate from those for being human. The emergence of personhood in the phylogenetic sense initially considered might then be equated with the emergence of humankind. That story has been the subject of intensive archaeological research in recent years. It has sometimes been called "the human revolution."

The Human Revolution

Before Sapiens Speciation (before 200,000 BP)

We should not forget that, before this "human revolution" of about 200-150,000 years ago, our hominin ancestors had achieved many things. They already had the bipedal gait, which made running easy and freed up the hands for skillful use (see Plate 9). They had evolved the prehensile grip appropriate for tool manufacture. They had, over more than two million years, practiced the manufacture of tools, including the "handaxes," which are the widespread artifact-type fossil — at least in Africa, Europe, and western Asia — of *Homo erectus.* The evidence is that they had already developed cooperative hunting skills: this hominin was already a social animal.

It was this ancestral species, evolving, it seems, in Africa and achieving its own out-of-Africa dispersal as early as 1.8 million years ago, as attested by finds at Dmanisi in Georgia. In Europe and western Asia, our cousins the Neanderthals subsequently developed this shared ancestry: they survived until well after 40,000 years ago in Europe before encountering our own species on its arrival in Europe. The Neanderthals later died out. And long before the evolution of *Homo sapiens,* these hominins had developed the use of fire. These are the presapient ancestors to whom, by apparently common consent, we today deny the status of "personhood." That should perhaps give cause for reflection, but it seems to be the unanimous view of the contributors to this book, and it is shared today by most archaeologists.

The Speciation Phase (200,000 to 60,000 BP)

The human revolution is now the subject of a vast literature. Initially the focus was on what I would call the *speciation phase:* that is, the emergence of

Homo sapiens from our earlier ancestors in Africa. The conclusion of the speciation phase may be set with the out-of-Africa dispersals of human populations of about 60,000 years ago (see below). Its beginnings are more difficult
to define, but may perhaps be set some 200,000 to 150,000 years earlier. This
has been dealt with by a number of writers (Mellars 1991; Stringer 2011; Tattersall, this volume). A couple of decades ago it was still possible to discuss
whether this process of speciation took place in Europe, or in western Asia,
or in Africa, or indeed — with the acceptance of some version of "multilinear
evolution" — in all of these.

It was the development of DNA analysis, applied to a wide range of
living humans, using first mitochondrial DNA and then Y-chromosome analysis, that led to the firm conclusion that the key aspects of human speciation
took place in Africa during the two hundred thousand years or so prior to
about 60,000 BP. Early DNA studies, applied to fossilized remains of Neanderthal hominins, clarified that these should not be regarded as ancestral to
our own species, but cousins, with a common ancestry in Africa some half a
million years ago. The early DNA analyses also indicated the African origins
of all living humans, that they were the product of a series of population
expansions from Africa from about 60,000 years ago.

These were cooperative hunters, and they now made artefacts of bone,
antler, and ivory, which also testifies to a skill in making clothing from animal skins. There was an increased tempo of technological change, and there
emerged an increased degree of regional diversification in material culture.
It is clear, for example, that these humans now buried their dead, often in
caves or rock shelters (Pettitt 2011). And by the time the speciation phase was
accomplished, they were, for the first time, making personal adornments,
notably shell beads, such as those seen in the Blombos Cave in South Africa,
that is, by 70,000 years ago (Henshilwood 2009). It is at this time also that
we see the first production of rhythmic patterning seen incised on objects
of red ochre, patterning that we could well term "decorative" (Renfrew and
Morley 2009, pl. IV).

The Dispersal Phase (60,000 to 12,000 BP)

The dispersal phase of our species seems relatively clear-cut. It begins with
the dispersal from Africa of the ancestors of all living humans (who include,
of course, those whose progenitors remained in Africa), around 60,000
years ago. The mapping of this process, using DNA from living human

societies, was established first using mitochondrial DNA (Forster 2004) and has been followed through by Y-chromosome analysis (Underhill et al. 2000; Renfrew et al. 2000). These humans are the "anatomically modern humans" of recent anthropological literature. It seems that there may have been somewhat earlier dispersals out of Africa of such anatomically modern humans, since their fossilized remains have been found at sites like Qafzeh and Skhul in Israel, dating to about 125,000 years ago. But they had no apparent survivors.

These DNA studies map out the relatively rapid human dispersals along the south coasts of Asia, reaching Australia as early as 50,000 years ago (Hadjuashov et al. 2007). Our species reached Europe rather later, only about 40,000 years ago, where they encountered the Neanderthals, their hominin cousins, the descendants of earlier out-of-Africa dispersals. That picture has been amplified — and complicated somewhat — by the recognition through ancient DNA studies of another hominin lineage, distinct both from the Neanderthals and *Homo sapiens* — called the Denisovans (Gibbons 2009) and identified via fossil remains found at Denisova in Siberia that date to some 40,000 years ago. It is clear that all these — Neanderthals, Denisovans, and sapient humans — were in their different ways capable of surviving in the cold climate of Siberia of 40,000 years ago; yet only our *Homo sapiens* ancestors have living descendants today.

The movement of the human population of the Americas across the Bering Straits seems to have taken place very much later, apparently after the Late Glacial Maximum cold period (about 26,000 to 20,000 years). As we shall see, this phase of early human dispersals may be said to have ended about 12,000 years ago, before the onset of neothermal conditions. By this time, most of the surface of the globe had been peopled, with only the majority of the Pacific Islands remaining uninhabited until the development of agriculture.

These were cooperative hunters and fishers, and the human diaspora is marked by their adaptation to a wide range of environments, to each of which they adapted their material culture. The increased tempo of technological change seen in the late speciation phase was maintained, and there was the increased degree of regional diversification in material culture. One of these adaptations, at least in some regions, was the development of seafaring.

The production of personal adornments, particularly beads, often of shell, heralded by the finds in Africa (e.g., Blombos) toward the end of the speciation phase, was now widely seen across the globe (well studied for

Upper Palaeolithic Europe by Vanhaeren and D'Errico 2006). But it seems strange that rock art did not really come into its own at a worldwide level until after the dispersal phase, after 12,000 years ago.

There was one regional "creative explosion" (Pfeiffer 1999) of great interest. This was the profusion of cave art in the Upper Paleolithic of France and Spain (and to a lesser extent in Italy), accompanied by the production of small human sculptures ("Venus figurines") across much of Europe and into Siberia. It is clear that cave art and rock art began also in Australia during the dispersal phase, and there are indications in other regions of the world as well, but the real global explosion of rock art, for instance in Africa, seems to have taken place after 12,000 BP (Bahn 2007). It is a popular misconception that cave art was a widespread phenomenon globally prior to 12,000 BP, during what we have termed the dispersal phase, in the Upper Paleolithic period. The "creative explosion" seen in the painted caves of France and Spain was a distinctly regional phenomenon. It was also a long-lasting one in that region, over some 20,000 years, but it faded away with little discernible aftermath, before the end of the dispersal phase.

The Sapient Paradox

This narrative of the origins and early development of the human species accounts well for the global distribution of our species, for the distribution of the human genotype. But it does not say much about human behavior. These resilient people were, as we have seen, cooperative hunter-gatherers who were capable of producing a variety of stone tools and who adapted well to a wide range of environments in different parts of the world. There was a striking regional diversification in their material culture. These sapient humans frequently buried their dead in a range of different circumstances. They often made personal adornments, which offer a rare and important clue to their own self-image. However, with the exception of the Franco-Cantabrian painted caves, like those at Grotte Chauvet or Lascaux or Altamira, there is little to excite the amazement of the outside observer at the achievements of this now widely dispersed species.

We shall come in a moment to the achievements of what may be called the *tectonic phase,* whose inceptions began at different dates in different parts of the world, but whose first beginnings may be set around 12,000 BP. It is clear that the genetic makeup of the human species was effectively established by well before this date of 12,000 BP. The humans of that time were not very different genetically from those of 50,000 years earlier, the time of the initial out-of-Africa dispersals of our species.

So here is the sapient paradox. What took so long? If our species was established perhaps by 100,000 BP in Africa and certainly by 60,000 BP, why did the new behaviors, which we associate with the tectonic phase and which led within a few thousand years to the rise of civilization and of literacy, take so long to emerge? It is a problem that has not yet been clearly answered and is overlooked by most existing accounts of the "human revolution."

The Tectonic Phase (from about 12,000 BP)

We have noted the new aspects of human behavior that emerged by the end of the sapient phase and were a general feature of the dispersal phase. These were summarized by Mellars (1991) and included changes in the production, techniques, and variety of stone tools; the use of artifacts of bone, antler, and ivory; an increase in the tempo of change and of regional diversification; and the early use of personal adornments — all of these together amounting to what Mellars regarded as significant cognitive changes. Others, such as Gamble (2007), have emphasized the significant changes in human behavior that must have accompanied these developments. Yet it remains fair to say that the developments seen in the succeeding early tectonic phase are rather more obvious.

It is in the tectonic phase that the first permanent houses are seen. Soon village communities were formed, the excavated fragmentary structures of which we can enter today (see Plates 10 and 11). The emergence of these permanent settled communities was accompanied in many parts of the world by the development of agriculture, with the exploitation of a wide range of domestic species: millet and rice in China, wheat and barley in western Asia and Europe, maize in Central America. In some areas, domesticated livestock had important roles, while in coastal Peru the abundant resources of the sea were crucial. The stability of permanent settlement and of the permanent occupation of the land implied new concepts of property and of ownership. They also gave scope for the development of new crafts and skills, notably in woodworking and weaving, and particularly in the field of pyrotechnology. Pottery was soon produced in most village communities, and later the skills of metallurgy developed, emphasizing the importance of procurement and thus of systematic trade.

A notable feature of the early tectonic phase is the development and construction of the first places of congregation. In some cases significant numbers of persons were needed for their construction as well as for the assembly. Early examples are offered by Göbekli Tepe in East Turkey (Schmidt 2007), by Caral and comparable sites in coastal Peru (Shady Solis et al. 2001), by the early stone structures of Malta (Evans 1971), and (at a rather later date) by Stonehenge in England (Cunliffe and Renfrew 1997). These were places of assembly, and thus presumably of pilgrimage. On a smaller scale there are also sometimes "shrines" associated with ritual practices relating to the dead. In some areas, for instance in neolithic Europe, there are also monumental structures often regarded as tombs (since they do often contain inhumation burials), but increasingly these are seen as places of ritual and assembly for local populations rather than as primarily funerary structures.

Many of these societies seem to have been relatively "egalitarian," in that they give little evidence for the spectacular accumulation of heritable wealth. And although there are various indications of what one may term ritual practices, there is little clear evidence for religion, if religion is defined as the worship or veneration of specific transcendent and immortal deities. These make their appearance in a subsequent phase (see below).

Later Social Processes (after 5000 BP)

In this discussion we shall avoid the generally later processes associated with the development of cities and the formation of state societies. These have their interest, and they must have transformed the circumstances of personal existence, and hence the nature of "personhood." But in most regions of the world the emergence of social stratification and of the state came several millennia after the inception of the tectonic phase, described above, and many millennia after the dispersal phase. If we wish to assess whether there was a "quantum leap" associated with the emergence of personhood, it is not necessary to look so late, since few would assert that humans of the early tectonic phase lacked the quality of personhood.

It is worth remarking, however, that it is often with the emergence of state societies that the first evidence is found for institutionalized religion, where that term is intended to mean the worship of transcendent deities. The iconography of the pantheon of ancient Egypt becomes explicit in the Early Dynastic period, shortly before 3000 BCE and cannot be identified in the earlier Predynastic period. The deities of Sumer and Akkad can perhaps be traced back to the Uruk period of Mesopotamia around 4000 BCE, but not as early as Göbekli Tepe or Jericho or Çatalhöyük. The fearsome presence of the *lanzon* at Chavín de Huantar in Peru (Burger 1992), whose divine status would not be questioned lightly, is some two thousand years later than early Caral. This may carry interesting implications for discussions about personhood and for the potential relationship sometimes claimed for its relationship to the divine.

Situating the Emergence of Personhood

So where, in this trajectory of development, along the three phases into which the "human revolution" can be divided, can we place the emergence of personhood? Certainly it is not easy to identify a "quantum leap" in the narrative offered above; instead, it may seem more appropriate to adopt a gradualist approach.

Questions of Language

So far in this discussion, I have said little about the use of language. But linguistic communication certainly seems an important component of personhood. For while one is aware of people who are mute, and whom we would certainly regard as persons, the converse is not so simple. Can one imagine holding a meaningful conversation with another living being — and not consider that being to be a person? This does, of course, bring the discussion close to issues of artificial intelligence, and it is already possible to have informative conversation with clever machines, just as it is not difficult to be defeated at chess by a computer. This leads — appropriately in the centenary year of the birth of Alan Turing (French 2012) — to ask whether it is conceivable that a machine could ever be considered a person. But that issue, like the possible personhood of extraterrestrial beings, lies outside the scope of this historical review.

The ability to talk, to understand, and to be understood is an important component of personhood. But in the longer view, it is very difficult, on the basis of the archaeological record, to locate with any precision the early origins of language. Most archaeologists would agree that those humans who participated in the out-of-Africa expansion of our species (about 60,000 years ago) shared a language capacity comparable to that of living humans today. But whether this capacity evolved gradually and continually over several million years, as some would argue (Hurford 2012), or whether it developed more rapidly in an evolutionary leap of the kind envisaged by Gould (Gould and Eldredge 1977 [discussion of punctuated equilibrium]; Borwick 2012) remains at present a matter for speculation. Such evidence as remains is in the material record (discussed above), though the increasing study of ancient DNA may yet have much more to reveal.

From the perspective developed here, it could be argued that the development of "humankind," associated with the emergence of *Homo sapiens,* is heavily involved with the development of the formidable linguistic capacity seen in today's descendants of all those human communities that participated in the out-of-Africa dispersal of our species some 60,000 years ago (as well as today's descendants of those who remained in Africa). It seems very plausible to correlate this sophisticated linguistic capacity with the symbolic practice documented by the use of the first shell beads at the outset of the Upper Paleolithic, and with the beginnings of decorative patterning as documented at the Blombos Cave (Henshilwood 2009; Vanhaeren and D'Errico 2006). Of course, the development of the linguistic capacities must have had deeper beginnings, but many scholars today might choose to situate their culmination with the emergence of *Homo sapiens* in Africa more than 100,000 years ago.

Personhood, however, may be another matter, with a focus on individuality and on forms of social behavior (including fidelity and affection) whose origins can be placed much earlier. We see aspects of these qualities already in some other species, as noted above. And we find them to a considerable degree among the great apes of today, especially the bonobos (Goodall 1986). So where in the trajectory outlined earlier might one place the emergence of "personhood"? Answering this question systematically would require a more formal and more thorough definition of personhood than I have attempted here, recognizing perhaps a polythetic definition that requires the fulfillment only of several of the criteria noted rather than the complete set.

A crucial test that will clearly emerge is whether we can imagine that a creature could be described as a person, with the attributes of personhood, who did not have that capacity for speech that we recognize in living humans. Those observers who insist that individuals possessing personhood must have that full symbolic and communicative facility that has been ascribed to *Homo sapiens* are effectively making the definitional decision that only humans can be persons. The discussion thus becomes tautologous: personhood equates with the defining qualities of *Homo sapiens,* of which

63

full speech capacity is the primary criterion. If, on the other hand, we can conceive of other species, including hominins now extinct, as possessing the quality of personhood, the question remains open.

It is not difficult to imagine a hominin predecessor possessing many of the defining qualities: *Homo habilis* perhaps, or *Homo erectus,* or an early contemporary, *Homo neandertalensis.* These could include individuality, fidelity, and affection for a life partner and for siblings as well as the possession of personal skills (e.g., a facility in tool-making) as well as communicative skills of the kind seen in other species (e.g., dolphins or bonobos). These would clearly be social animals, those who share a specific material culture and might possess special skills, such as the use of fire. While lacking developed syntactic language skills, they would probably be capable of answering to a vocal name and of assigning such names to conspecifics.

We can recognize that many of these qualities form the behavior and material traces of *Homo erectus,* and more perhaps from those of the Neanderthals. It would appear that to deny the quality of personhood to such hominins, just as to aliens from outer space (such as the fictional character E.T.), would be equivalent to the arbitrary decision to restrict the appellation to members of the species *Homo sapiens.*

Problems with the Soul

It may be worth referring at this point to one aspect of the Abrahamic religions as they developed in western Eurasia during the first millennium BCE. They are often interpreted as ascribing to each person the possession of an immortal soul, believed to continue to exist in some form after the death of the individual person. I was impressed at a Templeton discussion meeting devoted to the theme "Becoming Human" and focusing on the Upper Paleolithic period of Europe (Renfrew and Morley 2009) how the notion of the soul was not discussed with much vigor by the two invited discussants who participated, both of whom were speaking from a Christian perspective. It is easy to see why. If we follow the trajectory of development discussed above as a background for our discussion of personhood, the specific point of emergence of fully developed human beings is a key feature of the story, even if the position of its emergence along that trajectory of development is not easy to situate. From such a perspective it seems a reasonable question to ask just when the soul makes its first appearance in the evolutionary story. Yet to choose a specific moment in that long trajectory of development in response to this question would seem very difficult. It is not my intention here to trivialize the issue by referring to it so briefly. This is, however, a difficulty that may need to be addressed. Many theologians might be expected to take the view that "persons" have souls, and particularly that, in order to have a soul, it is a prior condition that one should be a person. That line of thought may represent a greater problem for a believer than it does for an agnostic. It underlies some of the discussions that resulted in the present volume, though the issue was not systematically addressed.

The Expansion of Personhood

The emergence of humankind from our earlier ancestral predecessors, as seemingly documented in the archaeological record, may better be conceived of, not as a "quantum leap," but instead from a gradualist standpoint. This would seem more readily supported by the archaeological data. The various components (or defining elements) of humankind that come together in the development of *Homo sapiens* were probably acquired by our ancestors at different times along the shared developmental trajectory. Perhaps, then, the notion of "personhood" should not automatically be associated exclusively with sapient humanity.

A further line of thought would lead us on to argue that personhood is a state of being that continues to develop at the present time with developing modes of communication and perhaps increasing degrees of communal awareness. It could certainly be argued that some aspects of personhood can develop fully only with the invention of writing, and with those special forms of self-reflection that only the use of writing makes possible: "Hypocrite lecteur, mon semblable, mon frère," as Baudelaire disconcertingly observed. Much of mathematics would not be possible without a written notation, and the same is true of several other sophisticated forms of thought. Epic narrative, like lyric poetry, did emerge in different cultural traditions before the local inception of literacy, but their continuing survival does depend upon that literacy. The developments of poetry, of drama, and especially of the novel have allowed new explorations and expressions of the person as never before. In such ways personhood in the sense of undergoing and communicating an enriching personal life experience continues to develop today. It is difficult to discern any quantum leap along the trajectory of development.

REFERENCES

Bahn, P. 2007. The earliest imagery around the globe. In *Image and imagination,* ed. C. Renfrew and I. Morley, 3-16. Cambridge: McDonald Institute.

Borwick, R. C. 2012. Me Tarzan, you Jane: Review of Hurford, *The Origins of Grammar. Science* 336: 158.

Burger, R. 1992. *Chavín and the origins of Andean civilisation.* New York: Thames and Hudson.

Burghardt, G. 2005. *The genesis of animal play.* Cambridge, MA: MIT Press.

Byrne, R. (contribution to this volume). The dividing line: What sets humans apart from our closest relatives?

Childe, V. G. 1936. *Man makes himself.* London: Watts.

Clark, J. G. D. 1961, *World prehistory, an Outline.* Cambridge: Cambridge University Press.

Cunliffe, B., and C. Renfrew, eds. 1997. *Science and Stonehenge.* London: British Academy.

Evans, J. D. 1971. *Prehistoric antiquities of the Maltese Islands.* London: Athlone Press.

Forster, P. 2004. Ice ages and the mitochondrial DNA chronology of human dispersals: A review. *Philosophical Transactions of the Royal Academy of London, Series B* 359: 255-64.

French, R. M. 2012. Dusting off the Turing test. *Science* 336: 164-65.

Gamble, C. 2007. *Origins and revolutions: Human identity in earliest prehistory.* Cambridge: Cambridge University Press.

Gibbons, A. 2009. Who were the Denisovans? *Science* 333: 1084-87.

Goodall, J. 1986. *The chimpanzees of Gombe: Patterns of behavior.* Boston: Belknap Press of Harvard University Press.

Gould, S. J., and N. Eldredge. 1977. Punctuated evolution, the tempo and mode of evolution reconsidered. *Paleobiology* 3, no. 2: 115-51.

Henshilwood, C. 2009. The origins of symbolism, spirituality and shamans: Exploring Middle Stone Age material in South Africa. In *Becoming human: Innovation in prehistoric material and spiritual culture,* ed. C. Renfrew and I. Morley, 29-49. Cambridge: Cambridge University Press.

Hudjashov, G., T. Kivisild, P. A. Underhill, et al. 2007. Revealing the prehistoric settlement of Australia by Y chromosome and mtDNA analysis. *Proceedings of the National Academy of Sciences of the USA* 104: 8726-30.

Hurford, J. R. 2012. *The origins of grammar, language in the light of evolution.* Oxford: Oxford University Press.

Malafouris, L. 2013. *How things shape the mind: Outline of a theory of material engagement.* Boston, MA: MIT Press.

Mellars, P. M. 1991. Cognitive changes and the emergence of modern humans in Europe. *Cambridge Archaeological Journal* 1: 63-76.

———. 2006. Why did modern human populations disperse from Africa ca. 60,000 years ago? A new model. *Proceedings of the Academy of Sciences of the USA* 103: 9831-36.

Mithen, S. J. 2005. *The singing Neanderthals: The origins of music, language, mind and body.* London: Weidenfeld and Nicolson.

Pettitt, P. 2011. *The Palaeolithic origins of human burial.* London: Routledge.

Pfeiffer, J. 1999. *The creative explosion: An inquiry into the origins of art and religion.* New York: Harper and Row.

Renfrew, C. 2007. *Prehistory, the making of the human mind.* London: Weidenfeld and Nicolson.

Renfrew, C., P. Forster, and M. Hurles. 2000. The past within us. *Nature Genetics* 26: 253-54.

Renfrew, C., and I. Morley, eds. 2009. *Becoming human: Innovation in prehistoric material and spiritual culture.* Cambridge: Cambridge University Press.

Renfrew, J. 2009. Neanderthal symbolic behavior. In *Becoming human: Innovation in prehistoric material and spiritual culture,* ed. C. Renfrew and I. Morley, 50-60. Cambridge: Cambridge University Press.

Schmidt, K. 2007. Die Steinkreise und die Reliefs des Göbekli Tepe. In *Badisches Landesmuseum: Die ältesten Monumente der Menschheit,* 83-85. Stuttgart: Konrad Theiss Verlag.

Shady Solis, R., J. Haas, and W. Creamer. 2001. Dating Caral, a preceramic site in the Supe valley of the central coast of Peru. *Science* 292: 723-26.

Stringer, C. 2011. *The origins of our species.* London: Allen Lane.

Tattersall, I. (contribution to this volume). Human evolution: Personhood and emergence.

Underhill, P. A., P. Shen, A. A. Lin, and L. Jin et al. 2000. Y-chromosome sequence variation and the history of human populations. *Nature Genetics* 26: 358-61.

Vanhaeren, M., and F. D'Errico. 2006. Aurignacian ethno-linguistic geography of Europe revealed by personal adornments. *Journal of Archaeological Science* 33: 1105-28.

Emergence of Personhood: Lessons from Self and Identity

Roy F. Baumeister

Within the context of the known universe, the human person is a unique being. How did this come to be? Some theological views may regard that as a process of divine intervention and creation of a human being endowed with distinctive traits. Scientific theories based on evolution must struggle to explain how standard, widespread causal processes can produce a novel and unique product. This chapter seeks to explain the emergence of the human person, and in particular the idiosyncratically powerful human versions of selfhood and identity, as adaptations to the requirements of social and cultural systems.

In a nutshell, humans share with all living things the constraints of natural selection. These reward and promote effective strategies for surviving and reproducing. What sets humans apart is the relatively novel and distinctive way that humans deal with those perennial problems. Culture, defined as a novel form of social life based on accumulating shared information (knowledge), systems of cooperation that use division of labor, and systems of economic trade, is the human species' strategy for solving the problems of survival and reproduction (Baumeister 2005). Human selfhood and identity, and indeed human personhood per se, can be understood as adaptations (or side effects of adaptations) that make culture possible.

The question posed to the contributors to this intellectual enterprise was whether the emergence of human personhood was a "quantum leap." Put another way, was there a highly unusual and discontinuous process that produced personhood, or was it merely the result of gradual, accumulating developments? In biological evolution, as in psychology generally, most phenomena exist on a continuum, and changes are gradual. Yet human selfhood and personhood are radically different from what has been observed elsewhere in nature. What might have produced such a radical discontinuity?

The contributors to this volume come from a dauntingly diverse array of expertise. My own background is in social psychology, with special emphasis in research on self and identity. Therefore, I shall use the emergence of self and identity as a suggestive guide to understanding the emergence of personhood per se. Self and identity share with personhood the facts of unity, singularity, differentiation from others, and specificity — plus possibly additional features. The challenge and purpose of this chapter, therefore, are to understand the emergence of selfhood and identity, as guides to illuminate the emergence of human personhood.

Body and Self

As with personhood, the possession of a distinct physical body is an important basis. Although a person and a self may consist of more than a physical body, they do not exist without one. Nor does any self (or person) have multiple bodies. A particular self, like a particular person, thus exists in isomorphic relationship to a particular physical body. But plainly it consists of plenty more than that. In my chapter I undertake to explain how the additional aspects emerge.

The human self thus starts with a biological fact, namely the organismic unity of the human animal. But it advances beyond that. The identity of an adult human is not just the specific reference to a particular body. It includes reputation, social security (or other national tax identification) number, membership in specific groups, credentials (e.g., educational degrees earned), accumulated career achievements, transient and negotiable (and renegotiable) memberships in various relationships to persons (e.g., marriage) and institutions (e.g., employment), and much more. The unity and integrity of the single human body are a start, but only a start, toward understanding the self. They do not make much of a self without all the other stuff.

Brain and Self

It is tempting to think that the self must be located somewhere in the brain. Indeed, the challenge of identifying just exactly where in the brain the self is located has attracted the attention of assorted brain laboratories. However, they have failed to settle on any single place. This has led some brain researchers to conclude that the self is an illusion (e.g., Metzinger 2009).

The self is real. But it is not in the brain. But the inability to localize it to a particular brain site or process is quite important. The brain may be the central controlling unit of the human body, but the brain itself does not have a central controlling unit. Instead, it seems organized on the basis of multiple sites and systems that operate in parallel and interact in mysterious, complicated ways.

To understand the self, therefore, it is essential to grasp how this collection of semi-independent, parallel parts and systems manages to produce a being that acts as a unity. The brain *operates* the self rather than containing it.

Solitary Selves?

The brain apparently does not need a "self" — or, indeed, any kind of central controlling unit. This is highly revealing. The brain doesn't need the self for its workings. It can function just fine without having a definite one. But when the body has to deal with other persons, suddenly selves become important, if not indispensable.

Indeed, I suggest that the need for self will prove elusive as long as conceptual arguments and research are focused on single beings (e.g., "the" brain). More broadly, it is instructive to consider how little a solitary creature would need any kind of self. A solitary being would not have much use for a name, address, job title, or other designation. Ownership would have no meaning or utility for it. It would have no reputation to build or protect. Moral responsibility, and hence moral agency, would be minimal. Self-knowledge would be sketchy at best, insofar as much self-knowledge comes by way of interactions with other people. (Moreover, a solitary being would not have language, so its knowledge of self could not be articulated in symbolic form.) Public self-consciousness, defined as awareness of how one is viewed by others, would be nonexistent. A solitary being would presumably have likes and dislikes and other opinions, but it would not know them as "my" opinions because there is no other source of opinions. Instead, it would probably regard the goodness and badness of external things as properties of those things rather than as opinions held by the self (so, again, the self would not seem to have content). The solitary being would have the same innate capacity for self-regulation that other, similar beings have, but it would not have most of the usual uses for it, such as for adjusting oneself to accommodate group norms and rules, to meet people's expectations, or to restrain one's impulses out of consideration for others.

Thus, the selfhood of a thoroughly solitary being would be quite limited. There might be a vague sense of bodily unity (as distinct from the physical environment), perhaps some awareness of feelings and capabilities, and some executive function. But most of what we know as a self would not exist without social interaction. The implication of this line of argument is that selves are needed more for social life than for the interior functioning of the brain and psyche. To understand the self, therefore, we must look outside the person and brain — at the social environment. In a sense, a human infant is not born with anything but the most rudimentary self. It acquires the self by means of socialization and by becoming part of a social group.

Context: Human Beings as Cultural Animals

Most discussions of the ultimate roots of human behavior and experience soon end up invoking either nature or culture, or both. For many theorists, this becomes an issue of deciding how to apportion causality between nature and culture. My own research, however, has led me to a more integrative approach. Rather than seeing nature and culture as alien — indeed somewhat opposing or independent — forces, I have come to understand *culture itself to be a biological strategy*. That is, the problem of sustaining life (by survival and reproduction) confronts all living things. Humans have developed a highly unusual strategy for solving that problem. Specifically, humans communicate and develop troves of shared information, perform tasks using group systems with interlocking sets of complementary roles, exchange goods and services to mutual benefit, and train newcomers to function within their systems. In a word, culture is how human beings deal with the challenges of survival and reproduction (Baumeister 2005).

Measured in terms of survival and reproduction, nature's harsh criteria for biological success, culture has been a remarkably successful strategy. While most mammals have seen their populations remain stagnant or decline, the human population has ballooned from a few small groups 200,000 years ago toward a predicted nine billion by the middle of this century. Moreover, unlike all other animals, humans have managed to triple their average life expectancy by dint of their research, health care, and public behavior (e.g., etiquette). Culture has pushed humankind ahead of other species. If anything, the biggest danger to the totality of life is the overweening superiority of humankind, which will overpopulate the planet, deplete its resources, crowd out the niches of most other mammals, and degrade the potential for mutually coexisting survival.

One might expect that such a successful strategy as culture would be used by many species, but it has not. Most other species use culture only slightly or not at all. The reason is presumably that most animals do not have the advanced psychological capabilities needed in order to create and sustain culture and make it work for them. For example, cooking is beneficial insofar as it improves the quality and caloric yield of food. Digesting raw food is an energy-intensive process, and the net caloric yield is small. Cooking food reduces the amount of energy lost in digestion, so the caloric yield is much greater. Cooked food is also healthier than raw food, because the cooking process kills some pathogens. Yet humankind is the only species that cooks its food. Many other animals seem to enjoy cooked food if humans cook it for them, but they are unable to figure out how to cook on their own. The reason is that cooking requires the accumulation of information from multiple sources, and animals do not share information like that. A single human, starting from scratch, would not get very far in developing cooking either; but by aggregating the results of many individuals' experiments with cooking, human cultures have been able to create healthy and satisfying ways to prepare food that are without any parallel at all in the rest of nature.

Cooking is thus a microcosm of the development of culture. A solitary mammal could not possibly develop the knowledge of how to cook; only by aggregating the sometimes painful experiments of many individuals can a reliable procedure of cooking be created. A social group that pools knowledge garnered from many individual experiences is thus a strong prerequisite for the development of cooking. Solitary and even social animals cannot do this. Only cultural animals can pool their learning to enable collective progress. Only cultural animals can invent cooking and reap its powerful benefits. Only humans resorted to this kind of collective pooling of information to adapt to their environment.

The broader point is that the unique features of human personhood likely reflect the evolution of traits suitable to maintain culture. By the theory of natural selection, traits flourish when the creatures possessing them survive and reproduce better than others. Among humans, the strategy for surviving and reproducing is essentially a matter of participating in culture, which means contributing to and benefiting from a social system based on shared information, performing complementary roles, and the like. No other species seems to have resorted to culture as its primary biological strategy. Therefore, human personhood emerges from our collective and individually competing efforts to participate in culture.

Hence my working assumption has come to be that most of the distinctively human traits are either *adaptations for culture* or the side effects of those adaptations (Baumeister 2005). When we seek to explain something that is unique (or nearly so) to humans, the place to start looking for explanations is in the requirements of highly complex, information-based social systems. How do animals change so as to be able to use these systems?

In this chapter I focus primarily on the emergence of human selfhood. However, it is intended as a powerful and central instance of the broader move toward personhood. As far as we can tell, no other being — mammal or other, animal or plant, living versus inanimate — has a self comparable to the human self. Selfhood is a crucial part of personhood. Therefore, the emergence of selfhood is potentially a powerful guide to understanding the emergence of human personhood.

Roots of Human Uniqueness

What makes us human? Many traits differentiate humans from the majority of animals (and certainly from most inanimate objects), but comparisons to the closest biological relatives (e.g., bonobos) yield severely fewer differences. The quest for the traits that define human uniqueness is thus a formidable and profound challenge.

The challenge to explain human uniqueness can be either formidably daunting or easy, depending on how one construes it. Human beings are animals and primates, and as such we undeniably possess all of the predispositions and preferences that are common to other primates: we want to eat and sleep, to have good sex and care for our offspring, to be safe, to prolong life, to get along with others, and so forth. Yet how we go about reaching those goals is unique. We constantly participate in culture, have meaningful identities defined by the collective institutions, earn respect by accumulated achievements, build reputations by moral and ethical actions, and the like.

The human project is thus tied up in how we participate in culture. Like other mammals, we seek to survive and reproduce by bolstering our standing in the social group. Unlike them, we use meaningful definitions to establish reputations, justify our actions, contribute to collective decision-making, and accumulate symbolic resources (e.g., a bank account) based on our aggregated rewards from culturally validated efforts.

Self, Identity, and Social Network

Identity can be understood as a position in the social network. It consists of roles, reputation, and other designations. Crucially, it is defined only in relation to others. The term "identity" is based on continuity and differentiation (Baumeister 1986). For example, an identification number, card, or bracelet signifies who one is, in contrast to others, and that designation remains stable across time, unless specific circumstances dictate some change (e.g., when someone leaves a job or graduates from an institution, whereupon the card is forfeited). Identity designates who you are in contrast to others. Identity is thus not inside the person but in the social matrix. The broader term "self" is typically used to refer to properties of the specific person, but these, too, mainly have meaning in contrast to others. For example, ownership of possessions entails that those things belong to one particular self and are thus not to be used by other selves without permission.

We can understand self as encompassing identity as well as subjective experience and physical body. The self is thus the combination of the inner and outer aspects: the subjectively aware animal and the node in the social network. Another way of putting this is that the self exists at the interface between the animal body and the cultural system. The self thus functions to connect the body (including its drives, needs, and vulnerabilities) to the social group (including its information and systems).

Each human being is in part a body existing in a physical environment. But it also exists in a social environment characterized by conceptual understandings that are shared by many people. In particular, each person's social group holds a concept of him or her. Crucially — and like it or not — the person's outcomes depend to a substantial degree on the evaluative content of that concept. Hence the person has ample reason to be concerned with his or her reputation and to exert him*self* or her*self* to keep it favorable. To put it another way, there is a concept (in other people's minds) with your name on it, and it behooves you to exert yourself so that that concept remains favorable. Your future outcomes will be better insofar as other people respect you and regard you favorably.

Social Basis of Self

Therefore, the human self is not present at birth nor even programmed to emerge in development. Rather, it comes into being in interaction with the social environment. Each baby is born as a full-fledged animal, but it only becomes a person by acquiring an identity from society. Subjectivity is not a property in the mind but is only recognized (and indeed only becomes meaningfully real) in distinction to others.

At a recent panel discussion at the New York Academy of Sciences, the moderator asked the group whether one first learns one's own self or the selves of others. The answer, I contended, is neither: the crucial step is learning that there is a distinction, such as that there are other minds with perspectives and knowledge that differ from one's own (Paulson et al. 2011). Thus the conceptual separation of self and other marks the beginning of knowing both. Communication is based on this, insofar as the essence of communication is information known by the sender and not, initially, by the receiver.

This learning of different perspectives is a vital and basic part of human development. In fact, I think it is the one thing the human mind is specifically designed for. The human mind and body are strongly and basically designed for communication. The vocal apparatus and the hearing apparatus are unique to humans, with the result that only humans can talk. The grammatically competent brain is another distinctively human trait; other animals who can learn words mostly cannot string them together, using grammar and syntax to create different meanings, as almost all humans do starting in early childhood. Although humans name their species *Homo sapiens* in honor of intelligence, the discovery of Australopithecus proved that upright posture preceded — and very possibly helped bring about — the expansion of brain size in evolution. Upright posture was in some views most likely an evolutionary advance that freed the hands for communication by gesture. (Other hypotheses link upright posture to raising the head to see farther and freeing the hands for making tools and carrying things.) Once humans began sharing information, the availability of increasing amounts of information would have created an environment that selected for brains that could process and store it. Thus, what set the evolution of humanity on its distinctive pathway was communication. Communicating led to the rise in intelligence.

Likewise, the self as point of reference or grammatical unit exists only as distinguished from others. As noted above, ownership is only meaningful on the basis of distinguishing the owner from others who might want to use the item. One can even argue that free will (in the sense of the distinctively human style of action control) only comes into being within the context of a culture. Insofar as free will involves using meaningful reasons (such as morality and planning) to guide one's actions — and these are learned from a culture — they only fully exist within a culture that sustains collective understanding of meaning.

The Role of Consciousness

Consciousness can be regarded as an adaptation for communication. Most theories of consciousness struggle with the question of what benefit there is from having thoughts in the mind be conscious. After all, unconscious thoughts can cause behavior, so why would nature go to the trouble of making them conscious? But consciousness serves communication. All talking is conscious, and people also need consciousness to understand other people's speech beyond single words (see Baumeister and Masicampo 2010; see also Baars 1997, 2002). The unconscious can process single words but not sentences.

   Consciousness does, however, have another function that facilitates the emergence of selfhood. Consciousness facilitates the integration of information scattered across different sites in the brain and mind, which is one reason why conflicting impulses for actions involving skeletomuscular movements invariably become conscious (Morsella 2005). If a stimulus from the environment went straight to one site in the brain, which produced a behavioral response (as happens with a reflex), consciousness might not be involved, nor would there be any need to invoke the self to explain such an automatic response. By contrast, if the person mentally rehearses the action before performing it, the mental simulation can elicit input from a wide assortment of relevant sites in the brain and mind that may contain helpful and relevant information. Such an action would thus be regarded as an expression of the full self. No doubt this is why premeditation figures prominently in moral and legal judgment: a premeditated action can be assumed to reflect the full person, acting as a moral agent. The function of consciousness in conducting these mental simulations is thus instrumental in enabling the self to emerge (Baumeister and Masicampo 2010).

The Role of Meaning

The most ambitious and far-reaching dimension of my analysis is probably the assertion of meaning as a causally efficacious but nonphysical reality (Baumeister 1991, 2008). At the conference from which this volume emerged, I aggressively asserted the (nonphysical) reality of meaning. Perhaps predictably, some attendees strongly concurred and affirmed this position, while others skeptically insisted that the only realities were physical realities.

The reality of meaning is partly dramatized by my heuristic characterization of the Whorf-Sapir hypothesis as the "wrongest idea in all the social sciences" (e.g., Baumeister 2008). Whorf and Sapir proposed that language determines thought. Because all languages are different, people in one culture think radically differently from people in other cultures (e.g., Whorf 1956). Carried to an extreme, it would be almost impossible under this hypothesis for members of one culture to fully understand the experiences and beliefs of members of different cultures.

In order to characterize the Whorf-Sapir hypothesis as the "wrongest idea" in all of social science, it is necessary to go beyond characterizing their hypothesis as wrong. To be sure, the evidentiary bases for their claims have all been discredited (e.g., Brown 1991); but that merely classifies their theory among the large set of discredited theories. What makes them wronger than other wrong theories? The extraordinary wrongness of the Whorf-Sapir theory is that the truly important and profound insight into human nature is contained precisely in the opposite of their claims. Instead of asserting that all thoughts are specific to a language and cultural context, it seems more correct to conclude that almost all thoughts can be expressed in almost all languages. The effectiveness of translation: almost every sentence or idea can be translated from one language into any other. I invite my fellow social scientists and philosophers to contemplate the profound implications of that fact.

One implication is that there is *one single universe of ideas.* With scattered exceptions, every language is based on that set of ideas. The seemingly extensive differences between ideas — I fully concede and appreciate that a fluent speaker of one language may be at a total loss in understanding a different language — arise simply because different languages use different sounds to express the same ideas. "Linguistic lacuna," a technical term of linguists, refers to the circumstance that a particular language lacks a specific term for a concept that is well articulated in other languages. The existence of such a designation reveals the assumption that there is a single, universal set of ideas, and each language expresses it. The universal set of ideas is the basis for language. It is thus a nonphysical reality that all human cultures have capitalized on, in order to accumulate shared knowledge, which is the foundation of culture.

In my view, a decisive step in human evolution — indeed, part and parcel of the emergence of personhood — was the appreciation and use of meaning. The capacity to express meaning in language is not unique to humans, but the de facto and extensive use of it is. As Pinker (1994) observed, a select few members of other species can be taught to use language in a limited sense, but they do so reluctantly and only under the influence of humans (see also Byrne's contribution to this volume). By contrast, humans are eager to use language to express, communicate, and develop thoughts. Pinker contrasts the grudging use of sign language among chimpanzees, who can master the signals (when mandated by human experimenters) to get what they need, to the astonishingly eager reception of sign language by deaf humans. When sign language was introduced to schools for the deaf, the children not only embraced it with alacrity but also quickly refined and improved it. The human mind, unlike the nonhuman ape mind, is strongly motivated to take up language to express, construct, and communicate thoughts.

It would be nice to think that meaning is ultimately just a physical event. It is not. I think in the English language, but the English language is not a feature of my brain processes, because if my brain processes ceased to exist (e.g., if I were killed), the English language would remain unchanged. Language and many other social realities are independent of any specific brain.

The central assumption is as follows. The distinctively human traits are adaptations for culture (Baumeister 2005). The evolved purpose and function of the human brain are to facilitate participation in the cultural group. In other words, the human brain evolved to pick up and tap into the information and systems that its group has. It evolved not so much to contain ideas but to acquire them from its social environment. Meaning is inherent in that common universe of ideas that forms the basis for all languages. Essentially, by working together in groups, humans have been able to learn how to use meaning for their benefit.

The implications for human personhood are profound. Each human is undeniably a biological entity. He or she is an animal with needs, wants, fears, vulnerabilities, and the like; he or she suffers pain and disease, rejoices with pleasure when his or her desires are satisfied, and seeks out food, safety, shelter, and the rest. But he or she also accesses the world of meanings, and so he or she has a concept of self, respects symbolic implications, communicates, cultivates a good reputation, and in extreme cases will risk or even sacrifice his or her life in defense of cultural values and other symbolic notions.

In one vivid example, in 2011 a young Tunisian man set himself aflame and burned to death as a way of expressing a symbolic protest against the oppressive regime that left too few opportunities for young people like himself. Such an act of self-immolation as symbolic protest would be unthinkable in any other species, and I am confident that no such act has ever been observed by animal researchers. It had profound impact: it was the beginning of the so-called "Arab spring" of mass protests and uprisings that overturned autocratic governments in multiple countries throughout the Middle East.

Elsewhere I have proposed that one viable theory of free will is the incorporation of meaning into the causation of action (Baumeister, forthcoming). Insofar as meaning is not inherently a physical reality — rather, it is something that physical beings represent and process — then its intrusion into the causal chain represents freedom from purely naturalistic, physical causation. Put more simply, basing action on meaning entails rising above purely physical causality and thus achieves a kind of freedom from purely physical causality.

The Nonphysical Reality of Meaning

My argument could be valid if one rejects the metaphysical reality of meaning, but it gains power if one accepts it. Accordingly, I recognize that this section will be extreme and controversial. The rest of the argument could stand without it; so I hope that readers who reject this portion of the argument will not reject all my discussion. But it all works better and more smoothly insofar as one accepts this (admittedly controversial) argument.

The gist is that human personhood is a blend of biology and meaning. Moreover, meaning is not, in the final analysis, a physical fact. I have come to think that meaning resides at least partly in the universe of concepts that forms the basis for all languages (see above). Human beings are physical animals who reached a level of sophistication that enabled them to use the universe of concepts to inform and improve their interactions.

Saying the word "table" is a physical event that involves emitting sound waves from the mouth that have a distinctive, recognizable physical sound. The link between that event and an actual physical table is not a physical reality. The link between that mutually understood sound and the physical entity (the table) brings one beyond purely physical causality. Physical entities evolved to the point at which they could represent and alter behavior based on nonphysical, immaterial realities, such as ideas, values, laws, norms, and the like. The emergence of the human person was intricately intertwined with the emergence of the biological capacity to direct behavior based on these nonphysical, immaterial realities (including, at the extreme, religious beliefs in supernatural deities and immaterial souls).

Asserting the reality of meaning is scientifically much less compromising than asserting the existence of souls, gods, and related factors. In my view, the universe of ideas was out there waiting for discovery, not entirely unlike how underground petroleum deposits lie in wait for people to develop an understanding of how to access and exploit them. At some point, human groups began to use the common universe of ideas to structure their social interactions and collective decisions, and this proved to be highly advantageous. Hominid groups that declined to use these methods lost out in competition with groups who embraced them and made effective use of them. Today's human population is thus descended from ancestors who figured out how to use the universe of possible ideas to facilitate communication, accumulate knowledge, and foster group action.

Returning to the rigorous constraints of natural selection, then, it is reasonable to speculate that hominid groups who incorporated the single universe of ideas into their social interactions outperformed the groups who did not. The emergence of the human person was thus a profoundly new integration of nature and culture, of physical reality and the immaterial reality of meanings. To be sure, a physical entity (in our case, a complex brain) is needed in order to use and process meanings. Probably meanings are best used not even by single brains but rather by brains that share assumptions and understandings with other brains, communicated by physical bodies. However, the physical systems that use meaning are not the same as the meaning itself, any more than the physical table is physically connected to the physically real sound waves in the spoken word "table." In other words, I readily concede that human animals process meaning physically. However, that processing is based on the independent reality of meaning, which is not a result of physical processes.

In that light, we may return to the questions of self and identity. Are they physical facts, or are they realities that consist in part of nonphysical realities, such as meaning? Is the identity of each person fully contained in his or her chemical and molecular structure, or is it rather a matter of conceptual reality as a node in a (nonphysical) conceptual framework based on shared understandings and abstract construals? I find the former untenable and the latter compelling. The human person is a blend of physical structures and cultural meanings.

The Jobs of the Self

What is the self for? I have said it exists at the interface between the animal body and the cultural society. Its tasks and functions are found there. At a basic level, facilitating survival and reproduction are the ultimate functions of all psychological processes. Humans survive and reproduce by means of participating in the cultural group. Therefore, being accepted by the social group is vital. The self is designed to seek meaningful social acceptance by others. Put another way, one of the self's basic functions is to induce other people to regard it as good.

There are several ways in which the self can be regarded as good, and these create the important motivational features of the self. The first — and arguably most basic — is to be liked, because liking promotes acceptance by social groups. Liking is a matter of getting other people to *feel* that you are good. The self will therefore adapt, change, and act so as to induce at least some other people to like it.

Being respected is a more complex form of being regarded as good (than being liked). Respect involves thinking more than feeling: others must *think* that you are good. This is normally based on performance of one's roles within the social system. Performance is evaluated on two dimensions: competence and morality. Therefore, one can take almost any role in society — parent, plumber, president, prostitute, porter, pundit, pilot, policeman, professor, painter — and evaluate how any given person performs it on those two dimensions. First, is the person moral, in the sense of being honest, reliable, trustworthy, and ethical in other respects? Second, is the person competent, in the sense of performing the tasks successfully? A person whose role performance lacks competence or morality is less likely to be kept on in that role than someone who is recognized as being good in both those respects. Hence the self learns to perform so as to earn respect — according to both dimensions. The self seeks to be validated by the social group as competent and as ethical.

Thus, the overarching job of the self is to secure social acceptance and the rewards that come with it. This is accomplished by being good. In human groups, being good means being liked and respected by others. Being respected means being regarded as competent and ethical.

The grander question of human free will is also relevant and implicated here. The integration of meaning into the causation of action is one viable definition of free will (Baumeister, forthcoming). Human beings are animals who have evolved to the point where they can incorporate consideration of immaterial, nonphysical realities, such as morality and complex rationality, into the causation of their acts. Such causal processes qualify as freedom insofar as the process of physical events is partly determined by nonphysical realities. The human person is thus a profound blend of nature and culture, or of physical and biological facts with immaterial, meaningful realities.

Conclusion

I have sought in this chapter to emphasize the social and cultural basis of selfhood and, by extension, of personhood. A human animal does not qualify as a person without self and identity. Moreover, self and identity are not contained in the physical reality of the human brain or body but rather link the individual physical entity to the social and cultural network. The unity and continuity of self are not built into the brain but rather are requirements of the social system. The central challenge for understanding the emergence of selfhood is to explain how parallel, distributed processes in the human brain and mind converge so as to create a being who acts as a responsible group member and moral agent and in other respects as a continuous, unified entity.

The human person is a mixture of physical entities (such as a body) and symbols (such as a name and reputation). Human physical bodies evolved to be able to work together in groups to use meaning to improve their collective lives. In the process, they created the human person.

REFERENCES

Baars, B. J. 1997. *In the theater of consciousness: The workspace of the mind.* New York: Oxford University Press.

———. 2002. The conscious access hypothesis: Origins and recent evidence. *Trends in Cognitive Science* 6: 47–52.

Baumeister, R. F. 1986. *Identity: Cultural change and the struggle for self.* New York: Oxford University Press.

————. 1991. *Meanings of life.* New York: Guilford Press.

————. 2005. *The cultural animal: Human nature, meaning, and social life.* New York: Oxford University Press.

————. 2008. Social reality and the hole in determinism. *Journal of Consumer Psychology* 18: 34-38.

————. (forthcoming). Constructing a scientific theory of free will. In *New directions in free will theory,* ed. W. Sinnott-Amstrong. Publisher to be determined.

Baumeister, R. F., and E. J. Masicampo. 2010. Conscious thought is for facilitating social and cultural interactions: How mental simulations serve the animal-culture interface. *Psychological Review* 117: 945-71.

Brown, D. E. 1991. *Human universals.* New York: McGraw-Hill.

Byrne, R. (contribution to this volume). The dividing line: What sets humans apart from our closest relatives?

Metzinger, T. 2009. *The ego tunnel: The science of mind and the myth of the self.* New York: Basic Books.

Morsella, E. 2005. The function of phenomenal states: Supramodular interaction theory. *Psychological Review* 112: 1000-1021.

Paulson, S., O. Flanagan, P. Bloom, and R. Baumeister. 2011. Quid pro quo: The ecology of the self. *Annals of the New York Academy of Sciences* 1234: 29-43.

Pinker, S. 1994. *The language instinct.* New York: HarperCollins.

Whorf, B. 1956. *Language, thought, and reality.* New York: Wiley.

Section Two

Morality and Personhood

Francisco J. Ayala

> *I fully subscribe to the judgment of those writers who maintain that of all the differences between man and the lower animals the moral sense or conscience is by far the most important.*
>
> CHARLES DARWIN (1871, 67)

The question whether ethical behavior is biologically determined may refer either to the *capacity* for ethics (i.e., the proclivity to judge human actions as either right or wrong), or to the moral *norms* accepted by human beings for guiding their actions. I propose: (1) that the capacity for ethics is a necessary attribute of human nature and thus an outcome of biological evolution; and (2) that moral norms are products of cultural evolution, not of biological evolution. Ethical behavior came about in evolution not because it is adaptive in itself, but as a necessary consequence of humans' eminent intellectual abilities, which are an attribute directly promoted by natural selection. That is, morality evolved as an exaptation, not as an adaptation.

Introduction

Humans are animals and have evolved from ancestors that were not human. But our "bodily frame," as well as the capacities that stem from it, show also that we are a unique kind of animal, a unique kind of ape, with distinctive features, of which the moral sense is one.

87

Two conspicuous human anatomical traits are erect posture and large brain. We are the only vertebrate species with a bipedal gait and erect posture; birds are bipedal, but their backbone stands horizontal rather than vertical (penguins are a trivial exception) and the bipedalism of kangaroos lacks erect posture and is drastically different from our own. Erect posture and bipedal gait entail morphological changes in the backbone, hipbone, feet, and other parts. Brain size in mammals is generally proportional to body size. Relative to body mass, humans have the largest brain. The chimpanzee brain has an approximate volume of 300 cubic centimeters (cc); a gorilla's is slightly larger. The human adult brain is more than three times larger, typically between 1300 cc and 1400 cc. The brain is not only larger in humans than in apes, but also much more complex. The cerebral cortex, where the higher cognitive functions are processed, is in humans, when compared to apes, proportionally much greater than the rest of the brain.

Erect posture and large brain are not the only anatomical features that distinguish us from nonhuman primates, even if they may be the most obvious. Other notable anatomical differences include the reduction of the size of the jaws and teeth and the remodeling of the face; reduction of body hair and changes in the skin and skin glands; modification of the vocal tract and larynx, with important implications for spoken language; opposing thumbs that allow precise manipulation of objects; and cryptic ovulation, which may have been associated with the evolution of the nuclear family, consisting of one mother and one father with their children.

Humans are notably different from the apes and all other animals in anatomy, but also — and no less importantly — in their functional capacities and behavior, both as individuals and socially. Most fundamental are the advanced intellectual faculties, which allow humans to categorize (to see individual objects as members of general classes); abstract thinking and forming images of realities that are not present (and thus anticipation of future events and planning future actions); and reasoning. Additional distinctive functional features are self-awareness and awareness of death; symbolic (creative) language; tool-making and technology; complex and extremely variable forms of cooperation and social organization; legal codes and political institutions; science, literature, and art; ethics and religion.

Humans live in groups that are socially organized; so do other primates, but their societies do not approach the complexity of human social organization. A distinctive human social trait is culture, which may be understood here as the set of human activities and creations that are not strictly biological. Culture in this sense includes social and political institutions, ways of doing things, religious and ethical traditions, language, common sense and scientific knowledge, art and literature, technology, and, in general, all the creations of the human mind. The advent of culture has brought with it cultural evolution, a superorganic mode of adaptation superimposed on the organic mode, which has, in the last few millennia, become the dominant mode of human evolution. Cultural evolution has come about because of cultural change and inheritance, a distinctively human mode of achieving adaptation to the environment and transmitting it through the generations.

Morality

I will define moral behavior for the present purposes as the actions of a person who takes into account in a sympathetic way the impact her actions have on others. A similar definition is advanced by David Copp in *The Oxford Handbook of Ethical Theory* (2006): "[W]e can take a person's moral beliefs to be the beliefs she has about how to live her life when she takes into account in a sympathetic way the impact of her life and decisions on others" (vol. 2, p. 4).

"Altruism" may be defined in a similar way as, for example, in the *Merriam Webster's Collegiate Dictionary* (10th ed., 1994): "unselfish regard for or devotion to the welfare of others." But altruism is usually taken to imply some cost to the altruist for the benefit of others. Moreover, "altruism" is also often attributed to the behavior of social insects and other animals, where no intentionality is involved — rather, it comes about as a result of genetically determined behaviors. A second definition of altruism in the *Webster's Collegiate Dictionary* is: "behavior by an animal that is not beneficial to or may be harmful to itself but that benefits others of its species." This is biological altruism, or altruism$_b$, in contrast to moral altruism, or altruism$_m$.

I will use the term "ethical behavior" as a synonym for "moral behavior," and "morality" and "ethics" as synonyms of each other — except when I explicitly note or it is contextually obvious that they are used with a somewhat different meaning. Actions that may be thought to be evil or sinful in some moral systems, such as masturbation or eating pork, will not be included in my use of "morality" so long as the actions have no consequences for others.

People have moral values: that is, they accept standards according to which their conduct is judged either right or wrong, good or evil. The particular norms by which moral actions are judged vary to some extent from individual to individual, and from culture to culture (though some norms, such as the prohibition of killing and stealing, and the mandate to honor one's parents, are widespread and perhaps universal), but value judgments concerning human behavior are passed in all cultures. This universality raises two related questions: whether the moral sense is part of human nature, one more dimension of our biological makeup; and whether ethical values may be products of biological evolution, rather than emerging from religious and other cultural traditions.

There are many theories concerned with the rational grounds for morality, such as deductive theories that seek to discover the axioms or fundamental principles that determine what is morally correct on the basis of direct moral intuition; or theories like logical positivism or existentialism, which negate rational foundations of morality, reducing moral principles to emotional decisions or to other irrational grounds. After the publication of Darwin's theory of evolution by natural selection, several philosophers, as well as some biologists, attempted to find in the evolutionary process the justification for moral behavior.

Aristotle and other philosophers of classical Greece and Rome, as well as many other philosophers through the centuries, held that humans hold moral values by nature. A human is not only *Homo sapiens,* but also *Homo moralis.* But biological evolution brings about two important issues: timing and causation.

We do not attribute ethical behavior to animals (not to all animals, certainly, and not to the same extent as to humans, in any case). Therefore, evolution raises distinctive questions about the origins and tenets of moral behavior. Is the moral sense determined by biological evolution? If so, when did ethical behavior come about in human evolution? Did modern humans have an ethical sense from the beginning? Did Neanderthals hold moral values? What about our ancestral species, *Homo erectus* and *Homo habilis?* And how did the moral sense evolve? Was it directly promoted by natural selection? Or did it come about as a byproduct of some other attribute (such as rationality, for example) that was the direct target of selection? Alternatively, is the moral sense an outcome of cultural evolution rather than of biological evolution?

Darwin and the Moral Sense

Two years after returning from his five-year trip in the HMS *Beagle* (1826-1831), Darwin gathered contemporaneous literature on human moral behavior, including such works as William Paley's *The Principles of Moral and Political Philosophy* (1785), which Darwin had encountered while he was a student at the University of Cambridge, and the multivolume *Illustrations of Political Economy,* by Harriet Martineau, published closer to his own time (1832-1834). These two philosophers, like other philosophers of the time, maintained that morality was a conventional attribute of humankind rather than a naturally determined human attribute. And they used an argument often exploited in our day: the diversity of moral codes.

The proliferation of ethnographic voyages had brought to light the great variety of moral customs and rules. This diversity is something Darwin had noticed when comparing the English norms to those of South American Indians and other native populations elsewhere. But this apparent dispersion had not distracted him. He would eventually develop a more complex and subtle theory of the moral sense than those contemporaneous authors: it was a theory that, implicitly at least, recognized moral behavior as a biologically determined human universal but with culturally evolved differences. For Darwin, the ethnographic diversity of moral customs and rules came about as an adaptive response to the environmental and historical conditions, unique in every different place, without necessarily implying that morality was an acquired, rather than natural, human trait.

A variable adaptive response could very well derive from some fundamental capacity, a common substrate, unique for the whole human race, but capable of becoming expressed in diverse directions. Darwin did not attribute the universality of morality to supernatural origin; rather, he saw it as a product of evolution by natural selection. The presence of a universal and common foundation, endowing humans with an ethical capacity, was for Darwin compatible with different cultures manifesting different stages of moral evolution and with different sets of moral norms.

Darwin belongs to an intellectual tradition, originating in the Scottish Enlightenment of the eighteenth and nineteenth centuries, that used the moral sense as a behavior that, largely based on sympathy (or "empathy," in modern terms), leads human ethical choice. In his account of the evolution of cooperative behavior, Darwin declares that an animal with well-defined social instincts — like parental and filial affections — "would inevitably acquire a moral sense or conscience, as soon as its intellectual powers had become as well developed, or nearly as well developed, as in man" (1871, 68-69). This is a hypothetical issue, because no other animal has ever reached the level of human mental faculties, language included. But this is an important statement because Darwin is affirming that the moral sense, or conscience, is a necessary consequence of high intellectual powers, such as exist in modern humans. Therefore, if our intelligence is an outcome of natural selection, so would be the moral sense. Darwin's statement further implies that the moral sense is not by itself directly conscripted by natural selection, but only indirectly as a consequence of high intellectual powers.

Darwin also says that, even if some other animal could achieve a human-equivalent degree of development of its intellectual faculties, we should not conclude that it would also acquire exactly the same moral sense as ours: "I do not wish to maintain that any strictly social animal, if its intellectual faculties were to become as active and as highly developed as in man, would acquire the same moral sense as ours. . . . [T]hey might have a sense of right and wrong, though led by it to follow widely different lines of conduct" (1871, 70). According to Darwin, having a moral sense does not by itself determine what the moral norms would be: which sorts of actions might be sanctioned by the norms and which ones would be condemned.

This distinction between moral sense and moral norms is important. Indeed, it is a distinction central to my thesis here. Much of the historical controversy, particularly between scientists and philosophers, as to whether the moral sense is or is not biologically determined has arisen because of a failure to make that distinction. Scientists often affirm that morality is a human biological attribute because they are thinking of the predisposition to pass moral judgment — that is, to judge some actions as good and others as evil. Some philosophers argue that morality is not biologically determined but instead comes from cultural traditions or from religious beliefs; this is because they are thinking about moral codes, the sets of norms that determine which actions are judged to be good and which are evil. They point out that moral codes vary from culture to culture — and thus are not biologically predetermined.

I consider this distinction fundamental. Therefore, I argue here that the question of whether ethical behavior is biologically determined may refer to either one of the following two questions. First, is the capacity for ethics — the proclivity to judge human actions as either right or wrong — determined by the biological nature of human beings? Second, are the systems or codes of ethical norms accepted by human beings biologically determined? A similar distinction can be made with respect to language. The question whether the capacity for symbolic creative language is determined by our biological nature is different from the question whether the particular language we speak — English, Spanish, Chinese, and so on — is biologically determined (in the case of language, it obviously is not).

The distinction between the *inclination* to judge certain kinds of actions as either morally good or evil and the *norms* according to which we determine which actions are good and which are evil, has some affinity with the distinction made by moral philosophers between *metaethics* and *normative ethics*. The subject of metaethics is *why* we should do what we should do; normative ethics tells us *what* we should do. I propose that the moral evaluation of actions emerges from human rationality or — in Darwin's terms — from our highly developed intellectual powers. Our high intelligence allows us to anticipate the consequences of our actions with respect to other people and, thus, to judge them as good or evil in terms of their consequences for others. But I argue that the norms according to which we decide which actions are good and which are evil are largely culturally determined, though conditioned by biological predispositions.

Darwinian Aftermath

Herbert Spencer (1820-1903) was among the first philosophers who sought to find the grounds of morality in biological evolution. In *The Principles of Ethics* (1893), Spencer seeks to discover values that have a natural foundation. Spencer argues that the theory of organic evolution implies certain ethical principles. Human conduct must be evaluated, like any biological activity whatsoever, according to whether it conforms to the life process; therefore, any acceptable moral code must be based on natural selection, the law of struggle for existence. According to Spencer, the most exalted form of conduct is that which leads to a greater duration, extension, and perfection of life. The morality of all human actions must be measured by that standard. Spencer proposes that, though exceptions exist, the general rule is that pleasure goes with what is biologically useful, whereas pain marks what is biologically harmful. This is an outcome of natural selection: while doing what brings them pleasure and avoiding what is painful, organisms improve their chances for survival. With respect to human behavior, according to Spencer, we see that we derive pleasure from virtuous behavior and pain from evil actions, associations indicating that the morality of human actions is also founded on biological nature.

Spencer proposes as the general rule of human behavior that anyone should be free to do anything that they want, so long as it does not interfere with the similar freedom to which others are entitled. The justification of this rule would be found in organic evolution: the success of an individual, plant or animal, depends on its ability to obtain what it needs. Consequently, Spencer reduces the role of the state to protecting the collective freedom of individuals so that they can do as they please. This laissez-faire form of government may seem ruthless, because individuals would seek their own welfare without any consideration for the welfare of others (except for respecting their freedom); but Spencer believes that it is consistent with traditional Christian values. I might add that, though Spencer sets the grounds of morality on biological nature and on nothing else, he admits that certain moral norms go beyond what is biologically determined. These are rules formulated by society and accepted by tradition.

Social Darwinism, in Spencer's version or in some variant form, was fashionable in European and American circles during the latter part of the nineteenth century and the early years of the twentieth century, but it has few or no distinguished intellectual followers at present. Spencer's critics include the evolutionists J. S. Huxley and C. H. Waddington, who, nevertheless, maintain that organic evolution provides grounds for a rational justification of ethical codes. For Huxley (1953; Huxley and Huxley 1947), the standard of morality is the contribution that actions make to evolutionary progress, which goes from "less advanced" to "more advanced" organisms. For Waddington (1960), the morality of actions must be evaluated by their contribution to human evolution.

The views of Huxley and Waddington are based on value judgments about what is or is not progressive in evolution. But, contrary to Huxley's claim, there is nothing objective in the evolutionary process itself, that is, outside human considerations (see Ayala 1982, 1987, 2010), that makes the success of bacteria, which have persisted as such for more than two billion years and which consist of a huge diversity of species and astronomical numbers of individuals, less valuable than that of the vertebrates, even though the latter are more complex. The same objection can be raised against Waddington's human evolution standard of biological progress. Are the insects, of which more than one million species exist, less successful or less valuable from a purely biological perspective than humans or any other mammal species? Waddington fails to demonstrate why the promotion of human biological evolution by itself should be the standard to measure what is morally good.

More recently, numerous philosophers, as well as scientists, have sought to give accounts of moral behavior as an evolutionary outcome (e.g., Blackmore 1999; Hauser 2006; Maienschein and Ruse 1999; Ruse 1995; Sober and Wilson 1998; Wilson 2012). Particularly notable are the early contributions of Edward O. Wilson (1975, 1978, 1998, 2012), the founder of sociobiology as an independent discipline engaged in discovering the biological foundations of all social behavior. Sociobiologists, as well as the derivative subdisciplines of evolutionary psychology (e.g., Barkow et al. 1992) and memetics (Blackmore 1999), have sought to solve the naturalistic fallacy by turning it on its head. They declare that moral behavior does not exist as something distinct from biological — or biologically determined — behavior (see also Churchland 2011). As Ruse and Wilson (1985) have observed, "Ethics is an *illusion* put in place by natural selection to make us good cooperators" (italics added).

Moral Behavior as Rational Behavior

I propose that the moral evaluation of actions emerges from human rationality or, in Darwin's terms, from our highly developed intellectual powers, and thus it is a necessary implication of our biological makeup. Our high intelligence allows us to anticipate the consequences of our actions with respect to other people and thus to judge them as good or evil in terms of their consequences for others. But I argue that the norms according to which we decide which actions are good and which are evil are largely culturally determined, though conditioned by biological predispositions, such as parental care, to give an obvious example.

The moral sense refers, first and foremost, to our predisposition to evaluate some actions as virtuous, or morally good, and others as evil, or morally bad. Morality, therefore, consists of the urge or predisposition to judge human actions as either right or wrong in terms of their consequences for other human beings. In this sense, humans are moral beings by nature because their biological constitution determines the presence in them of the three necessary conditions for ethical behavior: (i) the ability to anticipate the consequences of one's own actions; (ii) the ability to make value judgments; and (iii) the ability to choose between alternative courses of action. These abilities exist as a consequence of the eminent intellectual capacity of human beings.

The ability to anticipate the consequences of one's own actions is the most fundamental of the three conditions required for ethical behavior. Only if I can anticipate that pulling the trigger will shoot the bullet, which in turn will strike and kill my enemy, can the action of pulling the trigger be evaluated as nefarious. Pulling a trigger is not in itself a moral action; it becomes so by virtue of its relevant consequences. My action has an ethical dimension only if I do anticipate these consequences.

The ability to anticipate the consequences of one's actions is closely related to the ability to establish the connection between means and ends — that is, of seeing a means precisely as a means, as something that serves a particular end or purpose. This ability to establish the connection between means and their ends requires the ability to anticipate the future and to form mental images of realities not present or not yet in existence.

The ability to establish the connection between means and ends happens to be the fundamental intellectual capacity that has made possible the development of human culture and technology. An evolutionary scenario, seemingly the best hypothesis available, proposes that the remote evolutionary roots of this capacity to connect means with ends may be found in the evolution of bipedalism, which transformed the anterior limbs of our ancestors from organs of locomotion into organs of manipulation. The hands thereby gradually became organs adept for the construction and use of objects for hunting and other activities that improved survival and reproduction, that is, increased the reproductive fitness of their carriers. The construction of tools depends not only on manual dexterity but on perceiving them precisely as tools, as objects that help to perform certain actions; that is, as means that serve certain ends or purposes (which will occur only in the future): a knife for cutting, an arrow for hunting, an animal skin for protecting the body from the cold. According to this evolutionary scenario, natural selection promoted the intellectual capacity of our bipedal ancestors because increased intelligence facilitated the perception of tools as tools, and thus their construction and use, with the ensuing improvement of biological survival and reproduction.

The development of the intellectual abilities of our ancestors took place over several million years, gradually increasing the ability to connect means with their ends and hence the possibility of making ever-more complex tools serving more diverse and remote purposes. According to the hypothesis, the ability to anticipate the future, essential for ethical behavior, is thus closely associated with the development of the ability to construct tools, an ability that has produced the advanced technologies of modern societies and is largely responsible for the success of humans as a biological species.

A second condition for the existence of ethical behavior is the ability to make value judgments, to perceive certain objects or deeds as more desirable than others. Only if I can see the death of my enemy as preferable to his survival (or vice versa) can the action leading to his demise be thought of as moral. If the consequences of alternative actions are neutral with respect to value, an action cannot be characterized as ethical. Values are of many kinds: not only ethical, but also aesthetic, economic, political, gastronomic, and so on. But in all cases the ability to make value judgments depends on the capacity for abstraction — that is, on the capacity to perceive actions or objects as members of general classes. This makes it possible to compare objects or actions with one another and to perceive some as more desirable than others. The capacity for abstraction requires an advanced intelligence such as exists in humans and apparently in them alone.

I will note at this point that the model that I am advancing here does not necessarily imply the ethical theory known as utilitarianism (or, more generally, consequentialism). According to so-called act consequentialism, the rightness of an action is determined by the value of its consequences, so that the morally best action in a particular situation is the one whose consequences would have the most benefit to others. I am proposing that the morality of an action depends on our ability (1) to anticipate the consequences of our actions, and (2) to pass value judgments. But I am not declaring that the morality of actions is exclusively measured in terms of how beneficial their consequences will be to others.

A third condition necessary for ethical behavior is the ability to choose between alternative courses of actions. Pulling the trigger can be a moral action only if you have the option not to pull it. A necessary action beyond conscious control is not a moral action: the circulation of the blood or the process of digesting food are not moral actions. Whether there is free will is a question much discussed by philosophers, and their arguments are long and involved. Here I will advance two considerations that are commonsense evidence of the existence of free will. One is personal experience, which indicates that the possibility to choose between alternatives is genuine rather than only apparent: I may choose between writing or not writing this essay on morality. The second consideration is that when we confront a situation that requires action on our part, we are able mentally to explore alternative courses of action, thereby extending the field within which we can exercise our free will. In any case, if there were no free will, there would be no ethical behavior, and morality would be only an illusion. But I should make the point that free will is dependent on the existence of a well-developed intelligence, which makes it possible to explore alternative courses of action and to choose one or another in view of the anticipated consequences.

Adaptation versus Exaptation

I will now consider explicitly one issue that is largely implicit in the previous discussion. I propose that the moral sense emerges as a necessary implication of our high intellectual powers, which allow us to anticipate the consequences of our actions, to evaluate such consequences, and to choose accordingly how to act. But is it true that the moral sense may have been promoted by natural selection in itself and not only indirectly as a necessary consequence of our exalted intelligence? The question in evolutionary terms is whether the moral sense is an adaptation or, instead, an exaptation. Evolutionary biologists define exaptations as features of organisms that evolved because they served some function but are later co-opted to serve an additional or different function, one that was not originally the target of natural selection. The new function may replace the older function or coexist together with it. Feathers seem to have evolved first for conserving temperature; birds later co-opted them for flying. The beating of the human heart is an exaptation used by doctors to diagnose the state of health, though this is not why it evolved in our ancestors. The issue at hand is whether moral behavior was directly promoted by natural selection or, instead, is simply a consequence of our exalted intelligence, which was the target of natural selection (because it made possible the construction of tools, inter alia).

I will argue that the human moral sense is an exaptation, not an adaptation. The moral sense consists of *judging* certain actions as either right or wrong, not of choosing and carrying out some actions rather than others. It seems unlikely that making moral judgments would promote the reproductive fitness of those judging an action as good or evil; *acting* in one way or another might be of consequence in promoting fitness, but *passing judgment* by itself would seem unlikely to increase or decrease adaptive fitness. Nor does it seem likely that there might be some form of "incipient" ethical behavior that would then be further promoted by natural selection. Art, literature, religion, and many human cultural activities might also be seen as exaptations that came about as consequences of the evolution of high intelligence.

Rather, it seems that the target of natural selection was the development — which happened mostly through the Pleistocene — of advanced intellectual capacities. This was favored by natural selection because the construction and use of tools, made possible by advanced intelligence, improved the strategic position of our biped ancestors. Once bipedalism evolved and after tool-using and tool-making became practiced, those individuals who were more effective in these functions had a greater probability of biological success. The biological advantage provided by the design and use of tools persisted long enough so that intellectual abilities continued to increase, eventually yielding the eminent development of intelligence that is characteristic of *Homo sapiens.*

A related question is whether morality would benefit a social group within which it is practiced and would also indirectly benefit individuals who are members of the group. This seems likely to be the case, if indeed moral judgment would influence individuals to behave in ways that increase cooperation, or benefit the welfare of the social group in some way; for example, by reducing crime or protecting private property. Darwin would agree: "It must not be forgotten that, although a high standard of morality gives but a slight or no advantage to each individual man and his children over the other men of the same tribe, yet that an advancement in the standard of morality and an increase in the number of well-endowed men will certainly give an immense advantage to one tribe over another" (1871, 159).

That is, the moral sense that had evolved as an exaptation associated with high intelligence eventually became an adaptation — by favoring beneficial behaviors.

Mind to Morality

The capacity for ethics is an outcome of gradual evolution, but it is an attribute that exists only when the underlying attributes (i.e., the intellectual capacities) reach an advanced degree. The necessary conditions for ethical behavior only come about after the crossing of an evolutionary threshold. The approach is gradual, but the conditions only appear when a degree of intelligence is reached, such that the formation of abstract concepts and the anticipation of the future are possible and free will evolves, even though we may not be able to determine when the threshold was crossed. Thresholds occur in other evolutionary developments (e.g., in the origins of life, multicellularity, and sexual reproduction) as well as in the evolution of abstract thinking and self-awareness. Thresholds occur in the physical world as well. For example, water heats gradually, but at 100°C boiling begins and the transition from liquid to gas starts suddenly (and continues until the liquid water has fully vaporized). Surely, human intellectual capacities came about by gradual evolution.

When we look at the world of life as it exists today, it would seem that there is a radical breach between human intelligence and that of other animals. The rudimentary cultures that exist in chimpanzees do not imply advanced intelligence as it is required for moral behavior. Empathy, or the predisposition to mentally assimilate the feelings of other individuals, has recently been extensively discussed in the context of altruistic or moral behavior. Incipient forms of empathy seem to be present in other animals. In humans, increasing evidence indicates that we automatically simulate (mentally and emotionally) the experiences of other humans. Empathy is a common human phenomenon, surely associated with our advanced intelligence, which allows us to understand the harms or benefits that impact other humans, as well as their associated feelings. Empathic humans may consequently choose to behave according to how their behavior will impact those for whom we feel empathy. That is, human empathy occurs because of our advanced intelligence. Humans may then choose to behave altruistically or not — that is, morally or not — in terms of the anticipated consequences of their actions to others.

The question remains: When did morality emerge in the human lineage? Did *Homo habilis* or *Homo erectus* have morality? What about the Neanderthals *(Homo neanderthalensis)* or the recently discovered Denisovans in Siberia, seemingly different from both *Homo sapiens* and *Homo neanderthalensis,* though mentally quite developed? It is difficult to determine when in hominid evolution morality emerged. It may very well be that the advanced degree of rationality required for moral behavior may only have been reached at the time when creative language came about, and perhaps it was dependent on the development of creative language. This would likely have happened only after the evolution of our species, *Homo sapiens.*

Moral Codes

Moral behavior, I have proposed, is a biological attribute of *Homo sapiens* because it is a necessary consequence of our biological makeup, namely, our high intelligence. But moral codes, I argue, are not primary products of biological evolution, but of cultural evolution. I should note, however, that moral codes, like any other cultural systems, cannot survive for long if they prevailingly run in outright conflict with our biology. The norms of morality must be by and large consistent with human biological nature, because ethics can only exist in human individuals and in human societies. Therefore, one might also expect — and it is the case — that accepted norms of morality will often, or at least occasionally, promote behaviors that increase the biological fitness of those who behave according to them — for example, child care. But the correlation between moral norms and biological fitness is neither necessary nor indeed always the case: some moral precepts common in human societies have little or nothing to do with biological fitness, and some moral precepts are even contrary to fitness interest.

How do moral codes come about? The short answer is that moral codes are products of cultural evolution, a distinctive human mode of evolution that has surpassed the biological mode, because it is a more effective form of adaptation: it is faster than biological evolution, and it can be directed. Cultural evolution is based on cultural heredity, which is Lamarckian, rather than Mendelian, so that acquired characteristics are transmitted. Most important, cultural heredity does not depend on biological inheritance, from parents to children, but is also transmitted horizontally and without biological bounds. A cultural mutation, an invention — think of the laptop computer, the cell phone, or rock music — can be extended to millions and millions of individuals in less than one generation.

In chapter 5 of *The Descent of Man,* entitled "On the Development of the Intellectual and Moral Faculties during Primeval and Civilized Times," Darwin writes:

> There can be no doubt that a tribe including many members who, from possessing in a high degree the spirit of patriotism, fidelity, obedience, courage, and sympathy, were always ready to give aid to each other and to sacrifice themselves for the common good, would be victorious over most other tribes; and this would be natural selection. At all times throughout the world tribes have supplanted other tribes; and as morality is one element in their success, the standard of morality and the number of well-endowed men will thus everywhere tend to rise and increase. (1871, 159-60)

Darwin is making two important assertions: first, that morality may contribute to the success of some tribes over others, which is natural selection in the form of group selection; second, that the standards of morality will tend to improve over human history, because the higher the standards of a tribe, the more likely the success of the tribe. This assertion depends on which standards are thought to be "higher" than others. If the higher standards are defined by their contribution to the success of the tribe, then the assertion is circular. But Darwin asserts that there are some particular standards that, in his view, would contribute to tribal success: patriotism, fidelity, obedience, courage, and sympathy.

Moral codes arise in human societies by cultural evolution. Those moral codes that lead to successful societies tend to be widespread. Since time immemorial, human societies have experimented with moral systems. Some have succeeded and spread widely throughout humankind, such as the Ten Commandments, though other moral systems persist in different human societies. Many moral systems of the past have surely become extinct because they were replaced or because the societies that held them became extinct. The moral systems that are currently widespread in humankind are those that have been favored by cultural evolution. They were propagated within particular societies for reasons that might be difficult to fathom but that surely must have included the perception by individuals that a particular moral system was beneficial for them at least to the extent that it was beneficial to their society — that is, by promoting social stability and success.

Moral norms that are consistent with the biological interest of individuals, families, or societies are likely — and this has often been the case — to be incorporated into the moral systems of successful societies. One obvious example is the general perception of most societies that parents have a moral obligation to care for their children. Parental care, which is a behavior generally favored by natural selection, is present in virtually all codes of morality, from primitive to more advanced societies. There are other human behaviors sanctioned by moral norms that have biological correlates favored by natural selection. One example is monogamy, which occurs in some animal species but does not in many others. It is also sanctioned in many human cultures, but surely not in all. Polygamy is sanctioned in some current human cultures and was surely practiced more in the past than now. Food-sharing outside of a mother's feeding her young rarely occurs in primates, with the exception of chimpanzees and capuchin monkeys; but even in chimpanzees, food-sharing is highly selective and often associated with reciprocity. A more common form of mutual aid among primates is coalition formation: alliances are formed to fight other conspecifics, though these alliances are labile, with partners readily changing partners.

I should add that moral norms, similar to other elements of culture, are continuously evolving, often within a single generation. I should also point out that the acceptance by individuals or groups of particular sets of moral norms is often reinforced by civil authority (e.g., those who kill or steal with be punished) and by religious beliefs (God is watching, and you'll go to hell if you commit crimes, even if you are not caught).

REFERENCES

Ayala, F. J. 1982. The evolutionary concept of progress. In *Progress and its discontents,* ed. G. Almond, M. Chodorow, and R. Pearce, 106-24. Berkeley: University of California Press.

———. 1987. The biological roots of morality. *Biology and Philosophy* 2: 235-52.

———. 2010. What the biological sciences can and cannot contribute to ethics. In *Contemporary debates in philosophy of biology,* ed. F. J. Ayala and R. Arp, 316-36. Malden, MA: Wiley-Blackwell.

Barkow, J., L. Cosmides, and J. Tooby, eds. 1992. *The adapted mind: Evolutionary psychology and the generation of culture.* Oxford: Oxford University Press.

Blackmore, S. 1999. *The meme machine.* Oxford: Oxford University Press.

Churchland, P. S. 2011. *Braintrust: What neuroscience tells us about morality.* Princeton, NJ: Princeton University Press.

Copp, D. 2006. *The Oxford handbook of ethical theory.* Oxford: Oxford University Press.

Darwin, C. R. 1871. *The descent of man, and selection in relation to sex.* London: John Murray; New York: Appleton and Company.

Hauser, M. 2006. *Moral minds: How nature designed our universal sense of right and wrong.* New York: HarperCollins.

Huxley, J. S. 1953. *Evolution in action.* New York: Harper.

Huxley, T. H., and J. S. Huxley, 1947. *Touchstone for ethics.* New York: Harper.

Maienschein, J., and M. Ruse, eds. 1999. *Biology and the foundations of ethics.* Cambridge: Cambridge University Press.

Ruse, M. 1995. *Evolutionary naturalism.* London: Routledge.

Ruse, M., and E. O. Wilson. 1985. The evolution of ethics. *New Scientist* 108: 50-52.

Sober, E., and D. S. Wilson. 1998. *Unto others: The evolution and psychology of unselfish behavior.* Cambridge, MA: Harvard University Press.

Spencer, H. 1893. *The principles of ethics.* New York: D. Appleton.

Waddington, C. H. 1960. *The ethical animal.* London: Allen and Unwin.

Wilson, E. O. 1975. *Sociobiology, the new synthesis.* Cambridge, MA: Belknap Press.

———. 1978. *On human nature.* Cambridge, MA: Harvard University Press.

———. 1998. *Consilience: The unity of knowledge.* New York: Knopf.

———. 2012. *The social conquest of earth.* New York: Norton/Liveright.

Brain Connectivity and the Emergence of Capacities of Personhood: Reflections from Callosal Agenesis and Autism

Warren S. Brown and Lynn K. Paul

If the properties of personhood are rooted in physical processes and emergent, then core properties of humanness must emerge from complex patterns of physiological interactivity. Consequently, anything that reduces (or alters) brain connectivity will affect patterns of brain interactivity and, in turn, affect what can and does emerge. This is particularly true of connectivity within the cerebral cortex and the emergence of human cognitive and psychosocial characteristics. Thus, abnormalities of cerebral connectivity in children will have an impact on the cognitive and psychosocial capacities that develop, that is, will have an impact on the full emergence of personhood. This connectivity hypothesis is supported by the relationship between diminished long-range cortical-cortical connections and the psychosocial impairments found in two clinical syndromes: agenesis of the corpus callosum (ACC) and autism. ACC is a neuroanatomic abnormality of cortical connectivity involving congenital absence of the corpus callosum (the pathway that interconnects the right and left cerebral hemispheres). While the overall intelligence of individuals who have this syndrome can be in the normal range, they nonetheless have a pattern of consistent cognitive deficiencies, which affect their social interactions. The consequent behavioral profile of ACC overlaps notably with the social and cognitive deficits that constitute the behavioral diagnosis of autism. Much like ACC, autism has been shown to involve diminished long-range cortical connectivity (as well as increased local connectivity), a neural system disruption that likely contributes to the cognitive and psychosocial difficulties impacting personhood in these individuals. We also discuss the hypothesized relationship between connectivity and the emergence of the human capacities of personhood with respect to other domains of research and theory: (1) cortical connectivity and social capacity in nonhuman primates; (2) theories of interactivity and emergent properties in complex dynamic systems; and (3) the implications of patterns of connectivity within small-world networks.

Introduction

There are, roughly speaking, two options in looking for the source and essence of humanness and personhood: either human personhood is attributed to a nonmaterial component (as in a soul or mind), or one must explain how the functioning of physical systems and evolutionary processes come to constitute personhood. The best current physicalist hypothesis is that the basis of the distinctive characteristics of human persons cannot be attributed to (or reduced to) specific physical structures or physiological functions per se; rather, they are emergent from patterns of interaction between various systems and subsystems, particularly those within the cerebral cortex of the brain. From such interactivity emerge capacities with their own functional laws and their own forms of causal agency, and thus these capacities at least approximate what Tim O'Connor terms "strongly emergent" (in his contribution to the present volume).

The patterns of interaction and information flow, leading to the emergence of human characteristics such as would occur primarily over pathways of connectivity within the brain (especially the fast-conducting axonal pathways constituting cerebral white matter). Absence or alteration of these pathways would alter neural interactions and consequently the nature of properties that can emerge. For that reason, this chapter surveys clinical, empirical, and theoretical evidence generally in support of — but not necessarily proving — the following emergence-from-connectivity hypothesis:

> If the properties of humanness and personhood are emergent from complex patterns of physiological interactions, then neuropathology that reduces (or alters) the interactivity of brain regions, particularly within the cerebral cortex, will reduce (or alter) the nature of important human characteristics.

We will explore this emergence-from-connectivity hypothesis in this chapter with respect to: (1) the implications of the theory of complex dynamic systems; (2) the outcome of two disorders characterized by disrupted cortical connectivity with respect to impairments of human sociality: agenesis of the corpus callosum (ACC) and autism; (3) the comparative quantity of white matter in the brains of humans versus other primates; and (4) the information-processing consequences of different patterns of interconnectivity within small-world (scale-free) networks.

Dynamic Systems, Interactivity, and Emergence

The theory of complex nonlinear dynamical systems provides the most adequate current model for understanding how high-level human cognitive and social processes can emerge from the complexity and developmental self-organization of the brain, particularly the cerebral cortex (Juarrero 1999). The theory gives an account of how a large aggregate of interactive elements (e.g., neurons) can, in response to environmental pressure, self-organize into a *system* involving patterns of interelement (interneuronal) influence and constraint, and how such patterns of organization of the system become causal in their own right in meeting environmental pressures.

The properties that constitute a complex dynamic system, and that are necessary for self-organizational processes that give rise to the emergence of higher-order properties to occur, include: *complexity* (a very large number of elements, such as neurons); a high degree of *interconnectivity* (e.g., axons, dendrites, and synapses); *two-way interactions* (recurrent connections; feedback loops); and *nonlinear interactions,* which amplify small perturbations and small differences in initial conditions. The complex and massively interconnected neuronal network that is the cerebral cortex, with hundreds of millions of experience-modulated synapses, is well suited for the emergence of high-level causal properties-of-the-whole through dynamic self-organization, as described by this theory.

When pushed far from equilibrium by environmental pressures, large interactive aggregates self-organize into larger *patterns* that are constituted by *relational constraints between elements.* These patterns come to constitute a functional dynamic system that embodies new forms of interaction of the whole system (organism) with its environment. Once organized into a system, lower-level properties (e.g., the neurophysiology of individual neurons) interact bottom-up with the top-down relational constraints created by the higher-level pattern (for example, the large-scale processes necessary for comprehending the meaning of a sentence). Ongoing interactions of such systems with novel aspects of the environment can cause reorganizations of the system, such that increasingly more complex and higher-level forms of system organization evolve over time to meet the complex challenges of the environment. The theory of complex dynamic systems thus gives us a model for understanding how the highest levels of human cognitive and social capacities can be the product of the self-organization of a hypercomplex brain.

With respect to the extent and depth of self-organization (vs. genetically determined organization) in the human brain, it is particularly important to note the slow maturation of the human cerebral cortex relative to that of nonhuman primates. Even though the human cerebral cortex is only moderately different from that of other primates in its gross anatomy, the slower maturation process in humans results in a prolonged developmental period, during which its functional architecture remains relatively open. While genetically controlled structure lays the substrate of human brain organization, environmentally and socially driven self-organization builds the highest levels of functional capacities into the microstructure.

Accordingly, patterns of cellular and subsystem interactivity are the physical basis for the emergence of higher and higher system properties. To the degree that the brain is such a complex nonlinear dynamic system, the patterns of white matter axonal connectivity of the brain (particularly within the cerebral cortex) would be important in allowing for the kinds of interactivity that fosters the emergence of the human mind and personhood. Therefore, one might expect that changes in connectivity within the cortex, involving either reduction or proliferation of axonal connectivity, could adversely (or positively) affect cognitive development and the characteristics of the cognitive and social capacities that can emerge.

Ant Colonies, Communication, and Emergence

An ant colony is a helpful example that is often used to illustrate a *dynamic system* (Juarrero 1999; Johnson 2001). Think of each ant as one of the many *elements* and the colony as the whole *system*. Because of constant, ongoing interactions between the host of individual ants, the colony comes to function as a whole unified system, distributing activities in order to meet the colony's needs. Because it is a system rather than a loose assemblage of individual ants, the colony interacts with its surrounding environment as a single organism. The colony comes to have whole-system characteristics that cannot be entirely attributed to the characteristics of individual ants, just as human beings have characteristics of personhood that cannot be attributed to individual brain cells or even to isolated networks of intercellular connections. Colonies do things (such as building and maintaining nests or going on mass foraging expeditions) that are not the result of the plans or decisions of any individual ant. The characteristic action of the colony does not emerge entirely from characteristics of individual ants, but from the interactive patterns of inter-ant influence and constraint that come to characterize the colony. Colony behavior emerges from a massive quantity of small physical and chemical interactions across tens of thousands of individual ants.

The reason that a large quantity of individual ants can form and organize into a colony is related to the connectedness and ongoing communication between ants. Airborne interchange of hormone signals (called pheromones), as well as physical contact between ants, serve as communication signals that cause individual ants to do one thing versus another. These communications and interactions are what cause large numbers of ants to organize into patterns of activity recognizable as a colony rather than a mere swarm. For example, on the basis of such messages, an individual ant, or a smaller group of ants, might forage for food rather than work on building the structure of the nest or tending the queen. Consequently, colonies do things in the world that individual ants do not do. But if you eliminate or reduce inter-ant communication, a colony does not form, and we have merely an aggregate swarm of randomly scurrying ants.

If the human brain and body are just such a dynamic system — a "colony" of neurons rather than ants — then a self-organizing process (primarily during child development) of forming the higher-order properties of human mind and personhood is what one would expect. Human characteristics such as thinking, deciding, speaking, expressing emotions, and having inner experiences are thus not due to any particular neuron. Rather, these important characteristics depend on the patterns of activity that come to exist at any moment across the myriad interactions between hundreds of millions of neurons. These are properties of patterns of the ongoing activity of the entire brain and body, operating as a dynamic system.

The characteristics of such dynamic systems can help us understand the formation of personhood. For example, one important characteristic of dynamic systems is that they always retain the potential to reorganize in ways that result in new system characteristics. This happens whenever the system is destabilized by an inability to successfully interact with its surroundings. To continue, for the moment, the analogy of an ant colony, a change in the nature of the local food supply can cause the colony to adapt and learn (literally, "learn" as a system) new strategies for finding and gathering food. The characteristics of the colony change in ways that meet the new challenge. Similarly, we human beings, as complex dynamic systems (very much more complex than an ant colony), organize and reorganize in the process of interacting with our physical and social surroundings. It is interesting to note that newer (younger) dynamic systems (whether ant colonies or human bodies) reorganize readily, but older systems, though they are still capable of reorganization, are more robust and less likely to change significantly, except in the case of a major destabilization. Thus, though we continually adapt and incorporate new system characteristics through our ongoing life experiences as we get older, the reorganizations are generally less remarkable than those that occurred when we were younger.

Another important characteristic of dynamic systems is that the forms that can arise in self-organization are constrained (as well as opened to possibilities) by the physical and functional limitations of components and interactive channels (complexity, interconnectivity, recurrent feedback, and nonlinear interactions). For example, ants have a few genetically determined behavioral possibilities and a limited range of communication channels (that is, pheromones that are secreted and physical interactions on meeting one another as they move about). On the basis of this limited behavioral and communication repertoire, the colony as a whole continually adjusts its patterns of group activity to meet the challenges of a changing internal and external environment. Given current needs, varying quantities of ants will be foraging for food, clearing waste from the nest, tending the queen in her egg-laying, defending the nest from invaders, or building the nest itself. Likewise, as a dynamic system, the self-organization of each human brain is both constrained and open to potentialities by its history of interactivity and self-organization — whereas a colony of ants will never build a skyscraper or convene an academic convention.

Disorders of the Corpus Callosum and the Emergence of Personhood

Agenesis of the Corpus Callosum

For the past two decades, the authors and their students have been studying individuals born without a corpus callosum, the super-large axonal pathway that connects the right and left cerebral hemispheres. This congenital brain abnormality is called *agenesis of the corpus callosum* (ACC). Somewhat surprisingly, these individuals can have a normal-range IQ, despite the fact that approximately 200 million axons that would normally interconnect the right and left cerebral cortex are not making interhemispheric connections. They also can have intact basic capacities for perception, memory, executive function, simple problem-solving, motor control, and social comprehension (Paul et al. 2007; Brown and Paul 2000).

Nevertheless, the absence of interhemispheric connectivity results in a consistent pattern of subtle cognitive and psychosocial disabilities. Besides predictable difficulties in integrating information from the two visual fields or coordinating and synchronizing the activity of the two hands, we have found that these individuals also have diminished cognitive capacities in the areas of complex novel problem-solving, comprehension of nonliteral language, understanding of humor, detecting the subtleties of social interactions, and imagination and creativity. Thus, a major reduction in interhemispheric connectivity (for example, absence of the corpus callosum) results in mild to moderate deficits in these higher-order cognitive capacities that make important contributions to human functioning (Brown and Paul 2000; Mueller et al. 2010; Turk et al. 2010; Symington et al. 2010).

Two consequences of diminished connectivity seem to be core to the diminished capacities seen in ACC. First, *information-processing time is slow*. For example, we recently found deficits in ACC in a timed color-word interference test (Stroop test) that disappeared when controlling for simple word-reading time. What seemed to be a problem in executive function (resisting color-word interference) turned out to be mostly a more general problem in cognitive processing time. Slower cognitive processing may be related to delay in the sharing of information between hemispheres. A number of studies have demonstrated reduced interhemispheric transfer time in a simple visuomotor task in individuals with ACC (Jeeves 1969; Berlucchi et al. 1995).

Second, many of the deficits we have found in ACC seem to be explainable by a core deficit in *novel, complex, and rapid problem-solving* (Brown and Paul 2000; Brown et al. 2012). For example, problems seen in individuals with ACC in the comprehension of second-order meaning in language (including metaphors and jokes) may be related to difficulty rejecting the literal meaning of a statement in favor of a second-order meaning inferred from the context in which the statement is made — a complex and novel problem to be solved on the fly (Paul et al. 2003; Brown et al. 2005). It may be the case that rapid processing in complex and novel tasks is slower and less efficient when "running on a smaller computer," that is, being processed by a single isolated hemisphere rather than by two hemispheres connected by the very large "bus" that is the corpus callosum.

We have had extensive opportunity to interact socially with persons with ACC. Clearly, they are every bit *persons,* and many of them are interesting and accomplished in life. However, in these social interactions there is always a mild to moderate level of interpersonal naiveté, such that potentially rich dimensions of interpersonal relationships become compressed toward the concrete, losing some of the depth and richness of relatedness. Thus, reduced cortical interconnectivity as a result of the absence of the corpus callosum appears to limit the emergence of subtle dimensions of social functioning.

Autism

While ACC is diagnosed by an anatomical abnormality easily visible in an MRI, autism is diagnosed solely by abnormalities in behavior. The current standardized definition of autism requires behavioral abnormalities in two major domains: social communication, and restricted interests and repetitive behaviors (Volkmar et al. 2005). Behavioral symptoms overlap between autism and ACC, such that approximately 30 percent of adults with ACC and normal-range intellectual functioning exhibit an autism behavior profile (Paul et al. 2011).

Recently, autism research has called into question the expectation that autism has a singular cause, and some scientists are suggesting that autism may actually involve multiple independent (though interacting) domains of neurological impairment (Happe and Plomin 2006). Among the potential causes of autism symptoms, accumulating evidence exists that implicates abnormalities of cortical white matter, abnormalities that differ between early childhood and older childhood/adulthood. The relationship between developmental phase, brain connectivity, and autism is best understood against the backdrop of the development of connectivity in typically developing children.

In typical human development, the brain follows a clear developmental sequence, starting with early exuberant growth of neurons and connectivity, followed by maturational changes that facilitate differentiation of functional systems. In this latter phase, maturational changes, such as axonal myelination and synaptic stabilization, preserve and solidify connections within specific functional networks, while synaptic pruning decreases other connections (thereby decreasing global connectivity throughout the brain). In this way, the brain develops strong functional connections in networks that are important for human life and decreases connectivity within less important networks (Quartz and Sejnowski 1997; Kandel et al. 2000).

In contrast, the evidence to date indicates that young children with autism (< 5 years) exhibit generalized overgrowth of white matter tracts (including the corpus callosum), resulting in greater than expected long-range connections throughout the cerebrum. However, this pattern of overgrowth in autism appears to reverse over time. Possibly due to a disruption of axonal myelination and synaptic stabilization, white matter connections in autism do not mature at a normal rate through later childhood. Consequently, older children and adults with autism exhibit reduced volume and structural integrity of the longer cortical-cortical pathways. At the same time, what appears to be a disruption of pruning results in excessive local cortical connectivity (the "U-fibers" that constitute local cortical circuits) in older children and adults with autism (Muller et al. 2011).

Therefore, the typical pattern of functional interactions within the adult cerebral cortex is the product of two maturational systems, one that increases connectivity in networks for important functional systems and another that reduces extraneous connections. In autism, the pattern of connectivity is one of overgrowth during infancy, followed by a disruption in the maturational processes of differentiation. Specifically, the white matter connections that were overdeveloped in infancy do not mature normally, resulting in underconnectivity of long-range, task-relevant functional networks. Within local circuits, failure of pruning results in overconnectivity.

The outcome of this has been characterized in recent MRI studies of functional connectivity. Whole brain connectivity (examined in the resting state) suggests intact gross cortical connectivity, with some studies even showing greater than expected connectivity (likely due to early overgrowth and lack of pruning). However, task-driven connectivity seems to be reduced. The net effect of these changes with respect to information-processing suggests a reduction in the quantity and quality of task-relevant interactions between distant cortical areas, combined with a confusing plethora of local messages (Muller et al. 2011).

In summary, studies of autism provide clues about the importance of early neural growth and maturation to subsequent development of functional connections within the cortex. Disrupted connectivity or imbalance of connectivity across those networks results in the limitations of social communication seen in autism.

Connectivity in Human and Primate Brains

The Amount of Cortical White Matter

Comparative neuroanatomy has made it clear that, while humans do not have the largest brains, they have a relatively larger cerebral cortex, and, most markedly, a very much larger prefrontal cortex. The area of the prefrontal cortex is roughly 4 percent of the total cerebral cortex in a cat, 10 percent in a dog, 12 percent in a macaque, and 17 percent in a chimpanzee. But in the human brain, it has enlarged to 29 percent of the total cerebral cortex (Fuster 2002). Enlargement of the human prefrontal cortex is primarily the result of increased white matter. That is, there is a positive linear correlation in the white-to-gray-matter ratio across primate species. The human brain falls on this regression line for all nonfrontal neocortical areas. However, due to a disproportionate increase in prefrontal white matter, the human prefrontal cortex is well outside of what would be predicted by other species (Schoenemann et al. 2005). Therefore, the human prefrontal cortex is not simply larger than that of other primates; it is more intensely interconnected within itself and with other cortical and subcortical structures of the brain.

The "wiring diagram" of the prefrontal cortex is characterized by extensive two-way interactions with all of the motor, sensory, memory, and affective areas of the cerebral cortex, as well as a host of sub-cortical structures. More prefrontal white matter suggests, among other things, greater influence of the prefrontal cortex on the information-processing of much of the rest of the brain. Frontal interaction with other brain structures likely underlies the important role of the frontal lobe in such critical psychosocial capacities as focused attention, memory for serial order, temporal regulation of behavior, social information-processing, and language (Schoenemann et al. 2005).

Unlike the species-specific increase in frontal connectivity described above, humans appear to have relatively reduced interhemispheric connectivity. Cross-species comparisons among primates indicate that humans have the smallest corpus callosum relative to total cortical surface (Killing and Insel 1999). Across mammalian species, increases in cortical volume are positively correlated with increases in the area and number of fibers in the corpus callosum (Olivares et al. 2001; Killing and Insel 1999). However, the correlation is nonlinear, such that among primates, humans have the smallest corpus callosum relative to total cortical surface (Killing and Insel 1999). Reduced callosal size may facilitate hemispheric specialization of processing for uniquely human skills such as language (Ringo et al. 1994). Therefore, compared to other primates, humans have both greater prefrontal connectivity and lesser callosal (interhemispheric) connectivity.

Von Economo Neurons

Recent research has proposed another relatively distinct human enhancement in brain wiring that may be critical to our remarkable relational capacities: the proliferation of a special kind of nerve cell. These neurons are called Von Economo neurons (VENs) after the neuroscientist who discovered them. They are very large neurons that have very long branches (axons) that reach throughout the cerebral cortex. Some VENs originate in an area deep within the temporal lobe of the brain (the insula) that receives information about the visceral state of the body, such as those neurons involved in our body's emotional responses (e.g., changes in heart rate, blood-vessel dilation in blushing, etc.). Another adjacent area where these neurons originate is a part of the medial frontal lobe (the anterior cingulated cortex) that is involved in decision-making in uncertain conditions. The insula and anterior cingulated are parts of a deeper, more primitive cortex sometimes referred to as "limbic cortex." Both of these areas have been found, in brain imaging studies, to be markedly active during states of social emotion (e.g., empathy or shame), when detecting the mental and emotional states of others, and while making moral decisions. Therefore, it has been hypothesized that information about bodily emotional activity is detected in these brain areas, and then this information is spread throughout the cortex via the axons of VENs. Thus VENs may play a critical role in regulation of thought and behavior by distributing feedback from bodily states and emotions to multiple cognitive networks (Allman et al. 2001; Watson et al. 2007). Integration of thinking with information about bodily states is important for signaling the social significance of our actions and perceptions, providing us with the (mostly) unconscious "gut feelings" that modulate our social behavior.

VENs are relevant to our current discussion of personhood because they are relatively exclusive to humans. They are found in great abundance in the adult human brain, but they are few in number in chimpanzees and gorillas, and they are nonexistent in lower primates (Nimchinsky et al. 1999). Small numbers of these neurons are also found in a few other highly social nonprimate species (that is, elephants and some species of whales and dolphins). Most interestingly, these neurons are few in number in newborn human infants, but by the age of four they are as numerous as in adults. It is thus assumed that the progressive development of these neurons is critical for the burgeoning of personal and social capacities as infants grow into children.

The critical point to be made is that the differences between the human cerebral cortex and that of other primates appears to be significantly due to differences in the quantity and patterning of neuronal (particularly cortical) connectivity — both within and between the cerebral hemispheres. Therefore, we posit that the potential for the emergence of uniquely human intelligence and personhood depends, as least in part, on unique patterns of interconnections over white-matter axonal pathways.

Network Connectivity and Emergence

We have already described the critical role of interactivity (based on connectivity) as a basis for the emergence of higher-level properties in complex dynamic systems. Network theory — and particularly the theory of small worlds — provides a perspective on the relationship between patterns of connectivity and their outcome in information-sharing and processing.

Wherever one looks — from the worldwide web and social networks to international power and telephone grids, to networks of scientists, to nervous systems — one finds that complex systems organize into what are called "scale-free," "small-world," or "real-world" networks. Networks are composed of nodes and links: nodes can be persons, telephones, households, computers, or neurons; links are the ways the nodes are connected and communicate. Roughly speaking, small-world networks are characterized by small clusters of nodes with many strong local links, and a few longer links interconnecting clusters.

Linkages within small-world networks are characterized by a power law with respect to the proportion of local and long-distance linkages. This relationship is roughly captured by the 80/20 rule: 80 percent local links and 20 percent long-distance links. This distribution of connectivity is found in nearly every small-world network. If the ratio is skewed such that long-distance connections represent less than 20 percent, some long-distance communication has to be transferred via densely interconnected local networks (a more cumbersome, slow, and inaccurate process across long distances). On the other hand, if less than 80 percent of the links in a small-world network are local connections, then information flow is slowed such that information flow gets clogged with too many messages. Given the need to process information rapidly and efficiently, networks in dynamic systems tend to self-organize into just such small-world patterns.

The configuration of neural connectivity within the cerebral cortex is very much like that of a small-world network. At one level of observation, neurons are the nodes and the synaptic connections between neurons within cortical columns and the local clusters, while the white-matter pathways (at this level of analysis mostly the local U-fibers) create small-world configurations. Alternately applying the model at a more gross level, local clusters are formed by the local U-fiber connections between cortical columns (now the nodes), and the long-distance white-matter pathways are the more sparse distant links. Either way, what this neuroanatomy suggests is that the use of small-world theory to gain insights into relationships between brain connectivity and information-processing capacities is more than merely metaphorical.

To return to our clinical neuropsychological syndromes, individuals with ACC have significantly reduced long-distance (interhemispheric) links that appear to drop the dynamic system of the cerebral cortex below what is optimal for rapid, complex information-processing, at least in certain contexts. The fact that the overall cognitive impact of callosal agenesis is not as great as one might expect, given the absence of approximately 200 million linkages, suggests that either (a) these long-range connections are not very important to human functioning in the first place, or (b) interhemispheric connectivity is so important that the dynamic system reorganizes in response to this unusual characteristic (ACC). The former hypothesis is ruled out by research on adults who had the corpus callosum severed as treatment for epilepsy. While those surgical patients were remarkably typical in many ways, they exhibited dramatic deficits in bilateral sensory-motor coordination, as well as more subtle impairments in cognitive and social processing. Clearly, callosal connections are important.

Very recent studies have demonstrated that, despite a complete absence of callosal connections, resting activity patterns in the brains of adults with ACC are identical to the patterns in people with intact callosal connections — including coordinated bihemispheric activation (Tyszka et al. 2011). Through the processes of developmental functional organization, the acallosal system learns to utilize other, less direct, pathways for achieving interhemispheric communication networks; these alternative systems are sufficient for maintaining interhemispheric communication during periods of rest, but when challenged by specific tasks their limitations become evident. The acallosal dynamic system adapts to callosal absence as well as it can, but the structural limitations prevent it from functioning fully, as is evidenced by the slowed processing speed and deficiencies in solving complex novel problems seen in people with ACC.

In individuals with autism, the dynamic system appears to be disturbed by an increase in local connectivity (an overabundance of U-fibers). In that case, the small-world networks at the level of cortical columns and U-fiber links are too heavily connected, resulting in too many messages clogging up processing, while, at the same time, the more macrolevel networks involving the long-distance cortical white-matter pathways suffer from too few connections, reducing the efficiency of whole-cortex networks (somewhat similar to ACC).

Final Thoughts

In neither ACC nor autism are these network descriptions apt to capture the entire complex nature of the symptomatology. However, these clinical neuropsychological syndromes, coupled with dynamic systems and network theories, provide support for the hypothesis that the emergence of higher cognitive capacities in humankind is related, at least in part, to the patterns of connectivity present within the cerebral cortex of the brain.

In his chapter in the present book, Timothy O'Connor discusses the philosophical difference between strong and weak emergence. When dealing with neural systems in different species, or different systems within the human brain, it seems that this distinction cannot be unambiguously applied. It may be more physiologically helpful to think of a continuum of forms of emergence, with stronger and stronger emergence appearing as systems become larger, more complexly interactive, and more open to dynamic self-organization. Similarly, precisely what emerges is going to be a product of the patterns of organization that come to exist in the system.

REFERENCES

Allman, J. M., et al. 2001. The anterior cingulate cortex: The evolution of an interface between emotion and cognition. *Annals of the New York Academy of Science* 935: 107-17.

Berlucchi, G., S. Aglioti, C. A. Marzi, and G. Tassinari. 1995. Corpus callosum and simple visuomotor integration. *Neuropsychologia* 33, no. 8: 923-36.

Brown, Warren, and Lynn Paul. 2000. Psychosocial deficits in agenesis of the corpus callosum with normal intelligence. *Cognitive Neuropsychiatry* 5: 135-57.

Brown, W. S., L. K. Paul, M. Symington, and R. Dietrich. 2005. Comprehension of humor in primary agenesis of the corpus callosum. *Neuropsychologia* 43: 906-16.

Brown, W. S., L. Anderson, M. F. Symington, and L. K. Paul. 2012. Decision-making in agenesis of the corpus callosum: Expectancy-valence in the Iowa gambling task. *Archives of Clinical Neuropsychology* 27, no. 5: 532-44.

Fuster, Joaquín M. 2002. Frontal lobe and cognitive development. *Journal of Neurocytology* 31: 374-76.

Happe, F., A. Ronald, and R. Plomin. 2006. Time to give up on a single explanation for autism. *Nature Neuroscience* 9: 1218-20.

Jeeves, M. A. 1969. A comparison of interhemispheric transmission times in acallosals and normals. *Psychonomic Science* 16: 245-46.

Johnson, Steven. 2001. *Emergence: The connected lives of ants, brains, cities, and software.* New York: Scribner.

Juarrero, Alicia. 1999. *Dynamics in action: Intentional behavior as a complex system.* Cambridge, MA: MIT Press.

Kandel, E. R., T. M. Jessell, and J. R. Sanes. 2000. Sensory experience and the fine tuning of synaptic connections. In *Principles of neural science,* ed. E. R. Kandel, J. H. Schwartz, and T. M. Jessell, 1115-30. New York: Elsevier.

Killing, J., and T. Insel. 1999. Differential expansion of neural projection systems in primate brain evolution. *Neuroreport* 10: 1453-59.

Mueller, K. O., S. D. Marion, L. K. Paul, and W. S. Brown. 2010. Bimanual motor coordination in agenesis of the corpus callosum. *Behavioral Neuroscience* 123, no. 5: 1000-1011.

Muller, R. A., P. Shih, B. Keehn, J. R. Deyoe, K. M. Leyden, and D. K. Shukla. 2011. Underconnected, but how? A survey of functional connectivity MRI studies in autism spectrum disorders. *Cerebral Cortex* 21: 2233-43.

Nimchinsky, E. A., et al. 1999. A neuronal morphologic type unique to humans and great apes. *Proceedings of the National Academy of Science USA* 96, no. 9: 5268-73.

Olivares, R., J. Montiel, and F. Aboitiz. 2001. Species differences and similarities in the fine structure of the mammalian corpus callosum. *Brain, Behavior, and Evolution* 57, no. 2 (February): 98-105.

Paul, L. K., D. Van Lancker, B. Schieffer, and W. S. Brown. 2003. Communicative deficits in individuals with agenesis of the corpus callosum: Nonliteral language and affective prosody. *Brain and Language* 85: 313-24.

Paul, Lyn, Warren Brown, R. Adolphs, J. M. Tyszka, L. J. Richards, P. Mukher-

The study of great ape behavior, as described in Byrne's chapter, enables us to trace the point in human evolution at which some cognitive capacity entered the human lineage. For instance, if a trait is shared with only the two chimpanzee species, we might deduce a single origin in the most recent ancestor species we share with them, at 6 mya. But to find out what environmental or social conditions originally selected for the capacity, we need more than one case. That is why the study of distantly related species is also important in comparative cognition.

Here, an African elephant is being tested for the ability to understand human pointing, with no prior training to do so. Among primates, this ability seems to be unique to humans, so very recently evolved. But elephants have been found to share the ability (A. F. Smet and R. W. Byrne, "African Elephants Can Use Human Pointing Cues to Find Hidden Food," *Current Biology,* 2013, DOI 10.1016/j.cub.2013.08.037), showing that it arose "convergently" in their lineage. The most likely common factor that promoted the evolution of this capacity in elephants and humans is that both species live in highly complex societies where accurate reading of others' intentions pays dividends. *Photo: Anna Smet.*

Plate 2. Diorama figures in the American Museum of Natural History, representing early bipeds of the genus *Australopithecus* that lived about 3.5 million years ago. Although bipedal on the ground, these hominids retained substantial climbing abilities, and they had ape-like skull proportions with protruding faces and small braincases. *Photo: AMNH.*

Plate 3. "Acheulean" stone tools, of a type that began to be made at some time more than 1.5 million years ago. These were the first tools clearly made to an ideal that existed in the toolmaker's head; but, though sophisticated, they do not imply symbolic thought processes. *Photo: Ian Tattersall.*

Plate 4. Diorama figures in the American Museum of Natural History, representing *Homo ergaster,* the earliest hominid with essentially modern body proportions. Appearing at a little under 2 million years ago, the first *Homo ergaster* still used simple flake tools of the kind long made by their more archaically proportioned predecessors. *Photo: AMNH.*

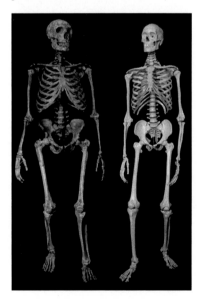

Plate 5. A reconstructed Neanderthal skeleton (left), compared with a modern human of similar stature. The Neanderthal skeleton retains many primitive bony features, and the contrast emphasizes the unusual slenderness of our modern body structure. *Photo: Ken Mowbray/Ian Tattersall.*

Plate 6. A deeply incised image of a horse, engraved on a block of limestone some 25 thousand years ago, at the Abri Labattut in western France. Beginning about 40 thousand years ago, artists in this part of the world produced some of the most compelling early evidence of fully symbolic thought processes. *Photo: AMNH.*

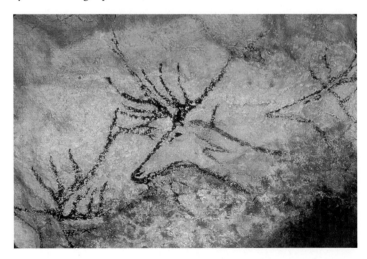

Plate 7. Drawing of a stag's head, made with a manganese crayon at Lascaux in western France some 17 thousand years ago. This deftly drawn head is one of a series thought to represent several stages of the animal's progress as it swam across a river. Early artists used many sophisticated conventions to suggest movement and perspective. *Photo of facsimile: AMNH.*

Plate 8. Three fragments of bone flutes found in cave deposits more than 30 thousand years old in the French Pyrenees. Instruments like these had very sophisticated sound capabilities and bear witness to the association of musical and artistic activities in the lives of the earliest modern humans known to occupy Europe. *Photo: Alain Roussot.*

Plate 9. First footsteps — in the volcanic ash, Laetoli, Tanzania, 3.6 million years ago. *Photo: Janet Root.*

Plate 10. Göbekli Tepe, east Turkey c. 10,000 BC. *Photo: Colin Renfrew.*

Plate 11. Detail from Göbekli
Tepe, east Turkey c. 10,000 BC.
Photo: Colin Renfrew.

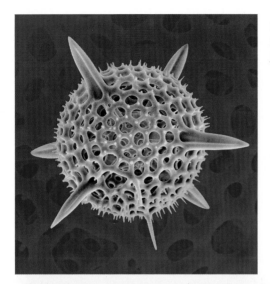

Plate 12. A unicellular organism, a radiolarian. *Photo: Dee Breger, Micrographic Arts.*

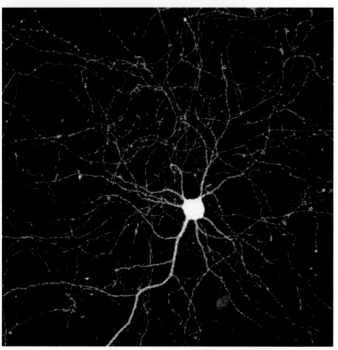

Plate 13. Another unicellular organism, a neuron, of which we carry around one hundred thousand million in our brains. *Photo: Paul De Koninck, Laval University, www.greenspine.ca.*

Plate 14. Monkeys show no self-recognition; they treat their reflection as another monkey. *Photo: Frans de Waal. Used by permission of Frans de Waal and Proceedings of the National Academy of Sciences.*

jee, and E. H. Sherr. 2007. Agenesis of the corpus callosum: Genetic, developmental, and functional aspects of connectivity. *Nature Reviews Neuroscience* 8: 287-99.

Paul, L. K., C. Corsello, D. P. Kennedy, D. Childress, B. Cheng, and R. Adolphs. 2011. Autism spectrum symptoms in agenesis of the corpus callosum. Presented at IMFAR 2011, San Diego, CA.

Quartz, S. R., and T. J. Sejnowski. 1997. The neural basis of cognitive development: A constructivist manifesto. *Behavioral Brain Science* 20: 537-96.

Ringo, J., R. Dory, S. Demeter, and P. Simard. 1994. Time is of the essence: A conjecture that hemispheric specialization arises from interhemispheric conduction delay. *Cerebral Cortex* 4, no. 4: 331-43.

Schoenemann, P. T., M. J. Sheehan, and L. D. Glotzer. 2005. Prefrontal white matter volume is disproportionately larger in humans than in other primates. *Nature: Neuroscience* 8, no. 2: 242-52.

Symington, S. H., W. S. Brown, M. Symington, M. Ono, and L. K. Paul. 2010. Social inference in individuals with agenesis of the corpus callosum. *Social Neuroscience* 5: 296-308.

Turk, A., W. S. Brown, M. Symington, and Lynn K. Paul. 2010. Social narratives in agenesis of the corpus callosum: Linguistic analysis of the thematic apperception test. *Neuropsychologia* 49: 43-50.

Tyszka, J. M., D. P. Kennedy, R. Adolphs, and L. K. Paul. 2011. Intact bilateral resting-state networks in the absence of the corpus callosum. *Journal of Neuroscience* 31: 15154-62.

Volkmar, Fred R., Rhea Paul, Ami Klin, and Donald J. Cohen, eds. 2005. *Handbook of autism and pervasive developmental disorders: Diagnosis, development, neurobiology, and behavior.* Vol. 1. Hoboken, NJ: John Wiley and Son.

Watson, K. K., et al. 2007. Brain activation during sight gags and language-dependent humor. *Cerebral Cortex* 17, no. 2: 314-24.

The Origins of Subjectivity

Adam Zeman

The distinction between subject and object is blurred in my body.
MERLEAU PONTY

"Subjectivity" is at the heart of human selfhood. While we are clearly objects, we are simultaneously subjects, centers of experience, capable of gaining knowledge from the unique viewpoints that our bodies afford. Our uniqueness and our "inwardness," our capacity for experience, can appear to be particularly mysterious elements of our being. This chapter describes several nested forms of subjectivity that emerged over the course of biological evolution, and that mature over the course of individual human development: (1) the capacity for sensorimotor responses; (2) the capacity for conscious perceptual experience; (3) the capacity to recognize our own bodies; (4) the capacity to think about our own and others' minds; (5) the capacity for mental time travel. This chapter reviews the biological basis of each of these capacities and the evolutionary advantage each may have conferred.

I have related my thoughts to linked ideas developed recently by other authors. While not denying that "hard questions" regarding the nature of experience and its relationship to our organic being remain unanswered, I will argue that the above five capacities, their neural bases and evolutionary functions, go a long way toward explaining the natural origins of subjec-

I am very grateful to Anthony David, Athena Demertzi, and David Mitchell for helpful comments in their discussion of this chapter.

tivity. I will discuss two misconceptions that contribute to a widespread reluctance to accept an explanation of this kind: the view that the brain is a passive machine and the view that the worlds of biology and culture are entirely separate and incommensurable. On the contrary, recent research has revealed that the brain is a constantly active, highly dynamic, autonomous organ, while culture provides human beings with the biological niche we have evolved to occupy: we are precisely "cultural creatures."

Subjects and Subjectivity

You and I are objects, and we inhabit a world of objects. But some objects, including ourselves, have a very special characteristic: we are simultaneously *subjects* — those who possess unique points of view from which we encounter the properties of objects. These include the looks, sounds, smells, tastes, and feels of things, and, just as important, properties of the objects that we subjects *are:* our states of being — thirst and hunger, pain and pleasure, love and loneliness — but also our capacity to act, our "agency."

Objects are accessible to investigation by the standard observational methods of science, but subjects appear, at least, to have some unusual qualities — particularly a kind of complex individuality and a mysterious inwardness that sets us apart from other things. This chapter will examine the nature, functions, and origins of subjectivity. It will interweave three guiding themes:

- The origins of subjectivity are natural, not magical — or, at least, they are no more magical than anything else in our magical universe.
- The varieties of subjectivity nest one within another, arising from recursive processes of growth.
- The relationship between object and subject, which we tend to regard as oppositional (and puzzling), is more accurately regarded as circular and mutually generative.

I will argue that the puzzling features of subjectivity are substantially explicable: the "individuality" I have highlighted is the natural result of having a viewpoint; the "complexity" results from our prodigious capacity to learn; the "inwardness" has to do with the fact that our bodies are the loci of much intricate and (normally) invisible processing that underpins all our experience. Before we are done, I will respond to some philosophical objections that often arise when proposals like mine are considered, and I will tackle two misunderstandings that can poison the wells for naturalistic theories of the self and subjectivity: the belief that the brain is robotic, and the view that biology and culture belong to separate, incompatible realms.

Types of Subjectivity

Subjects of experience are special because they are capable of gaining knowledge and acting on it. I will distinguish five kinds of knowledge — and corresponding forms of action — that are accessible to increasingly sophisticated kinds of subjects. The nested capacities to gain these kinds of knowledge develop during both ontogeny and phylogeny.

Knowing: The Protoself

In one of its several senses, a subject has been defined as "a person or thing that may be acted upon." In biological contexts, subjects must also be agents; otherwise, given that natural selection acts only on features of organisms that make an objective difference, subjectivity would never have evolved.

The process of being acted on, and acting in response, is the foundation of subjectivity in its most basic form. This is a succinct description of sensorimotor processing, as seen, for example, in the reflex that impels us to pull our hand away from a flame. The child who withdraws his hand from a flame in a famous illustration by Descartes, well before the arrival of the experience of pain, already has a certain basic "sensorimotor knowledge" of the flame: it is something noxious, best kept at a distance via a rapid escape. The child who withdraws his hand, of course, has a massively complex nervous system; and just after his act of withdrawal, his nervous system will announce the fact of pain, a vividly conscious, all-too-familiar form of human experience. But this kind of simple sensorimotor subjectivity does not require such a complex nervous system and, indeed, it may not require a nervous system at all.

The idea that a simple form of subjectivity may be found in creatures with relatively simple nervous systems has been raised by several authors recently, scientists seeking to understand the deeper roots of human selfhood. Panksepp (Panksepp and Northoff 2009), in particular, has discussed the "protoself" in some detail. He conceives of it as a preconscious, integrative system, centered in the mammalian upper brain stem. It is dependent on a set of neural representations of the body that relate organismic needs and states to environmental conditions via subsystems responsible for complex instinctual behavior, and in more sophisticated brains, for our basic emotions. The task of the protoself is to ensure basic behavioral coherence (see Table 1 for a summary of the confusing terminology of the self in use by different authors; a further set of linked insights into representations of the bodily self is emerging from work on the insular cortex and its connections [Critchley and Harrison 2013]).

Table 1: The terminology of consciousness and self

Panksepp (2009) / Damasio (2000)	Protoself	Core self	Reflective or cognitive or extended self		
Tulving (1985)	Anoetic awareness	Noetic awareness	Autonoetic awareness		
Edelman (1992)		Primary consciousness	Secondary consciousness		
Dehaene (2011)	subliminal	conscious			
Dunbar (2004)	First-order intentionality		Higher-order intentionality		
Rosenthal (1986)	First-order thought	Second-order thought	Higher-order thought		
Neisser (1988)		Ecological and interpersonal selves		Private self	Extended self
This chapter	knowing	Knowing that I know	MSR	TOM	MTT

This table sketches the differing use of similar terms by authors working in the area covered by this chapter. MSR stands for "mirror self-recognition"; TOM for "theory of mind"; and MTT for "mental time travel." It occurred to me while making this table that Freud's id, ego, and superego are surely lurking in the wings, alongside Mclean's reptilian, paleomammalian, and neomammalian brains (1990). Such distinctions remain highly topical (Carhart-Harris and Friston 2010).

Panksepp's proposal sketches a plausible precursor of more complex forms of human subjectivity. But while Panksepp restricts the protoself to creatures with "complex neural networks," another train of thought identifies elements of the protoself in the simplest creatures possible. Its point of departure is the observation that even single-celled organisms (see Plates 12 and 13) react to events and objects in their environments by active approach and withdrawal, indicating that these very simple creatures use and integrate "knowledge" of their surroundings to guide their behavior: they are, in this sense, primitive subjects.

Evan Thompson, the Canadian philosopher of biology and mind, has argued this case (2007), writing that *life* is already "beyond the gap" that separates matter from mind. He sees the precursors of subjectivity, "sense-making" and autonomy, in the characteristics of single-celled creatures: subjectivity is prefigured by the "interiority" of the world within the cell membrane, a boundary that the organism itself creates and that helps to create it. Sense-making (together with the attribution of significance, the growth of concern, and of purpose) is anticipated by the organism's orientation toward aspects of the environment that will satisfy its needs; autonomy is evident in the self-organizing, self-maintaining, and self-creating character of living things.

Recent research in "proteomics" has added a fascinating postscript to this view. The synapse, the point at which nerve cells communicate with one another by the release of chemical messengers, contains a huge array of proteins, the "synaptosome" (Bayes et al. 2011). Disturbances in the functioning of synaptosomes underlie a wide range of disorders in neurology and psychiatry alike. Many of these proteins can be traced back to ancestral forms in single-celled organisms, where they are often involved in communication and control within the cell. In other words, the lack of a nervous system in single-celled creatures may be misleading: these primitive subjects manage the jobs of command and control using systems that we have since elaborated into brains. The common assumption that nervous systems are a prerequisite for simple forms of subjectivity may be mistaken: "embodied cognition" began to emerge on earth in parallel with life.

At this juncture the reader may feel skeptical about the idea that "knowledge" is implicated at all in the very simple processes we are considering here, the reflex withdrawal of the hand from a flame or the movement of a protozoon toward a source of light or nutrients. Aren't these simply examples of action and reaction occurring for purely physiological or biochemical reasons in the absence of knowledge of any kind at all? These are indeed physiological and biochemical processes, but the cycle here is of stimulus and response rather than Newtonian action and reaction: through its response, the organism tells us something of itself, of its own needs and purposes, and of how these cause it to evaluate events around it, albeit on the basis of genetically transmitted capacities rather than individually acquired preferences. Its movement implies a primitive classification of the stimulus, and classification contains the beginnings of knowledge of the world.

The usefulness of this basic form of subjectivity is inarguable: the chances of survival and reproductive success are greatly enhanced by the pursuit of desirable goals — nutrition, safety, mates — and the avoidance of undesirable ones — harsh conditions, predators, toxins. But the kind of knowledge in question here is un-self-conscious in the extreme: it is "knowledge *in* the system" rather than "knowledge *for* the system." Creatures equipped with this kind of knowledge may "know" — but they don't yet know that they know. This second kind of knowledge has its uses, too.

Knowing That We Know: The Core Self

The step from "knowing" to "knowing that we know" is often identified with the genesis of "consciousness." It corresponds to a transition that all of us encounter once in a while — from automatic to reflective processing. Eating excellent ice cream provides a trivial but — to me at least — vivid example. I once found myself consuming some ice cream, successfully and with apparent enthusiasm, in the absence of any explicit consciousness at all, because I was absorbed by a conversation. Then the realization ("this is delicious") dawned on me, and the preconscious experience of its taste, which had somehow been present but unnoticed all along, came into my awareness. Part of my protoself (partial to good ice cream) had been fully engaged, while my "consciousness" was elsewhere. The etymology of consciousness supports this usage: in Latin the term — derived from *cum* (meaning "with") and *scio* (meaning "know") — was used in the context of knowledge *shared* with another or with oneself (Zeman 2002). The contrast between automatic eating and conscious delectation is nicely captured by the distinction between knowledge, confined to the hungry protoself, and knowledge shared fully with the wider self.

In a more serious vein, the contrast between "knowing" and "knowing that one knows" can be illustrated by an example of "blindsight" (Stoerig and Cowey 1997). Patients with damage to the primary visual cortex at the back of the brain who are, they genuinely believe, blind in the corresponding region of the visual field, can sometimes make accurate "guesses" about the presence, shape, movement, and other features of items in the blind field. Their success initially astonishes the patients themselves, but it is less mysterious than it might first appear, since visual information travels to several destinations in the brain besides the primary cortex. These patients, therefore, have visual knowledge of items in their blind fields, but they are unaware of their knowledge. Those of us with normal sight, by contrast, both see (as do patients with blindsight) and also *see* that we see: the knowledge *in* the system is now knowledge *for* the system. This "second-order," or "meta-cognitive," awareness allows us to do a great deal that first-order awareness (as in blindsight) does not: we can, for example, describe, embellish, and remember what we see.

There is suggestive evidence that monkeys, in whom the phenomenon of blindsight was first explored, are also capable of distinguishing blindsight from real sight (Cowey and Stoerig 1995). In other words, they can use blind-sight in just the same way as do human patients; and, like human patients, they do not classify the "experience" as visual — or, in fact, as different from the absence of experience. This suggests that they, like us, are capable of both knowing and of knowing that they know, and they can distinguish these two situations. Evidence from other sources supports this view.

In order to show that animals are capable of "metacognition," we must enable them to provide a "commentary" on their experience during psy-chological tasks, allowing them to do what we do so easily in words: to communicate to the researcher their degree of confidence in their per-formance, and to indicate when they are uncertain (Smith et al. 2003). One way of achieving this is to allow animals the option of declining to commit themselves when they judge that their chances of success in an experimental task are low. This approach has been taken in tests of percep-tion and of memory: it turns out that some intelligent animals, including monkeys and dolphins, can indeed monitor their chances of success in cognitively demanding tasks, and then can choose to opt out appropriately if the experimental paradigm is designed to allow them to do so. Rats and pigeons, in contrast, appear to be unable to make, or at least to convey, these metacognitive judgments.

Where in the brain does the transition from "knowing" to "knowing that we know," from implicit to explicit processing, occur? Larry Weiskrantz, the pioneer of blindsight, suggests that it must involve the "frontolimbic system" — with magisterial but prudent vagueness (Weiskrantz 1997). Two more detailed recent proposals deserve a mention.

Bernard Baars, Stanislas Dehaene, and others have suggested that the neurological distinction between conscious and unconscious processing, between explicit or implicit, hinges on whether that processing invades a "global neuronal workspace" that allows it to be broadcast through the brain, recruiting widespread resources to the leading task at hand. Exten-sive evidence indicates that the workspace is created by a network of highly connected brain regions in the frontal and parietal lobes — regions that forty years ago we would have described as belonging to "higher-order association cortex" because of their remoteness from direct sensory inputs or motor outputs. Once information has entered the global workspace, it can inform the full range of our cognitive processes, from perception through memory to the planning and control of our behavior. Information outside the global workspace can also influence behavior, just as blindsight does, but without any impact on conscious experience. Dehaene and Changeux (2011) have recently reviewed the evidence bearing on the "well-delimited" question of what distinguishes unconscious from conscious processing, with a focus on visual awareness: the primary research question here is what distinguishes a visible from an invisible — but neurally processed — visual event. Their current model emphasizes the role of "ignition" of the "global neuronal workspace" as before, but now also specifies that activation of the workspace leads to a late amplification of relevant sensory processing via feedback connections, synchronization, the augmentation of associated neuronal activity distributed across the brain, and the occurrence of the P3b, a distinctive electrical event occurring at around 300 milliseconds (one-third of a second) after the occurrence of the stimulus.

While Baars and Dehaene emphasize the distinction between two modes of information-processing, Panksepp and Northoff (2009) emphasize the connection between conscious processes and the biology of the self. In contrast to the preconscious "protoself," which depends primarily on neural systems in the upper brain stem, these authors locate the "core self," the subject of "primary consciousness," in a set of midline cortical regions, closely connected to the regions in the brain stem that sustain the protoself. These have been shown to become active in a range of "self-referential" tasks. Northoff describes the core self as a "sensorimotor, valuative, interoexteroceptive and subjective-affective experience integrator, a basic . . . tool for organisms to reach out to other organisms and objects."

Are these two current views of the genesis of primary consciousness compatible with one another? Baars, Dehaene, and Changuex are primarily concerned to define the mode of information-processing involved in consciousness, while Panksepp and Northoff emphasize the "self-centered" affective-motivational processes that, they believe, lie at the root of consciousness. The evidence considered by Dehaene and Changeux mainly considers the effects of stimuli impinging from the environment onto the organism, while Panksepp and Northoff direct their attention from the behaving organism to the milieu within. Yet, while their emphases are different, the two accounts have important commonalties. Both recognize that much neural processing occurs unconsciously, and conceptualizes the transition from conscious to unconscious processing in terms of a further, recursive phase of activity. Both locate this further phase in the neocortex. Both concur on the importance of a number of "associative" brain regions.

An aside on "knowledge" and "feeling" is in order here. To caricature the contrast between the Dehaene and Panksepp approaches, Dehaene seeks the key to consciousness in simple forms of *knowledge,* specifically perceptual knowledge of the world, while Panksepp seeks the key in simple forms of *feeling,* grounding experience of every kind in affect. It seems likely that, in simple forms of consciousness, "knowing" and "feeling" are inseparable, and it is of interest that we still use "feel" in a cognitive sense ("I feel you are wrong . . ."). A related clinical observation hints that we should expect to find some common ground in accounts of our awareness of our surroundings and of ourselves: pathologies that impair one often impair the other, so that "depersonalization," the psychopathology by which we lose our normal sense of our own personal existence, is often accompanied by derealization, the sense that our surroundings are no longer the solid and substantial world we once inhabited.

Whatever its anatomical basis, the process under consideration by Dehaene and Panksepp allows "knowledge in the system" to become "knowledge for the system," thereby rendering it available for flexible use in psychological functions, including, in the human brain, "verbal report, evaluation, memory, planning, and intentional action." This form of subjectivity moves beyond the implicit knowledge of the protoself to the explicit knowledge, the "primary consciousness," of the "core self." But knowing that we know does not tell us who we are: discovering this requires a further deepening of subjectivity.

Knowing Our Bodies: The Extended Self

In a wonderfully simple experiment, published in 1970, Gordon Gallup demonstrated that chimps, but not monkeys, rapidly became able to use a mirror to examine otherwise invisible parts of their own bodies (Gallup 1970). He also reported that chimps, unlike many other animals, came to use the mirror "for purposes of grooming and other forms of self-inspection." This suggested to him that chimps, but not monkeys, have a nascent self-awareness, at least an awareness of themselves as the possessors of bodies.

Human children begin to recognize themselves in mirrors at around eighteen months — the age at which they begin to use the first-person pronoun, to take an interest in self-adornment, to exchange roles in imaginative play, and to comfort others. Chimps and children are not alone; orangutans certainly, gorillas possibly, and dolphins also pass the "mirror test," reacting to the appearance of marks on their bodies, made visible by a mirror, in ways that make it clear they recognize that the body they can see in the mirror is their own (Reiss and Marino 2001). (See Plate 14.)

While it would be simplistic to suppose that there will be a linear *scala naturae* for cognition, it is interesting that the three types of subjectivity we have so far distinguished developed progressively in creatures with progressively more complex brains and behaviors. Very simple organisms arguably have knowledge of themselves and their surroundings, but it seems unlikely that they know that they know. Their knowledge is, as the term is generally understood, unconscious or preconscious. There is good evidence, as we have seen, that monkeys know that they know — that is, are conscious, have experience. But they do not appear to be able to include themselves in their mental inventory. Some of their most sophisticated cousins, including chimps, can incorporate themselves in their mental model of their world, taking a first step toward a concept of the "extended self." I will defer for the present the interesting question of whether this ability emerged as a byproduct of enlarging brains and developing intelligence or was selected for as an independently valuable capacity. But self-recognition, whether in chimp or in child — the awareness of self as *object* — does not imply the awareness of self as *subject,* which may be achieved securely, perhaps in some ways too securely, by just one species on earth.

Knowing Our Minds: The Extended Self

Between the ages of eighteen months and four or five years, children take a great intellectual stride that may be unique among animals. They come to realize that they, and others like themselves, view the world from uniquely personal points of view; that they acquire beliefs on the basis of limited evidence; that these beliefs may be mistaken; that it is possible to manipulate the thoughts of others by implanting false beliefs. More generally, they learn that somewhere within our visible bodies, invisible minds are at work. Besides beliefs, these invisible spaces are the loci of thoughts, desires, emotions, memories, dreams, and plans. The children who have learned these things have acquired, in the jargon, a "theory of mind," have learned to "mentalize." Crucially, in the terms of this chapter, this child has come to realize that she is not merely an object, but a subject also — a subject in a social universe of subjects. (See Figures 1 and 2 on p. 131.)

This realization is fundamental to mature human social existence. We constantly reflect on our own mental lives and those of our companions. We are capable, as Robin Dunbar and others have pointed out, of mastering many levels of "intentionality" in our thinking about thinking. Right now I am wondering whether you will or will not be able to follow what I am thinking about our mutual capacity for thought, an activity requiring third-level intentionality (I am thinking about what you are thinking about what I am thinking). Dunbar calculates that a novelist, seeking to manipulate his readers' beliefs about the beliefs that his characters entertain about one another, works close to the usual human limit of fifth-level intentionality (Dunbar 2004). Our ability to fathom the minds of others (at least to some extent) underlies our most distinctively human forms of behavior, including collaboration, teaching, learning, the use of language, and (since this powerful mind-reading ability can be used for good or ill) deception and manipulation, also peculiarly human activities in their deliberate forms. The inability to perform such feats of social cognition appears to be one of the keys to the grave disability of autism.

What do we know about the neural basis for this ability? Science is only just beginning to explore these high-level human abilities, but brain imaging techniques have started to shed some light on their anatomy. The most striking recent discovery has been that a network of brain regions — overlapping with the midline cortical regions linked earlier to the "core self" — is particularly active in the resting brain and in a set of functions that are all in some way linked to the human self. These include theory of mind, moral decision-making, recollecting the past, and imagining the future (Buckner et al. 2008). I will discuss this "default network" in greater detail below.

The "theory of mind" is well named, for the term reminds us that our knowledge of the mind is not straightforward. The concept of mind has a fascinating tendency to appropriate abiological qualities, such as immateriality and immortality. When we think about ourselves as subjects of awareness, we tend to forget the objects that we also are. I will return to this theme below. But first we need to consider a final kind of knowledge that can enrich our subjectivity — by allowing us to think about ourselves as travelers in time.

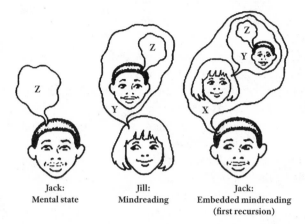

Jack:
Mental state

Jill:
Mindreading

Jack:
Embedded mindreading
(first recursion)

Figure 1. Theory of mind: three degrees of intentionality (Jack thinks, Jill thinks that Jack thinks, Jack thinks that Jill thinks that Jack thinks . . .).

This is Sally   This is Anne

Sally puts her ball in the basket

Sally goes away

Anne moves her ball to her box

Where will Sally look for her ball?

Figure 2. Theory of mind: the Sally and Anne test, which challenges children of three and older children with autism (Frith 1989).

ADAM ZEMAN

Knowing Ourselves: The Extended Self

Few, if any, of us remember what happened to us before the age of three. This is remarkable, and tantalizing, since so many of the events that shape us most powerfully, setting the direction of our future lives, occur during this unremembered period. Whether or not this amnesia reflects the difficulty of retrieving memories we acquired in such a different context than that of our subsequent self, the late maturation of the complex neural mechanisms required for autobiographical memory or prolific hippocampal neurogenesis in early life, by the time we approach our first school years we are beginning to lay down a more or less continuous record of events. From then on we can, with greater or lesser success, both revisit our past selves and project ourselves into imagined futures. Indeed, a rich seam of recent work in neuropsychology has shown that recollection of the past and imagination of the future depend on substantially similar processes in the brain. This capacity for "mental time travel," liberating us from the here and now, is crucial to our self-knowledge. It creates an "extended self" from the "core self," which is given to us in experience from one moment to the next. It expands our subjectivity into the fourth dimension. Tulving has referred to it in an influential set of distinctions as "autonoetic awareness" (Tulving 1985). (See Table 1 on p. 123.) It is also, perhaps self-evidently, the source of much inner conflict. Our ability to "time travel" allows us to recollect happiness and tragedy alike; it enables us to compare a painful present with a more contented past; to entertain future goals that energize us, but that may then poignantly elude our grasp. Conflicts between our current needs and our previous intentions are familiar to us all. Moreover, our remarkable memories are woefully imperfect, all the more so as time passes from the remembered event. Powerful as it is, recollection may be outdistanced by the increasing length of our lives.

A meta-analysis of the now quite numerous studies of brain activation by recollection of past episodes reveals the involvement of a network of brain regions, including many of those found in the default network (Svoboda et al. 2006). The medial temporal lobes are closely implicated in memory retrieval, the medial frontal regions in "self-related processing" and memory search, the medial posterior parietal lobes in tasks involving imagery, the lateral temporal lobes in the organization of "semantic" knowledge, and the temporoparietal junction in tasks requiring an understanding of the body in space.

The knowledge gained by the protoself is obviously useful: it enables the organism to approach whatever will help it to prosper and avoid whatever

132

threatens its well-being. The knowledge gained by the core self allows it to bring a wide range of cognitive resources to bear on its experience, allowing it to adapt to changing circumstances in the light of its history and future purposes. What are the uses of the knowledge gained by the extended self? Knowledge of other minds opens up possibilities of cooperation and Machiavellian manipulation; explicit recollection of the past enables a richer vision of the future; self-knowledge and insight enable us to monitor — and even sometimes change — ourselves.

Some Elephants in the Room

I have argued that human subjectivity is multilayered. At the center of our subjective being lies a knowledgeable but inarticulate — and probably preconscious — "protoself" that is charged with self-preservation, with powers that can be traced back to the very beginnings of life on earth. Our human protoself is enveloped by and interacts with a "core self," a later evolutionary arrival that elaborates implicit processes present in the protoself in such a way that they become known explicitly, and thereby become available for a range of psychological purposes. In very recent evolutionary time, the protoself and the core self have, in turn, become objects of knowledge — our knowledge of our bodies, minds, and histories, our knowledge of ourselves — giving rise to the "extended self." This account, incomplete as it surely is, helps me understand how I became a subject, one of the billions of loci of experience and agency with which I share the earth, and helps me understand what a subject is. But in telling this story, I have finessed (if I am generous to myself), or ignored (if I am less generous), some philosophical quandaries, the "elephants in the room." I should at least introduce these, even if in the present state of knowledge it is impossible to dispel them altogether.

The first objection likely to be offered is that I have sketched a naturalistic account of subjectivity that has, precisely, left out subjectivity. You came to my chapter, you may well feel, hoping for a satisfying explanation of how an object, your body, comes to be a subject, to have experiences — of how a rose comes to smell so sweet and its thorns to sting so bitterly, and indeed of why they smell and sting like anything at all. You may judge that I have failed to bridge — or even (so far) to recognize — the daunting "explanatory gap" between the kinds of natural processes that I have discussed and the phenomena of interest to us, experience and subjectivity. I sympathize with this reaction, since I have often been left with the same sense of dissatisfaction upon reading accounts of the general kind that I have offered. I will not be able to banish this reaction entirely, but let me try to mitigate it somewhat.

First, explanations of the kind that I have outlined surely give, at the least, an illuminating account of the key elements, the structure, of subjectivity. We *can* see the germs of interiority, autonomy, and purpose in the protoself. We *can* find in the brain — though I have not discussed this at any length here — the neural basis for the distinctions we draw in perception, the taxonomy of our emotions, the capacity of our memory, and so forth across the range of our psychological functions. Studies of neural activity *can* increasingly track the features of our experience, one by one. Theories of the core self *are* beginning to give an informative account of what distinguishes reportable from subliminal events in the brain. We *can* now glimpse the evolutionary steps and the associated transformations in the brain, required to supply us with the concept of our extended selves — our knowledge of our own bodies, our understanding of the workings of the minds of others, our recollections of the past and models of the future. All this surely makes at least a promising start toward an explanation of the occurrence and the qualities of consciousness.

Second, as a growing number of authors emphasize, we should not expect too much from the brain in providing us with an explanation for awareness. The provocative slogan of this line of thought is: "The mind is not in the head." Without embarking on a detailed discussion of such accounts, I can note that the broad thrust of the argument is that our brains exist not to mirror but to navigate the world. Understanding how they work — and their role in creating subjectivity — requires that we study the brain in action, a process of interaction between the brain and the body, and their physical, social, and cultural environments. By doing so, we may be able to shrink the explanatory gap between the matter we are made of and the experience it helps to sustain.

Third, the problem to which our attention is being drawn is essentially the "mind-brain" problem. It can easily seem that minds and brains are such very different kinds of things that there is little hope of understanding how one can give rise to the other (if, indeed, it does). It can seem utterly mysterious that intricate biological processes involving the firing of millions of neurons in our heads give rise to subjective experiences, such as at the sight of blood or upon a surge of joy. But we have to ask ourselves, in fairness, how sure we are that we know what the mind is — and what experience consists in. I suggest that our understanding of these is primitive, influenced by cultural traditions that may be inaccurate guides, and by a sense of polar opposition between mind and matter that is, frankly, mistaken. All the minds we know are vested in matter; all the matter we encounter is represented in our minds. This does not sound like an oppositional relationship, but rather a circular one. I am not a metaphysician, but the metaphysics relevant to the nature of mind appears to me sufficiently uncertain that we should not let it deter us from pursuing promising lines of scientific inquiry into the nature of the self.

A second general kind of objection warrants some discussion. Some have argued that naturalistic accounts of human behavior and experience are self-defeating, since they undermine the rational processes that are required to arrive at them. I have encountered the argument in two versions; they are formally similar. The first (A) attempts to refute determinism with respect to human thought; the second (B) does the same for evolutionary theory. They run as follows:

Version A

(1) Everything that happens is determined by a chain of physical events.
(2) Therefore, whether we conclude that a proposition is true or false is determined by a chain of physical processes.
(3) Therefore, the truth or falsity of a proposition does not determine whether we conclude that it is true or false.
(4) If so, rational consideration is futile: the initial claim can be rejected, since it is self-defeating.

Version B

(1) Everything in our nature, including the workings of our minds, has been conditioned by the selective advantage it confers in the course of evolution.
(2) Therefore, whether we conclude that a proposition is true or false is determined by our evolutionary history.
(3) Therefore, the truth or falsity of a proposition does not determine whether we conclude that it is true or false.
(4) If so, rational consideration is futile, and the initial claim can be rejected, since it is self-defeating.

These arguments are beguiling, but highly questionable. With respect to version A, consider the possibility that there is a dog in your garden as you look out of the kitchen window in the morning. A chain of causal processes (involving light, the optical properties of your eyes, processes within your visual system, activity in your language areas, and so forth) connects the presence of the dog in the garden with your seeing the dog in the garden and

135

your declaration (to someone) that indeed there is one there. In the absence of some such chain of causal processes, your judgment about the dog's location would surely be highly conjectural! The involvement of the causal chain does not *prevent* the truth or falsity of a proposition from influencing your decision: the chain *enables* you to judge truly. This is not to say, of course, that your judgments of truth and falsity will always be correct. Indeed, "cognitive illusions" that reliably induce people to judge incorrectly (at least initially) contribute to the evidence that such judgments are the outcome of a causal chain that can be biased by the quirks of our cognitive systems.

Just the same considerations apply to version B. Whether we judge that there is a dog in the garden or that a potential mate is attractive, the putative role played by our evolutionary history in enabling our judgment will not invalidate it. Indeed, just as a chain of external physical processes was required to enable judgments of truth and falsity about the presence of the dog, so a chain of evolutionary processes was required to create a cognitive system with the capacity to make them. Your eyes — the visual areas in your brain — and your language centers are all the outcome of countless ancient evolutionary events.

Moreover, it should not surprise us that our highly evolved brains are good at distinguishing truth from falsity. Evolution has a keen interest in truth: organisms that fail to track the way things really are in the world are doomed. It is true that the primary value of natural selection is not truth per se, but survival. This helps to explain why our minds are prone to shortcuts that can mislead us, in cognitive illusions. But we are able to identify and make good at least some of our errors because, though we cannot stand outside ourselves entirely, we can use one part of our evolved cognitive system to criticize and compensate for the failings of another.

We often get things wrong, but neither determinism nor evolutionary theory invalidates our efforts to get them right. The rival view — that judgments of truth and falsity can and must be made independently of causal processes or an evolved cognitive system — requires a starkly abstract and strangely disembodied view of thought.

Two Key Misunderstandings

Human subjects or selves have two conspicuous qualities that might make scientific accounts look like nonstarters. First, we are (at least on good days) dynamic, autonomous, creative entities; our brains, by contrast, are often compared to computers, which are invaluable tools but essentially passive ones, dependent, for all their animus, on us. Second, our subjectivity is suffused by human culture. It is likely that many of our most precious moments are spent in ways that rely on human traditions that may seem to have little connection with our biology — whether listening to Mozart or Snow Patrol, reading Proust or McEwan, contemplating the quantum universe or cooking Chinese food. In contrast to these views, I shall try to persuade you that the brain is itself dynamic, autonomous, creative, and quite at home with human culture.

Experimentalists often probe the brain with stimuli of various kinds and study its responses. Theoreticians often model the brain as a computational system. Both approaches are perfectly valid, but any inference that the brain is a quintessentially reactive organ or that its essential function is to run programs would be mistaken. Neuroscientific understanding of the brain is being transformed by recent discoveries that reveal its autonomy and dynamism. The simplest observation, but a key one, is that the brain is a voracious organ, consuming (at rest) 20 percent or so of the oxygen we breathe and the glucose we generate, though it contributes only around 2 percent to body weight (Gusnard and Raichle 2001). This level of consumption is maintained throughout day and night, with a fall of just one-fifth or so below its waking level in deep sleep, and a return to waking values during dreams. But, more than this, stimulating the brain — by showing it an exciting film or getting it to answer hard math questions — raises its fuel consumption by only a few percent. Most of its energy, in other words, is being expended on autonomous activity, and, as it turns out, that activity is primarily neuronal signaling (rather than housekeeping chores). Thus the brain is ceaselessly active, and most of its activity is endogenously driven.

This has been known for many years. Recent work has developed the theme dramatically. It turns out, quite unexpectedly (though in retrospect, in keeping with so many important discoveries, this might have been expected) that the entire functional architecture of the brain can be observed in its resting state (Smith et al. 2009). The approach that has shown this is simple in principle. Various forms of brain imaging, particularly functional MRI, can visualize the activity of brain regions while they are at rest. Once "rest state data" have been acquired across the whole brain, one can ask, of any small region, where else in the brain activity is correlated with activity there. Analyses based on such patterns of correlated activity turn out to reveal the functional systems of the working brain, for example, the visual and auditory systems, the language system, attentional systems, and a system that has attracted intense interest and research since its discovery, the "default system." We encountered this network of regions, which is particularly active in the "resting brain," earlier, since it is associated with theory of mind, recollection of the past, imagination of the future, and moral thinking. It contains most of the regions linked to "self-processing," and several of the areas involved in the "global neuronal workspace." It is a plausible candidate for the primary neuronal substrate of the self — and, like the self, it is constantly active in the background of our lives, indeed especially active when external demands and distractions fall away. These lines of evidence make the brain feel like a much more plausible and congenial home for subjectivity and selfhood than used to be the case. Like the human subject, while the brain can of course respond to events as they impinge, it is, by its nature, conspicuously autonomous, dynamic, and creative.

But still, the brain surely has little to do with the cultural matters that occupy much of our lives, the "ideas in which we live." At most, it provides the ignorant hardware that culture ingeniously programs with ideas for which our animal brains were never designed. This view, too, turns out to be a misconception (Zeman 2009). The period during which the specifically human features of our brains evolved, the past two million years — through successive species of *Homo habilis, Homo erectus,* and *Homo sapiens* — was the period over which human culture first appeared and gained momentum. While the main surviving relics from the earlier stages of this process are stone tools, and there is much uncertainty about the detailed timing of major developments, there is no doubt that during this period the key features of human culture began to appear: the family, division of labor, early forms of professional specialization, the production of a range of tools, the use of fire, the construction of dwellings, the use of the clothes, and, most controversially, language, religion, and art. The hominid brain roughly tripled in size while this was happening. It is highly likely that the emergence of culture, if only in its simpler forms, was a key source of the selection pressure that drove the rapid evolution of the brain, as intellect became the key resource in the struggle for survival. If so, culture is not the antithesis of biology, as it is often depicted, but one of its key elements, the niche that we inhabit. We are precisely cultural creatures.

Subjects and Objects

I have suggested that human subjectivity is a layered phenomenon, each layer enclosing and extending the last. The five layers this chapter has distinguished might be described along these lines, using knowledge broadly to encompass all the ways of apprehending the world distinguished in the course of this chapter:

Layer 1   knowing (as in blindsight)
Layer 2   knowing that I know (as in normal sight)
Layer 3   knowing that *I* know that I know (as when I look in a mirror)
Layer 4   knowing that I *know* that I know that I know (as when I reflect on the process of knowing)
Layer 5   knowing that I knew that I knew (as when I recollect what I once knew)

I do not mean to suggest that cognitive evolution must always move through these stages rigidly, nor that an animal's cognitive capacities could be fully described by placing it somewhere on this hierarchy. But these distinctions point to some key landmarks in both the ontogeny and the phylogeny of human cognition.

Subjectivity has everything to do with having a viewpoint. Viewpoints are by their nature unique: you, and only you, can occupy your given viewpoint at a given time. This simple physical constraint helps to explain the puzzle of our uniqueness. But there is a second element: human viewpoints are so distinctive because our huge brains become so different, one from another, over our long lifetimes, as each of us is exposed to subtly differing experiences. Substantial resources are available to code for our idiosyncrasies: the thousand million million malleable connections between the hundred thousand million neurons in our brains. We are poorly attuned to complexity: if we had a more sensitive complexity detector, we would be dazzled by our own.

Subjectivity involves more than being individual and idiosyncratic. It has connotations also of inwardness and privacy. These are at least partly explained by the intricacy of the recursive processes — Douglas Hofstadter's "strange loops" (Hofstadter 2007) — that take place within our brains to sustain the nested forms of selfhood just distinguished.

Subjectivity, according to the view I have advanced, is a natural property of nested processes within our brains. Historically, we have tended to regard our subjective selves as having properties that sharply distinguish them from the objects they inhabit — as immortal, immaterial inhabitants of mortal, material vessels. I have given three reasons why we should feel more relaxed about the proposition that our subjectivity arises from the objects that we are.

First, the relationship between objects and subjects is much less straight-forward than the abstract, oppositional contrast suggests. Arguably, their true relationship is circular: subjects are particular kinds of very complicated living objects. Objects exist in the experience of subjects. Mind arises from matter, while matter is conceived by mind. The "problem of subjectivity," or the "mystery of mind," tends to be formulated as if we knew everything there was to know about objectivity and matter. This is far from true. We understand the nature of mind and matter roughly equally well — or equally poorly. Second, the dominant computational model of the brain can obscure the fact that the brain is very much alive, intrinsically active, autonomous, creative, a natural host for the self. Third, the human brain was shaped by and for human culture: the contrast that is often drawn between the natural and the human world is to that extent misleading. Allowing that the scientific exploration of the self is at an early stage, it can offer some genuine insights into the natural origins of subjectivity. Neither its individuality nor its inwardness — both of which are, indeed, critical features of subjectivity — precludes this style of explanation.

REFERENCES

Baars, B. J., T. Z. Ramsoy, and S. Laureys. 2003. Brain, conscious experience, and the observing self. *Trends in Neuroscience* 26, no. 12: 671-75.

Bayes, A., L. N. van de Lagemaat, M. O. Collins, M. D. Croning, I. R. Whittle, J. S. Choudhary, and S. G. Grant. 2011. Characterization of the proteome, diseases and evolution of the human postsynaptic density. *Natural Neuroscience* 14: 19-21.

Buckner, R. L., J. R. Andrews-Hanna, and D. L. Schacter. 2008. The brain's default network: Anatomy, function, and relevance to disease. *Annals of the New York Academic Sciences* 1124: 1-38.

Carhart-Harris, R. L., and K. J. Friston. 2010. The default-mode, ego-functions and free-energy: A neurobiological account of Freudian ideas. *Brain* 133: 1265-83.

Cowey, A., and P. Stoerig. 1995. Blindsight in monkeys. *Nature* 373: 247-49.

Critchley, H. G., and N. A. Harrison. 2013. Visceral influences on brain and behaviour. *Neuron* 77: 624-37.

Damasio, A. 2000. *The feeling of what happens.* London: Vintage.

Dehaene, S., and J. P. Changeux. 2011. Experimental and theoretical approaches to conscious processing. *Neuron* 70: 200-227.

Dehaene, S., J.-P. Changeux, L. Naccache, et al. 2006. Conscious, preconscious, and subliminal processing: A testable taxonomy. *Trends in Cognitive Science* 10, no. 5: 204-11.

Dunbar, R. 2004. *The human story: A new history of mankind's evolution.* London: Faber and Faber.

Edelman, G. M. 1992. *Bright air, brilliant fire.* New York: Penguin Books.

Frith, U. 1989. *Autism: Explaining the engima.* Oxford: Basil Blackwell, Wiley.

Gallup, G. G. 1970. Chimpanzees: Self-recognition. *Science* 167: 86-87.

Gusnard, D. A., and M. E. Raichle. 2001. Searching for a baseline: Functional imaging and the resting human brain. *Natural Review of Neuroscience* 2: 685-94.

Hofstadter, D. R. 2007. *I am a strange loop.* New York: Basic Books.

Jones, S., R. D. Martin, and D. R. Pilbeam, eds., 1994. *The Cambridge Encyclopedia of Human Evolution.* Cambridge: Cambridge University Press.

Maclean, P. D. 1990. *The triune brain in evolution: Role in paleocerebral functions.* New York: Plenum Press.

Neisser, U. 1988. Five kinds of self-knowledge. *Philosophical Psychology* 1: 35-39.

Panksepp, J., and G. Northoff. 2009. The trans-species core SELF: The emergence of active cultural and neuro-ecological agents through self-related processing within subcortical-cortical midline networks. *Consciousness and Cognition* 18: 193-215.

Reiss, D., and L. Marino. 2001. Mirror self-recognition in the bottlenose dolphin: A case of cognitive convergence. *Proceedings of the National Academy of Science USA* 98: 5937-42.

Rosenthal, D. M. 1986. Two concepts of consciousness. *Philosophical Studies* 49: 329-59.

Smith, J. D., W. E. Shields, and D. A. Washburn. 2003. The comparative psychology of uncertainty monitoring and metacognition. *Behavioral Brain Science* 26: 317-39.

Smith, S. M., P. T. Fox, et al. 2009. Correspondence of the brain's functional architecture during activation and rest. *Proceedings of the National Academy of Science USA* 106: 13040-45.

Stoerig, P., and A. Cowey. 1997. Blindsight in man and monkey. *Brain* 120 (Pt 3): 535-59.

Svoboda, E., M. C. McKinnon, and B. Levine. 2006. The functional neuroanatomy of autobiographical memory: A meta-analysis. *Neuropsychologia* 44: 2189-2208.

Thompson, E. 2007. *Mind in life: Biology, phenomenology, and the sciences of mind.* Cambridge, MA: Harvard University Press.

Tulving, E. 1985. Memory and consciousness. *Canadian Psychology:* 1-12.

Weiskrantz, L. 1997. *Consciousness lost and found.* Oxford: Oxford University Press.

Zeman, A. 2002. *Consciousness: A user's guide.* London: Yale University Press.

———. 2009. Cultural creatures. *RSA Journal:* 16-17.

The Emergence of Personhood: Reflections on *The Game of Life*

Timothy O'Connor

The correlated terms "emergence" and "reduction" are used in several ways in discussions of human personhood, engendering confusion or talking at cross-purposes. I try to bring clarity to this discussion by reflecting on John Conway's cellular automaton *The Game of Life* and simple variations on it. We may think of such variants as toy models of our own world that, owing to their simplicity, enable us to see quite clearly, in general terms, two importantly distinct ways ("weak" and "strong") in which organized macroscopic phenomena might emerge from underlying microphysical processes. I will then consider the evidentiary standing for strong emergence associated with aspects of human life in the actual world, and I will argue that this has profound implications regarding the extent of (dis)continuity of human beings with the rest of nature and of our moral and/or theological significance within it.

Human beings are the most profound point of convergence of the world's basic forms of complexity: physico-chemical, biological, psychological, informational, social. We appear to be unique among living species in having the ability to engage in long-range individual and collective planning, or at least planning behavior that exceeds rudimentary foraging and storage behavior and is thought through. Standing out more dramatically are our abilities to partly control and manipulate the very biological and environmental conditions of our continued survival and to alter dramatically the circumstances of our day-to-day habitat. Furthermore, we think and act within complex moral and religious narratives, apart from which much of what we do would make no sense. A key question raised by the essays in this volume is whether these and other remarkable abilities and tendencies signal a discontinuity in the evolutionary processes that gave rise to us and, if so, to what extent and in what form.

Each of the many sciences that consider the phenomena of human life do so with different methodologies and from different "altitudes." Whether and how they mesh so as to provide a picture of a unitary whole is itself a substantive, open question. Some of the sciences have at best advanced to a midgame stage. It might well be that we are not currently in a position to see which of them merely offer useful models rather than more-or-less accurate maps of their domains.

A good place to consider how theories from different domains interrelate is in their characterization of organized complexity: phenomena that exhibit strikingly different kinds of robust patterns from those seen among their constituent elements when not so organized. Organized complexity is seen at a number of levels represented in living human beings. Theorists have described each of these patterned phenomena as exhibiting "emergent" (or sometimes "top-down") causation or control. It is tempting for specialists in one area to develop an abstract model of their favored phenomena and then to suggest that the model holds the key to thinking about naturally emergent phenomena generally. But it is rash to suppose at the outset that there is a *single* way to accurately and usefully apply a notion of emergence to all cases of interest. Maybe emergence is more "dramatic" or fundamentally significant in some cases of patterned complexity than in others.

In what follows I want to try to isolate two distinct senses of emergence, "weak" and "strong." The two notions are not orthogonal but rather of differing logical "strengths." Furthermore, they signal a basic division, on each side of which one may conceive variant forms, possibly such that one may think in terms of degrees of robustness. The contemporary sciences are very complicated and nuanced. This is good for the advancement of knowledge, since the world itself is complicated and nuanced, but it can make it difficult to see the fundamental issue I wish to raise. So I will invite us to consider a kind of toy world whose dynamics are quite transparent. It will be easy to isolate my two senses of emergence in relation to this kind of world and to grasp what kind of evidence would enable one to decide conclusively whether both notions, or merely the weaker one, have application. I will then consider the evidentiary standing for strong emergence associated with human life in the actual world, and I will argue that this has profound implications regarding the extent of (dis)continuity of human beings with the rest of nature and of our moral and/or theological significance within it.

The Game of Life and Two Forms of Emergence

Conveniently, my toy world has been supplied to us by the mathematician John Conway in the form of his cellular automaton *The Game of Life* (versions of *Game of Life* are readily available online; see http://conway-life.com/). *Life* is a dynamic and spatially and temporally discrete two-dimensional infinite grid. One sets an arbitrary initial state by assigning one of two basic properties, *live* or *dead,* to each of the square cells. Each subsequent state of the grid is wholly determined by applying the following three rules to every cell (which has eight "neighbors" in every direction, including diagonally):

> Birth: A dead cell with exactly three live neighbors becomes a live cell.
> Survival: A live cell with two or three live neighbors stays alive.
> Death: In all other cases, a cell dies or remains dead.

Over time, stable clusters of various kinds arise and exhibit macrolevel patterns of activity and interaction with other cluster types. (Apt names have been given to certain recurring sorts, such as "oscillator," "glider," "puffer," and "eater.") Once these clusters appear, their macrolevel behavior can be studied in ignorance of the three microlevel rules that underlie them. Interestingly, different kinds of high-level patterns are observed in games with different initial conditions.

If we think of Conway's 2-D grid as a kind of toy world (there are 3-D versions of it as well), the three basic rules and its initial state constitute its fundamental "physics." The high-level patterns can be thought of as its "chemistry" or "biology." These high-level patterns exhibit what I will term "weak" (or "physics-closed") emergence: they are emergent in the sense that one cannot — in any straightforward way — derive the high-level rules from the fundamental rules alone (though, at least for the case at hand, one could do so in principle, in a very laborious, roundabout way, from the low-level rules plus the initial conditions).

Weak Emergence=$_{\text{def}}$ Some aspects of the behavior of a specifiable type of composite, organized system that exhibit ongoing or recurrent lawlike patterns that, outside this organizational context, are neither exhibited by the system's components nor describable in terms of the concepts of the most compact theory that fully describes the component behavior.

The high-level rules of *Life* are only weakly emergent in that they do not in any way alter or supplement the basic dynamics that drive the world's evolution. The "physics" of a standard *Life* world is causally closed, with each total configuration of the grid at a time t_1 being strictly determined by its state at the previous time t_0 in accordance with the three basic rules.

Someone wishing to emphasize the significance of weak emergence might say that the high-level *theory* that applies under the right conditions to composites such as gliders and eaters is irreducible to the basic cellular theory and constitutes a relatively autonomous *explanatory* system: we can predict and explain macrolevel phenomena using only our knowledge of macrolevel laws and facts. (Absent the disruption of collisions with merely "physical" clusters, of course: just as in our world, biology is not going to tell you what will happen when a meteor strikes a biological niche.) Moreover, for certain purposes, an explanation of a configured state that is at once physical and biological in terms of biology is more illuminating than one in terms of physics. If we not only observe but intervene in a *Life* world by manipulating the value of one higher-level variable and holding other relevant factors constant, we can change the value of another higher-level variable in very predictable ways and in a variety of contexts. This indicates that we have not only high-level explanation, but also high-level *causal* explanation.

However, we should observe that this *theoretical/explanatory irreducibility* in standard *Life* worlds is matched by *physical reduction* in the following sense: first, the state of every stable cluster at any moment is wholly fixed and constituted by the properties of each of its cells; second, the cluster's evolution over time is fundamentally determined by the basic "physical" laws. If we think of the fundamental rules in *Life* as causal, then each macrolevel event (such as a glider's changing position over a time interval) has microlevel *causes,* the microlevel causes of its components' positions and behavior, and thus a microlevel causal explanation, in addition to the macrolevel explanation. The microlevel causation determines the macrolevel causation, not vice versa. Macrolevel events aren't doing anything "extra," that is, over and above what the microlevel events are doing, in order to bring about the positions and behavior of gliders, eaters, and the like. Macrolevel events, then, do not make a nonredundant causal difference to the behavior of the objects in such a *Life* world. Macrolevel objects and events in such worlds are weakly emergent only: theoretically/explanatorily irreducible, ontologically and causally derivative.

Once one gets used to looking at things in this way, physical reductionism can begin to seem inevitable — both in any imaginable variety of a *Life* world and in any law-governed physical world, notwithstanding the added complexity of three spatial dimensions, a richer inventory of basic properties, and continuity in space and time. Surely, *any* kind of organized complex phenomena must be grounded in comprehensive underlying patterns that hold without exception in every context?

Whatever is true with respect to comprehensive physical reduction in our own world, we can readily describe variations on standard *Life* worlds that enable us see that this *need not* be the case: that is, there exists a coherent form of alternative. Imagine that you are handed a tall stack of (very large!) numbered sheets of graph paper. On them are changing snapshots of a *Life* world (where the shaded squares are "live" cells). Your job is to figure out the basic transitional rules. After flipping through several pages, you hit upon the Birth, Survival, and Death rules as the most compact ways to capture all the transitions in each cell. Continuing to check subsequent pages to verify that the rules hold without exception, you hit upon a page where the result departs in a small way from what the rules predict. You observe that the divergence is restricted to a complex star-shaped cluster that first appeared on the previous page. Flipping ahead, you observe that as more of these star-shaped clusters appear, their subsequent evolution, too, departs from what the three basic rules predict. Further investigation reveals that the form the divergence takes is identical in each case.

You now can predict, upon seeing the emergence of the star shape, what the future world-states will be, using *modified, disjunctive* forms of the original rules. The new Birth rule, for example, has the form: A dead cell with exactly three live neighbors becomes a live cell, *except* when occurring within the bounds of, or immediately adjacent to, a star cluster, in which case. . . . Imagine that as star clusters come into contact, new modifications of the original rules are required to fully capture the way they interact. You find that the most compact way to capture the behavior is (1) to assign primitive new properties ("bright," "golden") to star clusters and then (2) to describe the precise impact of the emergent properties of the clusters on the "ordinary" microlevel dynamics via additional laws *that are no less fundamental* — even though they have application only in limited contexts.

The "world" you have been given to inspect exhibits what I will call "strong emergence":

Strong Emergence=$_{def}$ Some aspects of the behavior of a specifiable type of composite, organized system are such that (1) they cannot be fully described, even at a microphysical level of description, by compact low-level rules making no reference to macroscopic structures that *can* fully describe behavior outside certain situations of organized complexity, and (2) they can be fully described by rules that apply only in these contexts and that essentially involve reference to macroscopic structural properties.

Worlds manifesting strong emergence are plainly coherent possibilities. But are they objectionably strange (or "magical") ones that should offend the sensibilities of a properly empirically minded theorist? I don't see why — unless one is in the grips of a simple building-block picture of physical reality, treating the hypothesis that everything that happens is wholly fixed by compact microregularities without regard to macrocontext as some sort of a priori truth. It seems, rather, that there ought to be no presumption one way or another in advance of a sufficiently thorough investigation of the empirical facts. As the early twentieth-century emergentist Samuel Alexander put it, we should come to the world "with the 'natural piety' of the investigator" (1920, 47).

Perhaps you are thinking that a world with strong emergence is somehow fundamentally disunified. That might be a proper conclusion if departures from the simple rules happened willy-nilly. But in the scenario I've outlined, the new patterns, once they are discovered and the conditions of their appearance are learned, will become wholly predictable. There are sufficient conditions, involving organized complexity of a certain kind, for their appearance. Given that this is so, to make sense of such novel phenomena, we need only enrich our conception of the properties of the *fundamental* units (the cells), supposing that in addition to live and dead ones, whose dispositional profiles are largely captured by the original unmodified rules, they contain a set of dispositions toward cooperatively contributing to just such behavioral discontinuities, a disposition that is merely latent absent the requisite macrocircumstance. Unity within a physical world does not require causal continuity of *behavior,* only continuity of dispositional structure. In worlds that feature strong emergence, the seeds of every strongly emergent macroproperty and the behavior it manifests are found within the world's fundamental elements: latent dispositions awaiting only the right context for manifestation.

Strong Emergence and Consciousness

Armed with the basic distinction between weak and strong emergence, we can ask ourselves whether specific forms of organized complexity in our own world involve weak emergence only, or are instead forms of strong emergence. Surprisingly, there is quite good evidence for strong emergence at a very low level of complexity — within the domain of quantum mechanics itself. Well-confirmed theory indicates that some simple particle systems go into "mixed" states that cannot be decomposed into any mere "sum" of the states of the individual particles: they are "relational wholes." Outside this domain, the issue gets more difficult to adjudicate. Personally, I think that it is very difficult to establish strong emergence *or* its denial in any domain outside the mental. (More on the mental in a moment.)

Conway's standard *Game of Life* beautifully illustrates the consistency of striking and explanatorily irreducible macroscopic behavior with physical reduction, which two conditions constitute none other than our weak emergence. Note that "top-down causation," the term of choice for some theorists, likewise admits of weak and strong varieties. That there are top-down constraints on individual particle or molecule behavior is evident: a particle caught up in the motion of a wheel rolling down a hill; a molecule caught up in the life of a goal-driven organism as it moves through space. But these cases *may* be wholly a matter of low-level entities, so to speak, coming to "constrain themselves," entering into and collectively maintaining various kinds of stable boundary conditions merely by doing what they always do in their local interactions. (We should also recognize, however, that the simplicity of *Life* worlds can mask the fact that there can be different degrees of complexity of high-level patterns under the umbrella category of weak, or "physics-closed," emergence: the organizational complexity of a living animal moving through its habitat is much greater than that of a wheel rolling down a hill. While degree of complexity is *not* a bridge between weak and strong emergence, it is a theoretically significant feature for the study of complex systems and of interest in its own right.)

But my modified *Life* scenario shows that we can just as readily envision a stronger form of emergence. Unfortunately, once we are dealing with systems of great complexity relative to the microphysical level, it is unclear what feasible means are or could be available for deciding which form of emergence is being manifested. Obviously, it is a fantasy to suppose that we might someday apply fundamental physical laws directly to complex systems, tracking each of the many billions of physical factors constituting or impinging on them over a specified time interval, and see whether — and how — the laws prove incomplete. The best hope for making a case for a weak emergentist account of a domain's novel complexity is to use simplifying approximation techniques to develop reductive structural models of the target domain that prove to have some measure of empirical backing.

Some seem to think — wrongly, I would judge — that strong emergence, while possible, is inherently improbable, given the methods of science and especially the advances of physical and biological science from the beginning of the twentieth century (e.g., McLaughlin 1992). This keeps them from giving proper weight to the powerful evidence that we have for strong emergence that is right under our noses (which I will discuss shortly), in the form of our own conscious mental lives. I will make a couple of brief remarks intended to challenge these sources of built-up resistance to taking strong emergence seriously.

My first remark is historical. From the mid-nineteenth century to the early twentieth, there was a robust scientific-philosophical tradition in chemistry and biology, centered in Great Britain, that involved commitment to something like strong emergence in the sense that I have defined (McLaughlin 1992; O'Connor 1994). There was some measure of conceptual confusion in these discussions, making precise identification of their operative notion(s) difficult. The British emergentists had a neatly "layered" understanding of nature: there are discrete and isolated strata or levels within the most complex systems found in the natural world, and each level features a unified system with its own same-level properties and special laws governing their co-evolution over time. This picture was shown to be a failure by a raft of evidence in twentieth-century science, which showed that "lower-level" processes continuously and directly impinge on and partly regulate those at higher levels. In particular, specific biochemical processes are now known to regulate intercellular processes, which, on a large scale, constitute the functioning of biological organs. Even psychological processes are causally influenced in bottom-up fashion by subtle biochemical matters, such as chemical balance levels and neuronal receptor conditions that are implicated in clinical depression and schizophrenia, respectively.

But this kind of evidence from twentieth-century science can be taken to strongly disconfirm the strong emergentist view only if one conflates it with the particular account proposed by these earlier thinkers, an account that appears unnecessarily crude in hindsight. It is quite possible that higher-level features of a system have a "downward" causal influence on the evolving microstructure that sustains them, even as the lower-level processes play a vital dynamical role in the way emergent processes themselves unfold. In other words, we should replace the picture of mostly horizontal, or same-level, causal patterns within each level with one in which there is a complex web of myriad upward and downward causal influences that jointly (and nonredundantly) determine the system's evolution through time. Nothing in the successes of the more fundamental sciences in illuminating a vast array of higher-level phenomena precludes the applicability of this interactive kind of emergentist framework.

My second remark is that there is a tendency among some thinkers trained in the methods of empirical science to conflate what we have reason to believe is *true* with what we have *methodological* reason to take as the most fruitful starting hypothesis. Even if, for example, the mental is strongly emergent from the physical, if you wish to understand the details of just how mental features emerge and the difference they make to the overall functioning of the organism, you must have a thorough understanding of the purely physical processes from which they emerge. Thus, in practice, you should push a reductionist approach as far as you can, thereby isolating any emergent features there may be, allowing for highly specific descriptions of their character and function. Unlike the philosopher, the typical scientist does not spend much time thinking about what will turn out to be true at the end of scientific inquiry. Rather, she is thinking about what working hypotheses are most useful in advancing current understanding. It is easy but mistaken to slide from the quite proper methodological posture of looking for reducing explanations to drawing an evidential conclusion.

Each time we observe the world in some way, we are simultaneously aware of something else, namely, our *experience* of that bit of the world. We know our conscious experiences, not indirectly (i.e., not mediated by theory or even inner representation) but by direct acquaintance. I am presently visually aware of a large purple coffee cup next to my computer. This awareness consists in a certain kind of mental representational state, caused by a very rapid but complex processing of light reflections off the surface of the cup. By contrast, I am aware of the inner representational state itself simply by undergoing it. My acquaintance with it requires no causal or representational mediation; it is ontologically basic. My subjective experience of the cup consists in a unified package of "looks" of color, shape, relative size, and orientation (to me). These ways that the cup appears to me can change without the cup's undergoing any significant change at all, for instance, by dimming the light. These are changing intrinsic features of the experience, ones that I may not attend to at all — ordinarily my attention is on the cup — but they are directly present to me nonetheless.

My visual field is usually quite complex: right now it is filled with the appearances of a computer, a table, books and papers, and a window, beyond which are leafy trees amid patches of sunshine and shadows — just for starters. But this complexity is *surface* complexity: it is built up out of elements that are individually quite simple, for example, the "look" of a certain greenish hue in a certain smallish region of the field. These simpler elements of conscious experience cannot plausibly be identified with anything physical. The only candidates would be complex neural states, perhaps somewhat distributed, and the intrinsic properties of these states are not introspectively graspable and certainly do not have the structural simplicity that phenomenal greenness has. Indeed, as neuroscience and (further down) elementary particle physics progresses, the idea of any such empirical identification of an experiential quality with a physical state seems more and more fantastic: the layered structural complexity of any given smallish region of our brains is quite extraordinary!

What goes for visual experience goes for conscious mental phenomena generally, that is, other kinds of perceptual experiences and conscious thoughts, feelings, moods, beliefs, desires, and intentions. All of these have intrinsic aspects not describable in purely third-person terms. Thus the futility of conveying what the visual experience of greenness is like to a congenitally blind person, even one who is quite informed about the current state of the science of visual perception.

The foregoing reflections indicate that, while our conscious mental states undoubtedly have complex sustaining causes, the future identification of which is part of the business of neuroscience, the conscious states themselves are distinct. That is, they are caused by, but not identical to, structured physical states of the brain. If this is so, then the strong emergence of such states follows, given only the prima facie evident fact that these states are causally efficacious in all kinds of familiar ways. (My conscious visual experience of beer in the refrigerator causes my persisting belief that there is beer there, which, in the fullness of time, causally contributes to the movement of my legs in a fridge-ward direction.) Taking consciousness seriously means abandoning the ontologically reductionist dream in favor of a strong emergentist understanding on which the appearance of new basic properties within certain neurally complex physical systems must (to quote Samuel Alexander again) "be accepted with the 'natural piety' of the investigator." If so, the existence of such properties, while a fundamental fact, may nevertheless be fruitfully studied and eventually explained in detail in *non*reductive fashion, by spelling out the basic inventory of emergent properties, detailing the precise conditions under which physical systems give rise to them, and isolating the precise behavioral impact their presence has on the system. (Here I differ with Brown and Paul, and with Zeman: both chapters in the present volume give appropriate emphasis to the complexity of interactive processes in human brain activity; but, seeing no alternative to mind-body dualism and a thorough-going physicalism/materialism, they embrace the second alternative and opt for a weak emergentist account of human conscious states.)

Of course, there appears to be a radical, "illusionist" option — that of *not* taking consciousness seriously. That is, one might entertain the idea that we have a deeply illusory conception of our own conscious experience. For certain philosophers and scientists, reductionist physicalist metaphysics trumps, we might say, how the appearances appear to be. That is, they trump our intuitive phenomenal beliefs. But far from being a rigorously empiricist outlook, it puts the cart before the horse and thereby threatens the entire edifice of natural science. For we have greater rational warrant for our phenomenal beliefs than for our roughly reliable but fallible beliefs concerning even our physical environment — and, by extension, the physical world. Indeed, our beliefs concerning physical reality are grounded, in significant part, in our experiences. If beliefs concerning the physical world derived from the success of twentieth-century science (such as the shared material basis of all things, living and nonliving; the increasing interconnections of the sciences; and the rapid development of neuroscience) are used to call into question our grasp of our experiences themselves, they would thereby be undermining an important basis of their own justification. One can choose a more moderate stance that is deflationary, rather than eliminativist, regarding our awareness of the properties of our conscious states, a stance that lessens the severity of the epistemic problem I raise here. Pereboom (2011) explores the idea that, while we are reliably and noninferentially aware of the intrinsic properties of our conscious states, our awareness of them misrepresents them as being structurally simple, when in fact they are quite complex. I believe that there are deep problems associated with this view, too, though I cannot develop my argument for this claim here.

Strong Emergence and Free Will

A specific and important element of our conscious experience is our experience of *will*. We regularly have experiences of freely forming an intention to do some action while being aware of alternatives that were also available to us. To express it differently, these are experiences of being a purposely efficacious agent (and thus of holding an inner causal relationship between ourselves and our states of intention or choice). This raises the question: Are there cases of *mis*awareness of conscious willing, cases where we have experience as of willing but there is in fact no willing? How would these be identified as such? Supposing there can be such cases, if grasp of conscious willing is ordinarily a reflexive feature of conscious willing, can *mis*awarenesses have intrinsically identical phenomenal characteristics to genuine awarenesses? It would take me too far afield to explore these questions here.

If these experiences are veridical, then it cannot be the case that our actions are wholly determined by impersonal microphysical causes. If we have reason to believe these experiences are veridical, we have another source of strong emergence.

Some have suggested that here a radical, yet more targeted, illusionism is feasible, on which we deny that our experiences of being willing to do this or that are in fact *efficacious* (what philosopher Eddy Nahmias [2002] has dubbed "willusionism"). The most careful proponents of the doctrine allow that these experiences of control pretty reliably correlate with (and are likely caused by) wholly unconscious causal processes that are the real sources of our behavior (Wegner 2002, among many other recent authors). However, this kind of illusionism also has unstable underpinnings. Scientific theories, models, and results are themselves the products of scientific *activity:* of humans acting in certain coordinated, purposive ways and communicating their activities and results to one another. While the reality of reliably known, purposive action is not part of the theoretical content of (most) scientific theories, nor are those theories explicitly *inferred* from this belief, it is a *pragmatic* assumption of such science in the following sense: if we supposed it to be false, we would thereby have reason to doubt the trustworthiness of the outputs of such activity. It is reasonable to accept the trustworthiness of these outputs only insofar as we take them to have resulted from actions guided by the specific conscious purposes and beliefs that the actors report them to have been. Scientists must know what they are doing and why, to a significant extent, if the ideas that are based on the outputs of such actions are to be seen as more or less well supported. The lesson again is that well-grounded science cannot, in the end, *wholly* separate itself from our own self-understanding as humans, since that self-understanding is a foundational part of its evidentiary basis.

Having said that, I should note that a more moderate "willusionism" is not self-undermining. One may allow that we regularly consciously control our activity and are aware of our true purposes in so willing, and yet contend that the regularly accompanying belief that we are choosing *freely* is mistaken. And if we never choose freely, then neither are we morally responsible for our actions and their consequences. But why might one suppose that?

The direct empirical case for no-free-will is distinctly underwhelming. Some authors highlight studies that indicate that we can rather easily be induced to form unwittingly false ex-post-facto beliefs concerning *why* we did what we did (Delgado 1969; Gazzaniga 1994) or *that* we did something that we didn't do (Wegner 2002). Others note that we can be influenced in our decisions by hidden factors that we are unaware of, even nonrational physical factors (Brasil-Neto et al. 1992; Doris 2002). Taking the direct conclusions of such social and neuroscientific studies at face value, neither is in tension with the commonsense assumption that we often act freely upon known aims. The first category of studies merely indicates the malleability of our memories; the second indicates the imperfect nature of our own self-awareness, which doesn't threaten our belief in human freedom and moral responsibility if we allow (as we should) that freedom of choice need not be all or nothing — that it can come in degrees (I discuss these and other cases in O'Connor 2009). But the most widely discussed empirical basis for free-will skepticism stems from the work pioneered by neuroscientist Benjamin Libet (1985) on the timing of the felt experience of willing, which Libet and others took to indicate that a physical trigger or "unconscious decision" regularly precedes the conscious awareness of willing. There is not space to delve into the complexities of these studies here. It suffices to say, while they have independent scientific interest, there are deep methodological and substantive problems associated with them that undercut any argument from them to our lacking free will, a conclusion that is accepted by numerous authors of various philosophical opinions and sensibilities (see Mele 2009 and Clarke 2013 for very clear and thorough critical analyses).

If direct empirical evidence for the unreality of free will is weak, might there be a good indirect argument? Some authors seem to suppose that free will stands or falls with mind-body dualism, the view that we are, or have as an essential component, simple mental substances causally bound up with our bodies. Since contemporary science indicates that we are instead psychosomatic unities, free will is called into question. Even if our conscious psychological states (and thus our conscious choices) are strongly emergent, as I have argued, our choices must be causally determined by the underlying physical states that give rise to them.

I accept the philosophically controversial thesis that causal determinism is inconsistent with free will. But the strongly emergentist thesis that the existence and persistence of our capacity to choose is caused (or even causally *determined*, which is not the same) by organized physical states does not entail that the *output* of that capacity is likewise physically causally determined. There is no reason to make an a priori assumption that whatever kind of systemic capacity strongly emerges from the collective activity of an organized system of basic physical entities must be similar in kind, in specific respects, to the capacities that sustain it. Basic physical systems are ateleological, but it is an empirical question whether this is true of the capacities that emerge from them in certain organized contexts. Our experience of agency suggests that this is not universally true.

This simple reply will occasion an equally simple retort from a certain kind of "scientifically minded" thinker:

> All of your negative arguments may be correct, and yet you have provided us with no positive reason to think that we are free and responsible. The fact that we all *assume* this in practice is worthless. It's a mere prejudice of no more evidential weight than folk physics.

This kind of attitude is widespread among willusionists. I think it rests on a naïve conception of the underpinnings of scientific evidence and of human rationality generally. Descartes's heroic effort to doubt all his beliefs and rebuild from scratch notwithstanding, our beliefs about the world must start somewhere. Specifically, if we are to avoid total skepticism about knowledge in general (something that no one can sustain in practice), we must assume the rough reliability of our basic belief-forming capacities and the truth of our most foundational beliefs about reality.

Our basic cognitive capacities include the senses, memory, and basic forms of deductive and inductive reasoning. All of these are demonstrably fallible, but we learn about their limits and how to use them more critically *only* through using them. Our cognitively basic beliefs include such matters as the belief that the world has a causal or lawlike structure that will continue into the future (thereby permitting induction from past experience); that parts of the material world persist even when we're not observing them; that human bodies we observe are, like ourselves, animated by feeling, thinking, and purposive minds; and that our fundamental sociomoral belief that our seeming experience of freedom of choice is veridical. The reliability or truth of any of these items cannot be established by noncircular arguments. But that they are not reasonable is scarcely credible. Unlike other things we believe, they do not need to be inferred from evidence to be reasonable. As philosophers put it, these beliefs are properly *basic,* rationally speaking, including our belief that we are free and morally responsible. It is innocent until proven guilty. It is open for future science to make a solid case against this pervasive belief, but in the absence of such a case, and despite our ignorance of the details of how it "works" with respect to the massive physical information processing of the brain, it is perfectly rational for us to continue to believe it.

Strong Emergence from Social Processes?

I end by noting (without taking a stance on) the provocative suggestion, developed in quite different ways by Zeman and by Baumeister (in their chapters in the present volume), that certain important facets of human nature that we usually think of as wholly intrinsic characteristics may in fact be partly socially determined. Their suggestions are compatible with (and in Baumeister's case, seemingly indicative of) a claim that these characteristics strongly emerge not from purely physical underpinning but in part from external factors, whether a nonphysical realm of meaning (also emphasized by Tattersall in this volume) or social features of the human species. I make two points of connection: first, there is a nascent literature in cognitive science developing and exploring the thesis that some large, hierarchically organized human collectives constitute, for a time, group minds in the sense that the group possesses and processes informational states that none of the individuals possess. (Hutchins [1995] develops this thesis at length in his analysis of the complex, distributed behavior of several thousand people involved in the maneuvers of a modern naval ship.) How this idea fits with either of my two concepts of emergence is an open question (Theiner 2011; Theiner and O'Connor 2010). Second, and most pertinent to the present volume, the suggestion of a possible social dimension to emergence connects to Thistleton's and Torrance's (in their chapters in the present volume) *corporate* eschatological understanding of the Christian theological doctrine that human persons are divine image-bearers. While this takes us very far afield from scientific concerns, it serves to underscore how correctives to Enlightenment individualism are needed in multiple inquiries into what it means to be human.

Conclusion

I began by raising the question of whether the distinctive abilities and tendencies of mature human beings indicate a discontinuity in the evolutionary processes that gave rise to us. My way of addressing this question was through the abstract philosophical lenses of a pair of concepts of emergence. If human characteristics and behavior are merely weakly emergent, there is space for discontinuity at the level of psychology and its biological under- pinnings: capacities that have neither direct precedent in the terms of evolu- tionary anthropology nor equivalence in other known species. The still-open question is one of *degree* of dissimilarity to historical hominid precursors or contemporary mammalian intelligent species. However, weak emergence assumes strict continuity at the fundamental physical level. (In *The Game of Life,* fundamental patterns are universal and unchanging, even as they give rise to higher-order novel patterns of many forms within different varieties of stable structure.) In a merely weakly emergent world, there is nothing new under the sun — fundamentally speaking. But I have argued that capacities associated with human and other animal conscious awareness, and with the enhanced conscious feature of subjectivity — or having a point of view as a self — are not only weakly but also strongly emergent. If this is correct, then the historical and comparative psychological discontinuities that prove to be the case entail fundamental discontinuities: deeply novel characteristics on the world stage. To be human is to be made of the same substrate as every- thing else in the physical world and to be a product of a very long process of incremental biological change. Yet it is also to be a part of the world that transcends its constituting material by becoming aware of oneself as a self, separate from the rest of reality and acting in intentional ways that reflect that awareness. It is also to be rooted in a community of fellow beings, whose purposes and fortunes are deeply interwoven. What is the relationship of "we" to "I" and "you"? Is it always merely a conjunction, or are there respects in which we — in temporary, interacting communities or in its widest scope, encompassing all of humanity — constitute an ontological whole, making a fundamental difference as a whole to the way our corner of the world un- folds? This question is scientifically fascinating; it is also one whose answer has important philosophical and theological consequences.

REFERENCES

Alexander, Samuel. 1920. *Space, time, and deity.* 2 vols. New York: The Hu- manities Press.

Baumeister, Roy (contribution to this volume). Emergence of personhood: Lessons from self and identity.

Brasil-Neto, J. P., A. Pascual-Leone, J. Valls-Sole, L. G. Cohen, and M. Hallett. 1992. Focal transcranial magnetic stimulation and response bias in a forced choice task. *Journal of Neurology, Neurosurgery, and Psychiatry* 55: 964-66.

Brown, W., and L. K. Paul (contribution to this volume). Brain connectivity and the emergence of capacities of personhood: Reflections from callosal agenesis and autism.

Clarke, Peter G. H. 2013. The Libet Experiment and its implications for conscious will. The Faraday Institute for Science and Religion: Faraday Paper 17.

Delgado, J. M. R. 1969. *Physical control of the mind: Toward a psychocivilized society*. New York: Harper and Row.

Doris, J. 2002. *Lack of character: Personality and moral behavior*. Cambridge: Cambridge University Press.

Gazzaniga, M. S. 1994. Consciousness and the cerebral hemispheres. In *The cognitive neurosciences*, ed. M. S. Gazzaniga, 1391-99. Cambridge, MA: MIT Press.

Hutchins, E. 1995. *Cognition in the wild*. Cambridge, MA: MIT Press.

Libet, B. 1985. Unconscious cerebral initiative and the role of conscious will in voluntary action. *Behavioral and Brain Sciences* 8: 529-66.

McLaughlin, Brian. 1992. The rise and fall of British emergentism. In *Emergence or Reduction? Prospects for Nonreductive Physicalism*, ed. Ansgar Beckermann, Hans Flohr, and Jaegwon Kim. Berlin: De Gruyter.

Mele, Alfred. 2009. *Effective intentions: The power of conscious will*. Oxford: Oxford University Press.

Nahmias, Eddy. 2002. When consciousness matters: A critical review of Daniel Wegner's *The illusion of conscious will*. *Philosophical Psychology* 15, no. 4: 527-41.

O'Connor, Timothy. 1994. Emergent properties. *American Philosophical Quarterly* 31: 91-104.

———. 2009. Conscious willing and the emerging sciences of brain and behavior. In *Downward causation and the neurobiology of free will*, ed. George F. R. Ellis, Nancey Murphy, and Timothy O'Connor, 173-86. New York: Springer Publications.

Pereboom, Derk. 2011. Consciousness and the prospects of physicalism. Oxford: Oxford University Press.

Tattersall, Ian (contribution to this volume). Human evolution: Personhood and emergence.

Theiner, Georg. 2011. *Res cogitans extensa: A philosophical defense of the extended mind thesis*. Frankfurt: Peter Lang.

Theiner, Georg, and Timothy O'Connor. 2010. Emergence and the metaphysics of group cognition. In *Emergence in science and philosophy,* ed. Timothy O'Connor and Antonella Corradini, 78-117. Routledge Studies in the Philosophy of Science. London: Routledge.

Torrance, Alan J. (contribution to this volume). Retrieving the person: Theism, empirical science, and the question of scope.

Thiselton, Anthony (contribution to this volume). The image and the likeness of God: A theological approach.

Wegner, D. 2002. *The illusion of conscious will.* Cambridge, MA: MIT Press.

Zeman, Adam (contribution to this volume). The origins of subjectivity.

Section Three

Cognitive Evolution, Human Uniqueness, and the *Imago Dei*

Justin L. Barrett and Matthew J. Jarvinen

Current cognitive-evolutionary accounts of religion typically presume strong biological and cognitive continuity with ancestral species and with nonhuman primates. Further, in many of these accounts, religious thoughts are regarded as an evolutionary byproduct. Higher-order Theory of Mind (HO-ToM) activity frequently takes center stage as a key evolved capacity from which religious thoughts arise as a byproduct. Do such accounts, then, undercut the theological claim that human personhood is specially marked as being *imago Dei*, in the image or likeness of God? Being *imago Dei* entails a qualitative discontinuity from other species, something different that makes humans — but not any other animals — imagers. The fact that human cognition is descended continuously from nonhumans casts doubt on a possible incremental change in human ancestral lineage that suddenly leads to an importantly different being, does it not? We argue that, on the contrary, cognitive-evolutionary accounts provide fresh perspectives for understanding human uniqueness and *imago Dei*.

We begin this chapter with a case for HO-ToM as a distinct cognitive capacity that distinguishes humans from nonhumans, and, in particular, qualitatively distinguishes humans as *imago Dei*. We seek to do this by situating HO-ToM within an analysis of the other human capacities that have been offered as potential carriers of *imago Dei*, and we present a case for how HO-ToM sets humans apart. Then we examine HO-ToM from the perspective of evolutionary psychology and assess whether it is problematic for religious thoughts arising from HO-ToM to have developed as an evolutionary byproduct.

Human Capacities and Limitations

We begin with two assumptions regarding *imago Dei:* (1) all humans are *imago Dei* — we did not earn it and we cannot lose it; and (2) only humans (among animals) are *imago Dei*. Given these assumptions, what distinguishes humans as imagers? Anthony Thiselton (in his contribution to this volume) summarizes five human capacities that are representative of the image and likeness of God: (1) relationality; (2) rationality, wisdom, and intelligence; (3) dominion, or kingly rule; (4) freedom, morality, and creativity; and (5) love and relationality through communication.

Although varying degrees of these capacities effectively separate humans from nonhumans, Thiselton warns against isolating distinct capacities as essential to *imago Dei*. Rather, drawing from Vladimir Lossky, he argues that the biblical narrative points to no specific human capacities as characteristic of the image of God; rather, representing God occurs in our unified wholeness.

Attempts to situate the image of God in specific human characteristics have received a number of critiques, particularly with regard to its lack of universality on account of the various human disabilities. Regarding the human capacity to exercise dominion, Nicholas Wolterstorff says: "A good many human beings do not have the capacities necessary for exercising dominion. Those who are severely impaired mentally from birth never had them. Alzheimer's patients no longer possess them. Such human beings neither resemble God with respect to possessing those capacities nor can they implement the divine mandate or blessing by employing those capacities" (2008, 349). Alzheimer's patients and individuals who are severely mentally impaired may also lack the kind of rationality that is often deemed distinctive of humans in the divine likeness. Regarding morality, consider the case of Phineas Gage, regarded by many as the most influential case in the history of neuroscience. After a tamping spike went through his frontal lobes, his capacity for moral agency was markedly diminished. Malcolm Jeeves and Warren Brown have argued that Gage and others with similar brain damage "have difficulty regulating their behavior in order to abide by norms of socially acceptable or moral behavior. Such individuals may, capriciously and without malicious intent, violate social conventions, laws, ethical standards, or the rules of courtesy, civility, and regard for the benefit of others" (Jeeves and Brown 2009, 102).

Any definition of *imago Dei* that necessitates manifesting these capacities violates the first proposition made above — that is, that all humans bear the image and likeness of God. As Hans Reinders explains, "If the image is identified with uniqueness, as the first chapter of Genesis maintains, then all attempts to ground uniqueness in some quality to be found only in humans will sooner or later fail" (Reinders 2008, 238). How is it then, asks Reinders, that human uniqueness is to be adequately understood? Relationality.

Relationality

Relationality as a core human capacity is not without its own limitations. For example, individuals with conditions such as autism or agenesis of the corpus callosum — the nondevelopment of the major bundle of nerves that connects the two hemispheres of the brain — often have marked relational impairments. Limiting *imago Dei* to relationality still fails to include such individuals. However, relationality as Reinders understands it does not err in the same ways. Relationality necessitates more than one agent. It is not the inner human capacity in itself that is distinctive; rather, it is communion with God as modeled in the Trinity. Reinders says:

> From a theological point of view, the final end of being human is identified by the unique relationship that the triune God maintains with humanity through the economy of salvation. It starts with our being in his image, which does not refer to our nature as belonging to a particular species, even though our belonging to that species identifies us as humans, but the relationship God maintains with every human being. (2008, 273)

The locus of action is found within God. It is God who maintains and invites relationship. "The fact that humans differ with respect to the abilities and capacities characteristic of the human species does nothing to qualify or alter this unique relationship," Reinders continues. "God's love is unconditional and thus cannot be broken because of human limitations" (2008, 274). Such Christian anthropology maintains sufficient universality necessary to characterize *imago Dei*.

Many others share a similar affinity with relationality as a key characteristic of *imago Dei*. F. LeRon Shults chronicles how such a focus on relationality has emerged across disciplines — philosophy, theology, psychology, and even physics (Shults 2003). Many have grounded this relational emphasis within Trinitarian perspectives. For instance, Stanley Grenz posits that "the three Trinitarian persons are persons-in-relation and gain their personal

identity by means of their interrelationality," thus highlighting the fundamental human essence as persons-in-relation (Grenz 2001, 9). Similarly,
Jack Balswick, Pamela King, and Kevin Reimer (BKR) follow Karl Barth
in regarding *imago Dei* to be a relational concept. They advocate that as the
Trinitarian God necessarily combines both uniqueness of persons and unity
of the Godhead, so too are humans created to be unique individuals united
with God and with others, akin to the I-Thou relationships championed by
Barth and Martin Buber (BKR 2005, 38). Of those having I-Thou relationships, BKR write: "They would experience unity in their mutual recognition
of being Thou to each other but each remain personally distinct as I" (BKR
2005, 41). Further, they declare, "To live as beings made in the image of God
is to exist as reciprocating selves, as unique individuals living in relationships
with others . . . as a distinct human being in communion with God and other
in mutually giving and receiving relationships" (BKR 2005, 31). Thiselton,
too, regards a special kind of relational capacity as the most promising way
to understand *imago Dei,* particularly a relational capacity that allows us
to represent God on earth. As with Reinders, Thiselton maintains that this
relationality is initiated through the loving extension of God, allowing communion with God and subsequent communion with others in love.

Human Nature

In *Justice: Rights and Wrongs,* Wolterstorff takes a slightly different approach.
His critique of capacity-focused perspectives of *imago Dei* leads him to interpret the concept within a fundamental *human nature* rather than any actualized capacities. We understand him to be suggesting that there is something
like a grand design for what humans should be in fully realized form, a design
not necessarily present at all stages of development or in all humans, but
what humans should be in an ideal form. All human beings have the same
human nature, whether it is malformed or in the process of development.
Summarizing his argument, Wolterstorff contends:

> If we interpret the image of God along capacity-resemblance lines, then
> while those who bear the image do have a truly exalted status in the cos-
> mic scale of beings, not all human beings possess the image. If we more
> plausibly interpret image of God along nature-resemblance lines, then
> while all human beings possess the image, possessing it does not, as such,
> give its bearers a very exalted status; among those who possess the image

will be human beings who are seriously lacking in capacities on account of human nature being malformed in their case. (2008, 352)

On this note, Alasdair MacIntyre reminds us that "there is a scale of disability on which we all find ourselves. Disability is a matter of more or less, both in respect of degree of disability, and in respect of the time periods in which we are disabled" (2001, 73). Human dignity should not be separated into distinct categories of "disabled" and "not disabled," nor *imago Dei* and only "quasi-*imago Dei*." In addition, recognizing humans' relational nature, MacIntyre's challenge is to expand concepts of disability beyond the individual to include the community in which they belong. He claims: "What disability amounts to, that is, depends not just on the disabled individual, but on the groups of which that individual is a member" (2001, 75). Communities can serve to fill in the gaps where individuals lack certain capacities of *imago Dei,* opening up a richer embodiment of *imago Dei* through relational interaction.

What is this human nature, a nature that sets humans apart from other animals — who certainly have a nature, but not of a human kind? Wolterstorff does not elaborate on this point in great detail because doing so falls outside of his project — whether human rights may be grounded in the image of God — but he does situate essential human nature (and human worth) within God's love for us, particularly God's "bestowed worth" (2008, 357). In supporting this argument, he makes distinctions between three types of love, and those distinctions are helpful for our argument here.

Drawing from Augustine of Hippo, Wolterstorff distinguishes between love as attraction, love as benevolence, and love as attachment in the ways that worth can be bestowed on an object of love. First, he argues that love as attraction, a lover's "desire for engagement with the thing loved," recognizes and is drawn to worth, but does nothing to enhance it (2008, 359). Second, love as benevolence — if translated into benevolent action — would certainly enhance worth, but merely being the object of love as benevolence does not, as such, necessitate enhanced worth. The exception is love as attachment, which, through the establishment of a bond of friendship, bestows an enhanced worth. While these types of love likely often co-occur, Wolterstorff argues that the distinct relational quality of the love of attachment provides grounds for human nature to have a distinctive worth — a quality that he then uses to argue for natural human rights (2008, 359).

It is important to note that Wolterstorff's analysis provides an intellectual resource for affirming that all humans — regardless of the presence of mental impairments or pathology, or where they fall on the developmental lifespan — are *imago Dei* without grounding *imago Dei* in an arbitrary divine fiat. That resource is the notion of a human nature that all humans possess, even if they (currently) fail to manifest it (e.g., because of age or infirmity). In a way analogous to a plan, blueprint, or ideal, humans all possess such a nature, and it is by virtue of this nature — which is always potentially realizable, at least from God's perspective — that they are God's special love objects. Persons with severe autism or agenesis of the corpus callosum, who are unable to engage in full interpersonal loving relationships, still possess a human nature that could manifest — for instance, in the next life — such relational capacities. The person afflicted by Alzheimer's disease and hence impaired rationally, morally, or in terms of ability to exercise "dominion," would nevertheless have a human nature that includes the potential to manifest such traits.

Without appealing to a human nature, theological difficulties arise in trying to affirm that all humans (but only humans among the animals) are in God's image, even if *imago Dei* is relational. To avoid locating the image and likeness of God within nonuniversal human capacities, as sketched above, some have been tempted to transfer the decisive quality to the love of God. Some have gone so far as to effectively reject any aspect of human uniqueness as a criterion for *imago dei,* arguing that only the Hebrew notion of God's election is sufficient (Moritz 2011).

But among all the animals, why humans? Unless God's decision is entirely arbitrary and God could just have easily designated banana slugs as *imago Dei,* such a question inevitably transfers the locus back to humans, leaving us chronicling a list of capacities such as those we have previously discussed. Further, simply retreating to divine love neglects the critical biblical texts from which the doctrine of *imago Dei* springs:

> Then God said, "Let us make humankind in our image, according to our likeness; and let them have dominion over the fish of the sea, and over the birds of the air, and over the cattle, and over all the wild animals of the earth, and over every creeping thing that creeps upon the earth." So God created humankind in his image, in the image of God he created them; male and female he created them. (Gen. 1:26-27)

In this passage the image of God is also referred to as a likeness, some sense in which humans resemble God. Perhaps, from a Trinitarian perspective, the property of being loved by God is a sufficient resemblance to God to satisfy reasonable exegesis. But why, as Barth observed, the explicit mention of "male and female he created them"? If being the object of love was sufficient, why a reference to what appears to be the capacity for interpersonal relationship? And why does the passage place dominion over the other animals as part of this exalted status as being in God's image (see also Psalm 8)? Wolterstorff's emphasis on human nature revives the possibility that some trait or bundle of traits — even when not currently manifest — specify human uniqueness as imagers of God.

The Search for Convergence:
The Role of Higher-Order Theory of Mind

Our reading of Thiselton, Reinders, Wolterstorff, and others encourages us to find convergence among several commitments: (1) all humans are *imago Dei;* (2) only humans (among animals) are *imago Dei;* (3) *imago Dei* involves a divine relational choice to love humans in some special way; (4) humans are selected to be recipients of this special love because of some property or properties of their nature rather than any universally manifest property or properties; and (5) resembling a Trinitarian God, being created male and female, and being capable of exercising dominion are all pointers to the critical property or properties of human nature that enable humans to be *imago Dei.* Promising candidates for such properties include I-Thou relationality, rationality, and wisdom (which may require a level of linguistic competence not seen in nonhumans), and the ability to exercise moral judgment and volitional action.

If we emphasize the relational interpretation of *imago Dei,* part of the picture is God's choice to love humans in a special way; but some aspect of human nature that makes a reciprocal relationship of this kind possible appears to be required as well. Relational emphases, including "love as attachment," presume capacities that allow humans to open themselves up to the love of God knowingly, receiving it in unique ways through relational attachment. From this relational perspective, what distinguishes us as bearers of *imago Dei* is our capacity for receiving, experiencing, and being formed through God's love in a particular kind of way. What capacity allows for this? How might it have evolved? Alternatively, we may argue that exercising dominion requires rationality, the consideration of counterfactuals, and the ability to discern good and just alternatives from bad and unjust ones. What capacity allows for this exercise of dominion? How might it have evolved?

Rather than choose among the various properties as *the* locus of *imago*

Dei, we propose a property typically manifest in humans (which may be part of human nature and the nature of no other animal) that may play a role in all of the candidate properties: higher-order Theory of Mind (HO-ToM). Theory of Mind (ToM) is cognitive and developmental psychology jargon that refers to the typical way in which a human (or other sophisticated animal) attributes mental states and thinks about the interrelationships and roles of those mental states in directing action (also known as folk psychology). For instance, to understand that Mary Ann is gesturing with her empty glass because she wants Malcolm to pass the Merlot requires that we attribute to Mary Ann a specific desire and recognize that she intends to shape Malcolm's actions to satisfy her desire by a particular action (gesturing with the empty glass). This series of attributions and representations is the work of ToM.

Researchers concerned with the ontogenetic or phylogenetic development of ToM often distinguish between different types or levels of ToM. Analytically, we can think of proto-ToM as simply attributing rudimentary internal states to others that may bear on their actions, as in thinking that a garden snail has the goal of crossing the path to get at your lettuce. But since being "goal-directed" does not necessarily require the attribution of a mental state, the most basic true ToM is probably attributing states such as desires (Alan wants coffee) or percepts (Roy sees Tina) to another (accurately or not) and recognizing that these play some role in shaping actions (Alan wants coffee; he will act to get coffee provided he sees coffee). More sophisticated ToM (sometimes called belief-desire psychology) involves attributing beliefs and recognizing their role in shaping actions that are motivated by desires, as in: "Francisco knows that Brianna wants his pretzels, so he is hiding them so she won't know where they are." The litmus test for this sophisticated ToM has long been "passing" variants of the false-belief task (Wimmer and Perner 1983; Perner 1991). These tasks require someone to recognize that another person's belief differs from reality and is, therefore, false. Before making the distinction between beliefs and reality, it is not clear that beliefs are being fully understood as representational states about what could be true. "Belief" could simply refer to what is in fact the case (Dennett 1983). For this reason, such a ToM is sometimes called a "representational theory of mind," or is even simply regarded as ToM proper. Though some experiments suggest intuitions consistent with a representational ToM even in a human's second year of life, most experimental evidence points to humans acquiring this kind of ToM at about four or five years old, at least in a stable and verbally accessible form. Certainly, before this age we do not have any compelling evidence that children consciously reflect on the truth-value of another person's belief. That is, at age four or five years, most children begin to form representations (mental states) of representations (other people's mental states). That is, they meta-represent.

Sometimes these different levels of ToM are referred to as "orders of intentionality." The first order is to attribute some mental states to another, for example, "She wants to leave through the door." Second-order intentionality is to form a thought about the specific content of another's mental state, for example, "She believes the door is unlocked, but she is mistaken." Exercising third-order intentionality adds another layer of representation, as in forming a belief about a belief about a belief: "She thinks that I believe the door is unlocked, but she's mistaken." Of course, higher orders still are possible. Passing false-belief tasks (correctly and knowingly attributing a false belief to another) appears to require second-order intentionality as described here, and so we refer to these capacities as higher-order theory of mind (HO-ToM). Whether nonhumans (or even humans before age three or four) have HO-ToM is unsettled. Far less controversial is that adult humans commonly exercise third-order intentionality, and we have no reason to think that any nonhuman species does so.

The upshot of having HO-ToM is an entirely new type of social interaction. A community of people with HO-ToM would be able to be consciously aware of each other's thoughts, desires, and feelings. They would be able to know when another knows what they are thinking or feeling. Not only would they be able to know that the other has an internal life, but that such internal life could be about the other and it could be shared. Arguably, HO-ToM makes I-Thou relationships possible, both with other humans and with God.

Cognitive Science of Religion

An extrabiblical, nontheological clue to the importance of HO-ToM as critical to *imago Dei* comes from cognitive science of religion (CSR). As a scientific study of religious thoughts and actions, which draws upon the cognitive sciences and evolutionary psychology, CSR scholarship has begun to sound off on what cognitive mechanisms humans must have to conceptualize a god and to generate actions for interacting with that god. Recurrently, HO-ToM appears as a central player in these accounts.

A typical account of religion ("religion" here being shorthand for thought and action concerning or inspired by the believed existence of superhuman agents) from a CSR perspective would go something like this:

Humans' conceptions of the world around them are heavily dependent on early-developing cognitive predilections specific to numerous domains of things. For instance, in the first several months of life, babies give evidence that they expect bounded physical objects to have certain properties such as moving cohesively and continuously through space and time, requiring contact to be launched, and not being able to occupy the same place with another solid object at the same time. This group of expectations concerning physical objects is called *naive physics* and structures our learning about and interaction with physical objects throughout life (see Spelke and Kinzler 2007). Other domains for which people from about age five (or earlier) predictably evince relatively fixed intuitive expectations include numeracy, living things, and minded intentional agents (see Hirschfeld and Gelman 1994; Sperber et al. 1995; see McCauley [2011] for a treatment of the cognitive naturalness of religion without adopting a modularity approach). The tendency to have particular intuitions in various domains evolved under selection pressure to solve fitness-related problems in those domains.

A byproduct of this mental toolkit is that we find it easier to learn and talk about things that largely fit our intuitive expectations, and thus radically *counterintuitive* ideas are less likely to become widely shared or cultural. Slightly counterintuitive ideas, however, may attract special attention (Boyer 1994, 2001) — perhaps especially among young adults and adolescents — and be more successful cultural ideas than completely intuitive, mundane ideas, all else being equal (Gregory and Barrett 2009).

Furthermore, one feature of our maturationally natural cognitive equipment is that it eagerly attends to potential-minded agents in our midst, and readily generates inferences, explanations, and predictions regarding perceived intentional agency with respect to mental states, such as percepts, beliefs, desires, and emotions. The ToM system responsible for generating such inferences has evolved in such a way that it does not require the physical body of an intentional agent to be present to trigger its activation (Guthrie 1993; Barrett 2004). If it did, we could not speculate about the actions of unseen others (e.g., enemies hidden by camouflage or darkness, absent parties, etc.) or communicate with each other over distance (e.g., through symbolic communication). (Arguably, the evolutionary and developmental history and the input conditions of ToM are different enough from the conceptual systems concerned with living, physical bodies that it is harder to seamlessly integrate minds with bodies than divorce minds from bodies, rendering humans natural "intuitive dualists," and thereby helping to explain why it is so easy for people to entertain belief in ghosts, ancestors, and some kind of afterlife [Bloom 2004].) Consequently, humans are attracted to explanations of states-of-affairs and events surrounding them in terms of even unseen and mysterious intentional agency, particularly when mechanistic and biological folk causation does not appear satisfactory (Bering 2011; Guthrie 1993; Pyysiainen 2003). When humans (or other animals) appear insufficient, superhuman agency is entertained. Similarly, humans naturally attribute purpose and design to elements of the natural world, and hence find plausible intentional explanations that invoke superhuman agency to account for this perceived purpose (Kelemen 2004; Kelemen and Rosset 2009).

The possible actions of superhuman agents is further reinforced by their ability to account for cases of surprising fortune or misfortune, particularly when it appears to be compensation for morally relevant human actions (Boyer 2001). It requires little reflection or cultural elaboration for humans to be motivated to begin attempts to communicate and interact with these unseen, powerful — possibly knowledgeable and perhaps morally concerned — superhuman agents. Religious rituals, then, are subtle extensions or small tweaks on ordinary ToM applied to human/superhuman interactions instead of human/human interactions (McCauley and Lawson 2002). Once religious beliefs and the actions they spawn begin to coalesce in a population, they may prove adaptive in solving problems of human group living, such as trust, cooperation, and reputation management (Bering 2011; Sosis 2004). The entire gene-culture complex may then be selectively reinforced.

A few features of this CSR account of religion merit highlighting. First, these cognitive accounts typically presume strong biological and cognitive continuity with ancestral species and, by extension, with nonhuman primates thought to approximate human ancestors. Second, though conceding the possibility of later exaptation, cognitive accounts at their core are evolutionary byproduct accounts of religion. That is, the cognitive equipment that gives rise to religious expression is presumed to have evolved under selection pressures unrelated to religion or religious entities. Whereas the ease with which humans acquire fear of snakes presumably evolved in response to snakes themselves as a survival threat, the ease with which humans acquire belief in gods is not thought to have evolved in response to gods. Under these accounts, religious thoughts are an evolutionary byproduct and not an adaptation per se. (After their emergence, religious thoughts may have motivated religious actions, some of which were adaptive, and hence reinforced through natural selection. By these lights these forms of religious expression would be exaptations.) Third, many different cognitive subsystems, or "mental tools," cooperate to encourage religious beliefs and practices; belief in gods (or souls, the afterlife, etc.) are thus byproducts of multiple cognitive adaptations and not just one. Nevertheless, one "mental tool" takes center stage in these accounts: ToM.

The Problem

For the sake of argument, let us suppose that a CSR-type account is broadly accurate. Does such an account, then, undercut or cast doubt on the theological claim that human personhood is specially marked as being *imago Dei* — that is, in the image or likeness of God? Setting aside whether CSR-type claims constitute evidence against any and every god, are such accounts of religion particularly problematic for regarding humans as having a special place in the natural world in relation to a supreme creator deity (God)?

An affirmative answer may be argued in this way: It follows from (1) the fact that belief in God arises as an evolutionary byproduct (instead of an adaptation), plus (2) biological and cognitive continuity with other species, that (3) humans cannot reasonably be supposed to be in God's image. Being *imago Dei* entails a qualitative discontinuity from other species, something different that makes humans imagers — but no other animals. Surely, the something different is not a physical feature of humans (given that God does not have a physical form to be mimicked). Likely, then, the something different is part of human behavioral or cognitive nature. But the fact that human cognition is descended continuously from nonhumans casts doubt on a possible incremental change in human ancestral lineage that suddenly leads to an importantly different mental agent. If our natural disposition toward belief in a god were a product of an additional feature, an adaptation "for" belief in a god, then humans would have the something special that could make them possess *imago Dei*. Assuming byproduct accounts are accurate, then, there is no adaptation "for" belief in a god. Hence, the idea that humans (and only humans) are somehow special as in God's image appears implausible.

Even if one favors the view that *imago Dei* is not a distinctive cognitive or psychological capacity, but is a distinctive relationship between God and one species, the prerequisite equipment for such a relationship — a cognitive feature — seems likely to be unique to humans and human nature. (If not, why would God choose humans and not another animal with the requisite relational capacities? Would it be unjust favoritism?) Whether or not the cognitive capacities that make the right kind of relationality possible are unique to humans, by the lights of CSR, the capacity(-ies) that make the special relationship with God possible still amount to an evolutionary byproduct. Isn't that a problem? Along similar lines it could be argued that byproduct accounts of religion, as offered by CSR, pose a problem for at least some views of God. Is it consistent with God's character and properties to use an evolutionary byproduct as a primary vehicle for encouraging belief in God? If this seems improbable, the truth of any given byproduct account reduces the probability that God (of that sort) exists.

Regarding Evolutionary Byproducts

The alleged problem with byproduct accounts of religion cannot be because byproducts are somehow deficient in and of themselves. The mere fact of some kind of cultural expression — a belief, an act, an artifact — being an evolutionary byproduct of some cognitive system naturally selected because of its ability to solve a different kind of fitness problem says nothing about the cultural expression's goodness, truth, or value. Many things we regard as good, including art and music; many things we believe are truth-producing, such as our favorite branch of mathematics or philosophy; and many things we value as useful, such as clothing and fishing tackle — all are evolutionary byproducts in a comparable respect. Recognizing modern science as an evolutionary byproduct, Chomsky says: "The experiences that shaped the course of evolution offer no hint of the problems to be faced in the sciences, and the ability to solve these problems could hardly have been a factor in evolution" (Chomsky 1987, 158).

Perhaps the status of religion (or theism) as a byproduct is concerning because being a byproduct seems to imply that it could have been otherwise, that it is an "accident," a term Paul Bloom has used in casting doubt on theism because of its alleged byproduct status (Bloom 2009). But as Peter van Inwagen has observed (contra Bloom), an evolutionary byproduct could very well be intentional and not an "accident" at all. That is, God could have selected this universe out of any number of possible ones because it featured in one species a tendency toward theism as one (by)product of evolution (van Inwagen 2009). Furthermore, unless we wish to personify natural selection

— from a naturalistic perspective — all adaptations, as well as all byproducts, are unintended accidents, the products of arbitrary mutations that did not happen to kill the host organism and were successfully passed on to offspring.

Suppose humans' natural disposition toward religion were incidental as a part of our evolution, that it might not have evolved because it did not confer any special selective advantage as byproduct accounts suggest. From a naturalistic perspective, it was highly improbable that humans evolved with such a byproduct. What accounts for this improbable state of affairs? Certainly not ordinary selection pressure. This is a *by*product after all. Given God, such an improbable state of affairs is more probable than given no-God. Hence, this improbable state of affairs (the religious byproduct) amounts to evidence for God. We do not offer this suggestion because we are committed to the success of such an argument, only to observe that it is not obvious that being an evolutionary byproduct is problematic for all religious beliefs or for the notion that humans are created in God's image.

Consider an adaptationist alternative. Suppose that humans evolved to their current form, and then a religious instinct or *sensus divinitatis* evolved as an adaptation on top of the complete biological and psychological suite of features that makes us behaviorally modern humans. Would we then be concerned that the tendency to believe in a god is an extra, an add-on, something unnecessary that need not have appeared but only did because it "happened" to be useful? Perhaps the concerns would not be so different. If so, can it really be that byproduct versus adaptationist explanations are an issue?

We find it more theologically palatable to find that the bundle of features that makes us behaviorally modern humans has the intrinsic, emergent property that humans are drawn to believe in at least one god (Barrett 2012). This tendency is inextricable from our humanness and personhood — and not a mere addendum. Such a suggestion, too, is consonant with Thiselton's argument for *imago Dei* being identifiable with the wholeness of human being and not manifest in some specific capacity that is additional to our human nature.

Regarding Evolutionary Continuity

We do not see that the alleged fact that humans have a religious or theistic predilection as a byproduct of evolved cognitive faculties is a problem for the notion of humans being *imago Dei*. Perhaps, however, the mere evolutionary continuity with other species is a problem by itself. That is, if humans are biologically and cognitively just tiny steps removed from some ancestors that presumably were not possessors of *imago Dei,* then is it credible to claim that humans have some capacity that creates a radical enough qualitative break from other species such that humans can be said to be in God's image but other animals (including now extinct ancestral ones) cannot be? To put it another way, is it plausible that a child in God's image had a parent that was not?

A solution to this problem is suggested by CSR accounts themselves. Repeatedly, we see in the CSR literature the pivotal role of ToM in driving religious intuitions. Often tacit in these presentations is that what is presumed in terms of human ToM is importantly different from what is likely present in other species. Arguably (but controversially), at least chimpanzees and bonobos — and possibly some other nonhuman animals — have some kind of rudimentary, lower-level ToM, in that they attribute percepts and goals to others and perhaps even basic beliefs (Call and Tomasello 2008; but see Povinelli and Vonk 2003). But as sketched above, traditionally in the cognitive developmental literature the defining feature of human ToM is a degree of meta-representation: being able to have thoughts about thoughts, particularly another's. For instance, if Malcolm thinks Warren believes X, but knows that X is false, Malcolm has formed a representation about another's representation, a meta-representation, and is using a higher-order ToM (HO-ToM). Similarly, if Mary knows that Colin knows that Mary and he are both attending to Tim, Mary is using HO-ToM, specifically joint-attention. Michael Tomasello has argued convincingly that it is joint-attention (knowing that another person knows you are both attending to the same thing) that makes much cultural learning, including mature language learning, possible (Tomasello 1999). Robin Dunbar has noted that it is this kind of joint attention that characterizes corporate religion: we each know that the other has a relationship with the same god (Dunbar 2004). In addition, beyond markedly enhanced relationality, such meta-representation seems critical for the other cognitive capacities that are often cited as evidence of *imago Dei,* such as reason/rationality and morality. One must be able to consciously form representations of candidate propositions (moral or otherwise) and to form representations about the truth or error of such propositions, to reason or to make moral judgments about possible future actions. (For more on the evolution of meta-representation, see Barrett 2011.)

Could it be that this HO-ToM — an incremental step beyond an ancestral precursor ToM — fills the bill for a cognitive capacity affording a very special status for humans in relationship with God? It looks promising.

As individuals possessing HO-ToM, we can have thoughts about what God desires for us and from us. God can communicate with us and not just behaviorally modify us. In contrast, we can train dogs to get them to behave in one way or another via commands, but we cannot inform them the way we can inform other humans. Presumably, God could have the kind of relationship with other animals that we can with dogs, but not the quality of relationship that God could have with humans — because humans possess HO-ToM. Further, HO-ToM gives us the capacity to collaborate with God and not merely cooperate. Similarly, humans can also enjoy joint relationships with God, knowing that other humans are thinking, feeling, or desiring something in common with regard to God.

Perhaps, then, HO-ToM is the key feature of human nature that makes humans the kind of creature that God would opt to engage with in a special I-Thou relationship. Though only incrementally different from that in other species, HO-ToM yields a radical change in the quality of the organism humans are and the quality of their potential relationship with God. Once an organism with HO-ToM evolved — even as an adaptation for managing more complex social interactions with other humans and not necessarily with God — it would have the additional qualities that make it capable of special status before God: *imago Dei*. An entirely different defense is open to theists of various stripes: If God (or spirits, devils, angels, ancestors, etc.) exist and really act on the world, then arguably there would have been selective pressure to detect the presence and activity of these superhuman agents. Having a cognitive system that is tuned to detecting gods, then, would have been an adaptation and not a byproduct at all.

One potential weakness of such a perspective of *imago Dei* is that HO-ToM appears to develop. Though evidence of some kind of joint attention and maybe even meta-representation appears in infancy (Onishi and Baillargeon 2005; see also Perner and Ruffman 2005), ToM does not appear in a robust form until about the age of four or five years (Wellman et al. 2001). Would we want to say infants and toddlers do not possess God's image? Perhaps. Alternatively, following Wolterstorff's arguments concerning human nature, it may be that being in "God's image" is a status assigned by virtue of potential qualities rather than actual ones. Infants may be *imago Dei* even if they have not yet manifested the capacities that have led God to designate humans as imagers because their nature possesses the right properties. With development, they will typically grow into the fullness of being as individuals capable of the special I-Thou relationship with God that God intended for them. Perhaps such development requires relational inputs. That is, basic human capacities, plus the right kind of relationships, with already developed humans or with God, may be required to fully develop our nature as I-Thou relational beings with HO-ToM. Indeed, as Malcolm Jeeves and Warren Brown plausibly suggest, off-line meta-representation and abstraction may require "social scaffolding" to develop (Jeeves and Brown 2009, 51-52). A point in favor of Jeeves and Brown's suggestion is that those individual nonhumans that provide the most compelling evidence for sophisticated ToM and symbolism approaching human levels have been heavily socialized through interactions with humans (e.g., the bonobo Kanzi). Analogously, merely possessing a native language acquisition device may be insufficient for full-blown linguistic competence. Being exposed to other language users, particularly in the first six years of life, may be critical. Such social scaffolding may enhance the capacity for HO-ToM, and thus may enhance the capacities for engaging in the kinds of relationship that qualifies us as full imagers. Similarly, our ancestor who first possessed the capacity for higher-order ToM may have required socialization, but socialization by whom? God?

Consider the following scenario. Steve and Jane had a rudimentary ToM system, perhaps more advanced than that of chimpanzees or bonobos, but significantly less advanced than modern adult humans. Steve had the meta-cognitive abilities to reflect on the existence of his thoughts, but nothing further. When interacting with Jane, he only had a vague idea that Jane might have her own mental states. Otherwise, their interactions were largely based simply on reinforcement contingencies and careful behavioral observation. ToM researchers would classify Steve within first-order intentionality (Kinderman et al. 1998). (Zero-order intentionality would be simply a behavioral response to stimuli, without any recognition of one's mental states.) However, Steve and Jane's child, Adam, had a mutation for second-order intentionality, or what is commonly understood as basic ToM and what we have been calling HO-ToM. (We have no convincing evidence that any other species has this kind of higher-order Theory of Mind, though it seems likely that some kind of rudimentary precursor exists in chimpanzees and bonobos. Some have suggested that great apes and monkeys do not reach full ToM, but may aspire to level 1.5 intentionality [Byrne 1995].) Adam was able to postulate the content of mental states of others and make inferences and predictions about their roles in driving actions. One day Adam came across Eve, a woman who had a similar capacity for second-order intentionality. During their interaction, they realized that they shared this cognitive ability. They were able to jointly comprehend that they understood each other's thoughts. The result was a level of relationality that had never occurred in the history of the world — resulting in an incredibly adaptive social bond. They were able to develop communicative sounds and gestures that had substantially more complex meaning and were able to understand each other on a completely new level. The resulting socialization allowed for a substantial jump in levels of intentionality, such that Adam could think (1) about what Eve was thinking (2) about Adam's thoughts (3) regarding Eve's ideas (4) about Adam's (5) . . . (and so on). Robin Dunbar has argued that these levels of intentionality may be implicitly reflexive, such that they form an embedded hierarchy that is unending (2007). While this may be true in theory, it seems that humans have a difficult time with comprehension past the fifth level (see Kinderman et al. 1998).

These ToM systems allowed Adam and Eve to not only consider the mental states of each other, but jointly consider the thoughts of others, both present and not present — including God. They were able to alternate their behaviors based on perceived thoughts of others, anticipate the intentions of others, even commune with God together in a unique way: they could think about what God was thinking about, and they could do so together. Such expanding socialization could have only served to heighten the presently stimulated ToM capacities. Expressed within the terminology of Barth and Buber, Adam and Eve were able to transcend I-it relationships, responding to each other in an I-Thou way. Moral outcomes greatly expanded as they were able to consider various actions and the outcomes they inferred from those actions. They were also able to engage in a whole new level of empathy through an ability to understand the thoughts and feelings of others.

The previous hypothetical scenario has outlined just a small sample of the entirely novel ways of living that emerge from the interactions of those with HO-ToM. We maintain that such unique relationality with God and others could have represented a qualitative distinction with all previous humans, and could have served as the basis for bearing the *imago Dei*. Such an account also succeeds in finding resonance with evolutionary accounts of the development of personhood.

Conclusion

HO-ToM is a capacity that makes possible a qualitatively different kind of interpersonal relationship, and it represents an incremental development beyond the lower-order theory of mind that may be present in nonhuman species and infant humans. Furthermore, HO-ToM may serve as the lynchpin for not just a new type of sociality, morality, and even symbolic communication, but also a new type of religious thought and experience, markedly different from ancestral species that did not have this capacity. Incremental change in ToM capacity could have been the key for the emergence of an importantly different being, a being capable of a personal but shared relationship with the divine. With HO-ToM, two individuals can share an interpersonal relationship with the same god. The development of HO-ToM could be the central mechanism that made possible the development of the kind of love and communion, both with God and with others, that Thiselton esteems as most noteworthy about our role as bearers of *imago Dei*.

REFERENCES

Balswick, Jack O., Pamela Ebstyne King, and Kevin S. Reimer. 2005. *The reciprocating self: Human development in theological perspective.* Downers Grove: InterVarsity Academic.

Barrett, Justin L. 2004. *Why would anyone believe in God?* Walnut Creek, CA: AltaMira Press.

———. 2011. Meta-representation, *Homo religiosus,* and *Homo symbolicus.* In *Homo symbolicus: The dawn of language, imagination, and spirituality,* ed. Christopher S. Henshilwood and Francesco D'Errico, 205-24. Amsterdam: John Benjamins.

———. 2012. *Born believers: The science of children's religious belief.* New York: The Free Press.

Bering, Jesse M. 2011. *The belief instinct: The psychology of souls, destiny, and the meaning of life.* New York: W. W. Norton and Company.

Bloom, Paul. 2004. *Descartes' baby: How the science of child development explains what makes us human.* New York: Basic Books.

———. 2009. Religious belief as an evolutionary accident. In *The believing primate: Scientific, philosophical, and theological reflections on the origin of religion,* ed. Michael Murray and Jeffrey Schloss, 118-27. New York: Oxford University Press.

Boyer, Pascal. 1994. *The naturalness of religious ideas: A cognitive theory of religion.* Berkeley: University of California Press.

———. 2001. *Religion explained: The evolutionary origins of religious thought.* New York: Basic Books.

Byrne, Richard W. 1995. *The thinking ape: Evolutionary origins of intelligence.* Oxford: Oxford University Press.

Call, Joseph, and Michael Tomasello. 2008. Does the chimpanzee have a theory of mind? 30 Years Later. *Trends in Cognitive Sciences* 12: 187-92.

Chomsky, Noam. 1987. *Language and problems of knowledge: The Managua Lectures.* Cambridge, MA: MIT Press.

Dennett, Daniel C. 1983. Intentional systems in cognitive ethology: The "Panglossian paradigm" defended. *Behavioral and Brain Sciences* 6: 343-90.

Dunbar, Robin I. M. 2004. *The human story.* London: Faber and Faber.

————. 2007. The social brain hypothesis and its relevance to social psychology. In *Evolution and the social mind,* ed. Joseph P. Forgas, Martie G. Haselton, and William von Hippel, 21-33. New York: Psychology Press.

Gregory, Justin, and Justin L. Barrett. 2009. Epistemology and counterintuitiveness: Role and relationship in epidemiology of cultural representations. *Journal of Cognition and Culture* 9: 289-314.

Grenz, Stanley J. 2001. *The social God and the relational self.* Louisville: Westminster John Knox Press.

Guthrie, Stewart. 1993. *Faces in the clouds: A new theory of religion.* New York: Oxford University Press.

Hirschfeld, Lawrence A., and Susan A. Gelman, eds. 1994. *Mapping the mind: Domain specificity in cognition and culture.* Cambridge: Cambridge University Press.

Jeeves, Malcolm, and Warren S. Brown. 2009. *Neuroscience, psychology, and religion: Illusions, delusions, and realities about human nature.* West Conshohocken, PA: Templeton Press.

Kelemen, Deborah. 2004. Are children "intuitive theists"? Reasoning about purpose and design in nature. *Psychological Science* 15: 295-301.

Kelemen, Deborah, and Evelyn Rosset. 2009. The human function compunction: Teleological explanation in adults. *Cognition* 111: 138-43.

Kinderman, Peter, Robin Dunbar, and Richard P. Bentall. 1998. Theory-of-mind deficits and causal attributions. *British Journal of Psychology* 89, no. 2: 191.

MacIntyre, Alasdair. 2001. *Dependent rational animals: Why human beings need the virtues.* New York: Open Court.

McCauley, Robert N. 2011. *Why religion is natural and science is not.* New York: Oxford University Press.

McCauley, Robert N., and E. Thomas Lawson. 2002. *Bringing ritual to mind: Psychological foundations of cultural forms.* Cambridge: Cambridge University Press.

Moritz, Joshua M. 2011. Evolution, the end of human uniqueness, and the election of the imago Dei. *Theology and Science* 9, no. 3: 307-39.

Onishi, Kristine H., and Renée Baillargeon. 2005. Do 15-month-old infants understand false beliefs? *Science* 308: 255-58.

Perner, Josef. 1991. *Understanding the representational mind.* Cambridge, MA: Bradford Books, MIT Press.

Perner, Josef, and Ted Ruffman. 2005. Infants' insight into the mind: How deep? *Science* 308: 214-16.

Povinelli, Daniel J., and Jennifer Vonk. 2003. Chimpanzee minds: Suspiciously human? *Trends in Cognitive Science* 7: 157-60.

Pyysiainen, Ilkka. 2003. *How religion works: Towards a new cognitive science of religion.* Leiden: Brill.

Reinders, Hans S. 2008. *Receiving the gift of friendship: Profound disability, theological anthropology, and ethics.* Grand Rapids: Eerdmans.

Shults, F. LeRon. 2003. *Reforming theological anthropology: After the philosophical turn to relationality.* Grand Rapids: Eerdmans.

Sosis, Richard. 2004. The adaptive value of religious ritual: Rituals promote group cohesion by requiring members to engage in behavior that is too costly to fake. *American Scientist* 92: 166-74.

Spelke, Elizabeth S., and Katherine D. Kinzler. 2007. Core knowledge. *Developmental Science* 10, no. 1: 89-96.

Sperber, Dan, David Premack, and Ann J. Premack, eds. 1995. *Causal cognition: A multidisciplinary debate.* New York: Oxford University Press.

Tomasello, Michael. 1999. *The cultural origins of human cognition.* Cambridge, MA: Harvard University Press.

van Inwagen, Peter. 2009. Explaining belief in the supernatural: Some thoughts on Paul Bloom's "Religious Belief as an Evolutionary Accident." In *The believing primate: Scientific, philosophical, and theological reflections on the origin of religion,* ed. J. Schloss and M. J. Murray, 128-38. New York: Oxford University Press.

Wellman, Henry, David Cross, and Julanne Watson. 2001. Meta-analysis of theory of mind development: The truth about false-belief. *Child Development* 72: 655-84.

Wimmer, Heinz, and Josef Perner. 1983. Beliefs about beliefs: Representation and constraining function of wrong beliefs in young children's understanding of deception. *Cognition* 53: 45-57.

Wolterstorff, Nicholas. 2008. *Justice: Rights and wrongs.* Princeton: Princeton University Press.

The Image and the Likeness of God: A Theological Approach

Anthony C. Thiselton

Main Thesis, Its Relationship to Other Chapters, and Three Popular Misconceptions

The John Templeton Foundation letterhead carries this slogan: "Supporting science — investing in the big questions." But while physics and other sciences explore the "big question" of *how* the universe came into being, Christian theology investigates the even bigger question of *why* the universe came into being. The nearest formulation to the truth of the mystery may well be, at its simplest: "Because it is the very nature of God to reach beyond himself and to *engage in love with a universe he has chosen to create.*" The major thesis of this chapter is that to fulfill the vocation of representing God as his image and likeness, humankind is called to reach *beyond the self in love and communion* with God and the other, which includes other human beings.

At a secondary level this may involve language, address, and communication, as Richard Byrne has indicated, but also especially community and relationality, as Roy Baumeister, Warren Brown, and Justin Barrett have indicated. Further, as Francisco Ayala has argued, "personhood" is closely related to moral responsibility. For this, too, belongs to the very nature of God. Because God is righteous and faithful, as well as loving, humans cannot truly "represent" God without an understanding of what this involves for their way of living.

Justin Barrett and Roy Baumeister also raise relevant questions about human habits, dispositions, and character. The uniqueness of a person does not emerge solely in terms of such physical properties as weight, height, skin color, hair color, eye color, or stature of the body. In the striking terms suggested by the Russian Orthodox theologian Vladimir Lossky, a human being remains no more than an "individual" when he or she is regarded as part of "nature." When that individual receives divine grace to participate in the nature of God — or to represent God — he or she becomes a "person" in the strict meaning of the term. Lossky explicitly argues: "Individual and person mean opposite things" (Lossky 1991, 121). From Lossky's viewpoint, the "individual" belongs only to nature — to the empirical chain of cause and effect in which the individual defensively sets the self off from the other. It thereby establishes a particular exclusive identity, like the self-contained individual ego of Descartes. Person, however, expresses personhood by a relationship with God and the other, in which giving and receiving take place in love, communication, and mutuality. This is why "image of God" has to include subjectivity, as Adam Zenan observes in his chapter. If "image and likeness of God" represents or even mirrors the nature of God, self-giving, loving, and engagement with others must remain central to this vocation.

When we consider God as Holy Trinity, this approach becomes all the more unavoidable. From all eternity God acts cooperatively as Father, Son, and Holy Spirit. The church fathers spoke of God's internal *perichōresis* relations: an interpretation or internal relationality that did not merely come about with the creation of the universe. The fathers also agreed that creation itself was a cooperative act within the Godhead. By way of example, I would cite the second-century writer Irenaeus, who was rooted in both East and West: "By the hands of the Father, that is the Son and the Holy Spirit, man . . . was made in the likeness of God" (*Against Heresies* 5.6.1). He adds: "Throughout all time, man, having been molded at the beginning by the hands of God, that is, of the Son and the Spirit, is made after the image and likeness of God" (*Against Heresies* 5.28.4). I might also cite Athanasius (c. 296-373): "The Spirit [is involved] in the act of creation. For the Father creates all things through the Word [Christ] in the Spirit; for where the Word is there is the Spirit also" (Athanasius, *Letter to Serapion* 3.5).

John Zizioulas, the foremost contemporary theologian of the Greek Orthodox Church, goes even further than do these fathers and Lossky. Indeed, some may understandably accuse him of exaggeration. But in *Being as Communion* he says: "God is a relational Being: without the concept of communion it would not be possible to speak of the being of God . . . . 'God' has no ontological context, no true being, apart from communion" (1997, 17-18). But we are not obliged to depend on Eastern Orthodox theologians for this approach. The Scottish Presbyterian David Cairns, of Aberdeen, declares: "It is the individual-in-the-community . . . that is in the image of God" (1973, 44). The Baptist evangelical Stanley Grenz emphasizes relationality and communion in his book *The Social God and the Relational Self: A Trinitarian Theology of the Imago Dei* (2001). He argues that "the image of God" in humankind has nothing to do with "an inward turn," but is constructed "*extra se in Christo* by the Holy Spirit," and "finds identity through participation in the divine dynamic of love" (2001, 332).

I conclude this introduction by defining my position and thesis over against three popular misconceptions of the "image of God." First, in the ancient world images of a deity did *not* constitute *reflections* or kinships with the deity, but *representations* of the invisible divine figure. Humankind was originally called to *represent* God to the world. Images of wood or stone were denied to Israel, because to construct an image out of inanimate objects was to construct a false substitute to Israel's task of representing God in their life, habits, and conduct. This was to include representing God's kingship or dominion, his righteousness and faithfulness, his wisdom, his creative freedom, and his going forth out of himself in love and relationality. Representation is an active vocation or calling; reflection, or mirroring, suggests a human capacity or potential.

We shall discuss this crucial point further. However, for the present we may note two facts. First, the representative significance of "image and likeness" finds expression in two modern writers in particular, Jürgen Moltmann and David Clines. Moltmann urges that the prohibition of images, the second commandment of the Decalogue (Exod. 20:4), arises "because he himself [humankind] and *only he* is intended to *represent* the image and likeness of God upon earth" (Moltmann 1971, 109; italics added). David Clines has provided a meticulous and comprehensive survey of the subject in a research article of fifty pages, which he delivered as the Tyndale Old Testament lecture in 1967 (Clines 1968, 53-103). He rightly challenges the traditional translation of Genesis 1:26: "Let us make humankind *in* our image," arguing that the Hebrew *b*ᵉ (beth) is "the *beth* of essence, meaning 'as,' 'in the capacity of'; *as* our image" (1968, 75). On the basis of careful research into "image," Clines concludes that the function of the image is to be "*representative* of one who is really or spiritually present, though physically absent" (1968, 87).

Second, this explains how in the New Testament Christ is said to be the true image and likeness of God, whereas humankind failed in this vocation. Hebrews 2:6-9 makes this explicit, quoting Psalm 8:4-8, which begins: "What are human beings that you are mindful of them?" The Hebrews text then rehearses God's intention to let humans have dominion over the earth.

But the writer adds: "As it is, we do not yet see everything in subjection to them, but we do see Jesus . . . now crowned with glory and honor" (Heb. 2:9). In Colossians 1:15, Paul declares: "He [Christ] is the image of the invisible God" (Greek: *eikōn tou Theou tou aoratou*). In the judgment of theologian Eberhard Jüngel, in Christ "God's being is *thinkable again*" (1983, 111; italics in original). In Christ, Jüngel continues, "God defined himself as love on the cross of Jesus, God *is* love (1 John 4:8)." He adds: "The word of the cross is the self-definition of God in human language" (1983, 220, 229).

This brings us to the second popular misunderstanding. Many identify the image and likeness of God with specific qualities or dispositions that they see in humankind and also in God. The favorite candidates down the centuries have been rationality, or wisdom; kingship, or dominion over the earth; freedom, or the ability to make decisions in self-determination; the ability to communicate, to address, or to use language; and the capacity to enjoy relationships with others, or relationality. Vladimir Lossky considers these qualities or dispositions, but comments: "The number of these definitions and their variety show us that the fathers refrain from confining the image of God to any one part of man. In fact, the biblical narrative gives no precise account of the nature of the image" (1991, 116). The unified wholeness of the image, he argues, can be seen in Irenaeus, Gregory of Nyssa, and Gregory Palamas.

Second Corinthians 4:4 anticipates Colossians 1:15. We see, Paul declares, "the light of the gospel of the glory of Christ, which is the image of God" [Greek: *tou Christou, hos estin eikōn tou Theou*]. It is a commonplace of the Greek fathers, as Lossky insists, that Jesus represents and reveals God: "Proclamation of the image of God manifested in Christ, the God-Man, makes use . . . of the Biblical writings" (1974, 137).

This brings us to a third problem. Lossky constantly quotes from Irenaeus, Athanasius, Gregory of Nazianzus, and Gregory of Nyssa: "God made Himself man, that man might become God" (1974, 97). The Eastern Orthodox Church follows the fathers of the Eastern Church in making much of "deification," or *theōsis*. Where Western writers might speak of "sanctification," the Eastern Orthodox speak of transformation into the likeness of God, in a sense which is related to the "exchange formula" of Irenaeus, Athanasius, and Gregory. The concept is not idolatrous or naturalistic. Indeed, it is taken up by the Protestant Pentecostal Veli-Matti Kärkkäinen in his book *One with God: Salvation as Deification and Justification* (2004). Second Peter 1:4 calls Christians "partakers of the divine nature," and that is based on adoption, not on natural birth (Rom. 8:15-17, 23; Gal. 4:5). The first formal definition of deification comes from Pseudo-Dionysius (fifth to sixth centuries CE), who calls it "the attaining of likeness to God and union with him as far as possible" (1.3.376 A). Hence Lossky comments: "Thus creation in the image and likeness of God implies the idea of participation in the divine Being, of communion with God. That is to say, it presupposes grace" (1991, 118).

The "misconception" that I have referred to is that this participation in God does not arise from the natural capacities of human beings. Sharing this likeness to God depends on receiving the grace of God to enable humans to fulfill their vocation as the image and likeness of God. Lossky expresses this bluntly: "Creation in the image of God would contradict the Christian teaching that man is a creature called to *attain* to union with God, to *become* god by grace, but in no way god by virtue of his origin" (1991, 117; italics in original). We are called to become persons who share likeness with God, and to be raised above "nature," in which we are merely "individuals" (1991, 20-34). The "confusion," Lossky suggests, is caused by taking fallen humanity as our starting point. "It is not part of our nature which corresponds to the image of God in us" (1991, 122).

Image of God as Representation: A Closer Look at Biblical Passages

I have noted that Clines and Moltmann are two of the most explicit and emphatic writers to emphasize the representational character of image and likeness. We may first dismiss the mistaken notion that *image* (Hebrew: *tselem;* Greek: *eikōn*) differs significantly in meaning from *likeness* (Hebrew: *dēmuth;* Greek: *homoiōsis*). These words occur in the Hebrew text and Greek Septuagint of Genesis 1:26. A distinction between the two is often ascribed to Irenaeus, but as James Purves argues, this was not his primary concern (Purves 1996, 99-120). Genesis 5:2, then, refers to the "likeness of God," while Genesis 9:6 urges the sanctity of life: "for God made man in his own image." Today, after generations of study of Hebrew poetic parallelism, it is clear that often a second phrase with a new synonym merely explains or repeats what has been expressed in the first phrase or sentence. Thus "likeness" almost certainly expounds and unpacks "image" in Genesis 1:26-27.

In research before about 1940, as Clines has indicated, scholars tended to explain "image" and "likeness" in four or five specific ways: (1) as self-consciousness or self-determination (Delitzsch); (2) as capacity for rational thought and understanding (Dillmann and Heinisch, following Aquinas);

(3) as human rule or dominion over fellow creatures (Holzinger and Koehler, also following Aquinas); (4) as immediate relationship between God and man (Vischer); (5) as some correspondence of form (Gunkel, von Rad). After 1940, Paul Humbert argued for *tselem* as physical form or embodiment, as in an upright statue of the deity in pagan religions (Humbert 1940, 153-75; Stamm 1956, 84-98; Migliore 1991, 120-29).

The significant contribution of Humbert was to explore the three-dimensional physical images of invisible or mythological deities. The upright posture of the image does not *mirror,* or reflect, the deity; it *represents* the deity. Thus Edmond Jacob writes: "*Tselem* means a fashioned image, a shaped and *representative* figure (2 Kings 11:8; Amos 5:26; Ezek. 23:14). Something eminently concrete . . . the term *dēmut* can have the same concrete sense as *tselem*" (e.g., Isa. 40:13). Jacob continues: "The ancient orient shows us with ever increasing clarity that the purpose and function of an image consists in representing someone. An image . . . a statue of a god, is the real presence of this god" (Jacob 1958, 166-67). Often a king, for example, set up his image in a remote province, which he could not visit in person, to represent him, his prestige, and his authority. Many inscriptions provide evidence of this, for instance, those of Assyria and Egypt. The phrase "image of God" appeared in ancient Egypt to convey the notion of the king as vizier, or vice regent, of God on earth. Jacob confirms, in effect, Lossky's comment: "Man is a representative by his entire being," that is, not by means of some specific quality, "for Israelite thought always views man in his totality" (1958, 168). Vriezen seems to travel halfway. He recognizes that the image of God entails humankind's "vocation to be God's vice regent on earth"; but he also speaks of "reflecting" the nature of God (1962, 208). Jacob and Eichrodt both recognize that "likeness" *(dēmut)* provides an "explanation" of image *(tselem)* and that, as Humbert argues, image is a concrete "representation," such as a statue (Eichrodt 1961/1967, 1:122-23). Eichrodt enlarges on "representation," or even "substitute": in this sense a son may "represent" his father and be like him.

In spite of the warning from Lossky and Jacob about specific parts or functions of humankind, Hans Walter Wolff sees Psalm 8:4-9 as an explication of Genesis 1:26-27, in which human beings are called to "rule" over the world as those whose vocation is to be in God's image. "Rule" does not mean mere mastery or domination. Like a responsible king, humankind is to be God's steward, who cares for the universe. The Hebrew for *rule* in Psalm 8:5-6 is *m-š-l,* and the addressee in Genesis 1:26-27 is not an individual but *'ādām,* humankind. Wolff urges: "The context makes it clear that no individual at all is meant. . . . Thus *'ādām* is unquestionably to be understood in a collective sense . . . the community" (Wolff 1974, 161). Without splitting apart human functions, Wolff interweaves stewardship with the capacity to be addressed and to converse, and the capacity to relate to God and to others. He concludes with the interaction between male and female: "Be fruitful and multiply" (Gen. 1:28). When we leave the realm of Old Testament scholarship, we shall note again that Lossky, Zizioulas, and Grenz relate this to the plurality-in-oneness of God as Trinity.

We may recall the theme in Clines and Moltmann that the prohibition against images in the Decalogue arose because God willed that his people alone would represent him as his image and likeness, and not seek a false substitute for the task in wood or stone. Gerhard von Rad goes a long way toward recognizing this in his long discussion of the prohibition of images (1962/1965, 1:212-19). The notion that God cannot be represented visibly, he insists, is "quite inapplicable" to the Old Testament (1962/1965, 1:213). The image is an affront to God, because it seeks to make God "at man's disposal" rather than as the recipient of revelation, where and when God chooses.

We cannot exclude the concepts of relationality and community from that of the image and likeness of God. Even the use of the plural in Genesis 1:26 may be significant. We may discount a number of explanations for the plural, including the Trinitarian one, for this is part of the Old Testament. Some see the plural as suggesting cooperation with creation; others see it as a plural of majesty (cf. Isa. 6:8: "Who will go for us?"). Still others see it as an address to the heavenly court, some as the notion of an as-yet-undefined plurality within the Godhead. We cannot be certain. What is important is Clines's proposal that "in our image" *(be tselem)* could better be translated "*as* our image," by *be* by regarding *be* as a "*beth* of essence" (1968, 75). "I appeared as *(beth)* El Shaddai" (Exod. 6:3) offers a parallel, and Clines appeals to Gesenius's *Hebrew Grammar.* Thus we return to the "representational quality" of the image of God. Again, Egypt, Mesopotamia, and Assyria provide parallels.

Human embodiment is also important here. The Old Testament knows little to nothing of a mind-body dualism. From the point of view of Pauline theology and the New Testament, few have expressed the matter as eloquently as Ernst Käsemann does. He declares that, by "body," Paul means "that piece of world which we ourselves are, and for which we bear responsibility. . . . It signifies man in his worldliness and therefore in his ability to communicate. . . . In the bodily obedience of the Christian, carried out in the service of God in the world of every day, the lordship of Christ finds visible expression, and only when this visible expression takes personal shape in us does the whole thing become credible as Gospel message" (1969, 135).

Jesus Christ as Image and Likeness of God, and Relationality in Ricoeur and Lossky

It is probable that the New Testament ascribes being in the image or likeness of God more frequently and more decisively than the image or likeness of God is ascribed to humankind in the Old Testament. The significant terms in the Greek Testament are *eikōn,* image; *homoiōsis,* likeness; *morphē,* form; and *charaktēr,* representation or exact imprint. I have noted that believers see "the light of the knowledge of the glory of God in the face of Jesus Christ, who is the image of God" in 2 Corinthians 4:4; Christ is "the image of the invisible God" (Col. 1:15). In John's language, "He who has seen me has seen the Father" (John 12:45; 14:9). In Hebrews, Christ is "the reflection of God's glory, and the exact imprint of God's very being" (Heb. 1:3; Greek: *hos ōn apaugasma tēs doxēs, kai charaktēr tēs hypostaseās autou*).

Hugh Montefiore comments on the *charaktēr:* it "suggests an engraving. . . . The Son does not merely resemble certain aspects of his Father: he is the exact representation of his essence, that is, of what God is that makes God be God" (1964, 35). He adds that this is virtually a synonym for "image," and he notes that *apaugasma* may mean "radiance" just as well as "reflection." He further comments that, in Hebrews 2:5-6, it is the Son who has dominion proper to the image of God, not humankind or angels, quoting B. F. Westcott: "[Humankind] has lost his capacity for receiving that for which he was created," and emphasizing that image of God, Christ's self-offering, is "congruous with the generosity of a self-effacing Creator . . . self-emptying, self-effacement, self-denial by him in whom lies all the fullness of infinite being" (Montefiore 1964, 60). Harold Attridge agrees that the two terms *apaugasma* and *charaktēr* are best translated as "effulgence" and "imprint." He also sees the reference to "perfection" in Hebrews 2:10 in terms of "relationship to God" and "a vocational process" (Attridge 1989, 41, 86).

On Christ as "the image of the invisible God" *(eikōn tou theou aoratou),* Charles F. D. Moule observes: "Christ is claimed to gather up in his own person that manifestation of the invisible God, which was to be found . . . in Man (Gen. 1:26; 1 Cor. 11:7; 2 Cor. 3:18)" (1957/1962, 62). The term *eikōn,* Moule adds, was familiar in the wisdom tradition and in Philo. He compares it with 2 Corinthians 4:4 and Hebrews 1:3. Commenting on "image" in

2 Corinthians 4:4, Victor Furnish observes: "The concept of Christ as God's image already had a firm place in the church's liturgical tradition. . . . Each describes that by which and in which the original is truly *represented*" (1984, 248; italics added). Verse 4 is the supreme climax of the whole passage. We may compare it with Philippians 2:6-11, where Christ is in "the form of God."

If Jesus Christ more truly represents God than any human being, what characterizes God as he is revealed in Christ most decisively? Clearly, Jesus conveyed both the love of God and the kingdom or reign of God more decisively than any other theme: "God so loved the world that he gave his Son" (John 3:16). On "kingdom" (more accurately, "rule" or "reign"), James D. G. Dunn says: "The centrality of the kingdom of God *(basileia tou theou)* in Jesus' preaching is one of the least disputable, or disputed, facts about Jesus (Mark 1:14-15). . . . The heart of that gospel is precisely Jesus' preaching of the kingdom of God" (Dunn 2003, 383-84; cf. 761-62). Again, in Jüngel's words, "God defined himself as love on the cross of Christ. God is love (1 John 4:8)." For God and for Jesus, he continues: " 'Inner being' *is* itself a turning toward what is 'outside.' God communicates with himself without *withholding* himself from others." Relationality is encapsulated in these words: "Who can separate us from the love of God which is in Christ Jesus?" (Rom. 8:38-39). Jüngel repeats: "Paul unmistakably identifies the being of God concretely with love: God's love in Jesus Christ. . . . God happens as love in the death of Jesus" (1983, 220-21).

This precisely coheres with what Paul Ricoeur and Vladimir Lossky say about *personhood.* Ricoeur writes from the consciously limited perspective of philosophy; Lossky writes from the unlimited viewpoint of theology. From the theological viewpoint, Lossky says: "Creation in the image and likeness of God implies the idea of participation in the divine Being, of communion with God. That is to say, it presupposes grace" (Lossky 1991, 118). Without the transforming grace of God, humankind cannot fully represent God. A human being may certainly be an individual — but not, in the fullest sense, a person.

Paul Ricoeur takes this theme of relationality and otherness as far as he can — that is, without explicitly resorting to theology. He begins by engaging with Descartes and Hume. Descartes, the father of rationalism, leaves the self as isolated and individual. Hume, the empiricist, sees the self as a bundle of successive perceptions, which Ricoeur counters by searching for some continuity or "sameness": for the immutability of the *idem,* or the self-constancy of the *ipse.* But this does not provide self-identity. The "other" is presupposed from the outset, not as a mere object of thought, but as subjective "personalities of a higher order," who "maintain myself in my identity" (Ricoeur 1992, 332). Through many chapters and many philosophers he traces a series of thinkers who improve on Descartes, Locke, and Hume, but never quite reach full personhood based on relationality and otherness. P. F. Strawson, speech-act theorists, and several others in this area still end by reducing "Who?" to "What?" They failed to overcome "the paradoxes of self-identity," though the nearest to a solution begins with an appeal to "narrative identity" (Ricoeur 1988, 244-49). *Narrative,* or telling stories, helps to uncover the uniqueness of the self as a person, including a person's eccentricities, decisions, and character. Ricoeur makes a "plea on behalf of the irreducibility of . . . 'mineness' and selfhood," in which we may discover "a moment of self-dispossession essential to authentic personhood" (1988, 138).

"Dispossession of the self" denotes expressing the self "in its dialectic with otherness" (1988, 297). Without relationality with another, we lack "the ethics of reciprocity" (1988, 180, 187). The self requires self-esteem, justice, and practical wisdom, but these, in turn, depend on otherness. Otherness is not an add-on to the self; it belongs to the ontological constitution of selfhood. One of the few philosophers to take this argument seriously is the Jewish thinker Emmanuel Lévinas. But Lévinas may go too far in reaching "the substitution of the 'I' for the 'Other'"; ethical responsibility involves what Ricoeur calls a "for the Other" stance (Lévinas 1981, 102, 112-13, 118, 135-36; cf. Ricoeur 1992, 238-41). In plain language, it presupposes a to-and-fro with the other in mutuality and reciprocity, which includes giving of the self.

This fits admirably with Lossky's argument about the self and personhood. He insists that the individual is different from the person: indeed, "individual and person mean opposite things" (1991, 121). An individual becomes a person only when the self opens up itself to give and receive from the other. To Lossky, a mere individual is part of *nature;* "while person, on the other hand, means that which distinguishes it from nature." He insists that the image and likeness of God is that to which "we are called to *attain . . .* to *become* god by grace, but in no way god by virtue of his origin" (1991, 121, 117; italics in original). Union with God, or sharing God's likeness, becomes possible only on the basis of redemption, salvation, and "deification." He derives this from Irenaeus, Gregory of Nyssa, Gregory Palamas, and ultimately from Scripture. If humans are to *represent God,* their self-giving love and reciprocity with the other "subject" must in some measure reproduce the love of God.

To Lossky, this relationality finds expression in communion with God and with the other. As an individual, the self walls itself up defensively and in exclusivity, to mark off self-identity and difference from others. As a person, the self becomes open to others in inclusivity. In his book *The Image and Likeness of God,* Lossky declares: "Personal existence supposes a relation to the other . . . . A person can be fully personal only insofar as he has nothing that he seeks to possess for himself to the exclusion of others . . . . Otherwise we are in the presence of individuals." Elsewhere in the book he observes: "The philosopher's *persona* becomes the theologian's *relatio.*" "Persons, as such, are not parts of nature." But when we consider God, "the Son is therefore a concise declaration of the nature of the Father" (1974, 106, 116, 107, 135).

The ultimate foundation of all this, for Lossky, is that of intrarelations within the Holy Trinity. It is almost a truism of patristic, medieval, and classical Reformation theology that in every act of creation and redemption the three persons of the Trinity cooperate together in bringing about a desired effect. Wolfhart Pannenberg, Jürgen Moltmann, and Eugene Rogers have illustrated this, for example, with reference to the narratives of the Gospels. In the baptism of Jesus, says Rogers (2005, 135-71), the Father "sends" the Son, and expresses delight through the voice from heaven; the Holy Spirit descends on Jesus in visible form; the Son undergoes the rite of baptism (Mark 1:9-13, and parallels). Moltmann insists: "The New Testament talks about God by proclaiming in narrative the relationships of the Father, the Son, and the Spirit, which are relationships of fellowship and open to the world" (1992, 64). Pannenberg similarly declares that the revelation of God in Christ involves *"the reciprocal self-distinction of the Father, Son, and Spirit; as the common concrete form of Trinitarian relations"* (1991-1998, 1:308; italics in original). He argues further (1991-1998, 3:10), following Paul, that the Father and the Holy Spirit work cooperatively in the resurrection of Jesus Christ (Rom. 8:11). All three of these writers emphasize the importance of this for relationality. Moltmann also observes that the Holy Spirit inspires Jesus to pray to the Father, arguing that "subjectivity is intersubjectivity" (1992, 289).

John Zizioulas, as we have seen, goes further. In *Being as Communion,* he declares: "God is a relational being. . . . 'God' has no ontological content, no true being, apart from communion. . . . Nothing exists as an 'individual'" (1997, 17, 18). Some may think that Zizioulas goes too far; but he restores the balance after Enlightenment individualism. Stanley Grenz cites "the near consensus that person is a relational concept" (2001, 9). But if we are considering what it is to be like God, or to represent God, Grenz, like Lossky, argues from the nature of the Trinitarian God to the image of God in humankind, rather than from humankind to God. He concludes on this basis: "In the final analysis, then, the *imago Dei* is not merely relational. . . . It is ultimately communal": it involves "the quest for completeness that draws humans out of isolation into bonded relationships" (2001, 303).

Implications Relating to More Traditional Characteristics of the Image of God

To emphasize, as we have done, the three aspects of relationality, representation, and vocation (or attainment) does not suggest the irrelevance of more traditional work on derived or secondary characteristics of the image and likeness of God. To represent God, or to bear his likeness, includes not only love and reciprocity, but also kingship, righteousness (or faithfulness), and wisdom (or intelligence). To talk about such qualities is not "wrong" in the context of relationality, representation, and vocation. Furthermore, these necessary entailments enhance cross-references to other chapters in this volume.

Relationality

Relationality has always found a place among the more traditional attempts to explain "image of God." One of the best surveys of these attempts can be found in brief in Daniel Migliore's work (1991, 120-38). He lists five more traditional answers to questions about the image of God, which include reason (or wisdom), dominion (or rule), freedom, and relationality. On the last he comments: "Being created in the image of God means that humans find their true identity in coexistence with each other and with all other creatures. . . . Human existence is not individualistic but communal" (1991, 125). In his contribution to the present volume, Justin Barrett asks whether current evolutionary accounts of religion undercut theological claims about relationality, and he answers firmly in the negative. He rightly emphasizes the relationships with others that God may choose to establish.

Barrett's account of continuity within a relational framework also coheres well with Paul Ricoeur's defense of the self against Hume, which I have discussed above. Barrett's appeal to theories of mind remains entirely relevant. C. A. Campbell has pointed out that, on the basis of Hume's theory of the self as mere successive perceptions, we might perceive the striking of a clock ten times as a tenfold repetition of its striking one o'clock, where continuity of a stable mind would interpret this as striking ten o'clock! (Campbell 1957, 76-79). Barrett's emphasis on potential qualities rather than actual ones also coheres with my emphasis on vocation and attainment. Francisco Ayala's account of the moral and the ethical also offers close resonance with my references to Ricoeur. Roy Baumeister and Warren Brown have indicated, along with Barrett and this chapter, that the self does not denote an isolated individual. The importance of relationality and communion is not limited to theology alone. Baumeister devotes a section of his chapter to the question "Solitary Selves?" and declares: "The selfhood of a thoroughly solitary being would be quite limited." He adds: "Identity is thus not inside the person but in the social matrix."

Rationality, Wisdom, or Intelligence

Proverbs and James are not alone among the biblical books that commend wisdom as a God-like quality. It is a widespread popular mistake today to follow the secular Enlightenment in confusing wisdom as *phronēsis* with mere knowledge or information. In *Jesus the Sage* (1994), Ben Witherington has shown that this emphasis characterizes the teaching of Jesus, and I have recently discussed the nature and importance of wisdom in the Old and New Testaments (2011-2012, 163-72, 260-68). The philosopher Hans-Georg Gadamer has also sharply distinguished between the individualist and rationalist tradition of Descartes and the communal and wisdom-related tradition of Giambattista Vico, in promoting practical wisdom rather than bare instrumental reason (1989, 9-35). If there is any hostility toward "reason" in Paul, Luther, or Barth, this is only against *instrumental* reason, not against *rationality (logos),* reasonableness, or argued reason (Stowers 1990, 253-86). As Pannenberg and others have argued, Paul deliberately used argumentation, logic, and reason in his epistles, rather than exclaiming, "Thus says the Lord." Indeed, Origen viewed reason, or mind, as a distinctive human quality. The mind, he says, "receives reasons and assertions"; it contemplates "the reason for things, perceiving and understanding divine truths" (Origen, *De Principiis* 1.1.7).

This also has communal and moral dimensions. Augustine gave a preeminent place to mind (*City of God* 12.24), and Gregory of Nyssa believed that "word, understanding . . . and mind" were part of the image of God in humankind (*On the Making of Man* 5). In the medieval period, Thomas Aquinas emphasized the positive view of reason, and argued that humans differ from animals in their use of reason and will (ST, 2a, Q. 3, Art. 7; Q. 1, Art. 1). John Calvin says: "Man was created in the image of God. . . . [The mind] distinguishes and separates us from the lower animals. . . . The primary seat of the divine image was in the mind and the heart" (*Institutes,* 1.15.3). In our modern era, Reinhold Niebuhr declares: "The rational and intellectual . . . is made after the image of God . . . able to use reason in the understanding and beholding of God" (1941, 1:165-66).

Dominion, or Kingly Rule

This is explicit in Genesis 1:26, Psalm 8:4-8, and Hebrews 2:5-9. It also corresponds with qualities in God, and the central proclamation by Jesus of the kingdom of God, or more accurately of his "reign," or "rule," as we noted in Dunn and others.

However, Moltmann, Lossky, Niebuhr, van den Brink, and many other theologians have pointed out that God's reign is not to be conceived of as one of brute force, but of care, stewardship, and providence. Gijsbert van den Brink has argued convincingly that God's almighty rule must be conceived in terms of power *for* or power *to,* rather than as power *over* (1993, 119-34, 159-84). Power *over* suggests mastery and domination; power *to* or *for* suggests empowerment and enabling. As the one example of a perfect representation of God, Jesus renounced the way of brute force. The dominion entrusted to humankind at creation does not imply the exploitation of the world solely for the sake of human needs or wealth. To quote Moltmann again: "God created human beings '*to be* his image.' . . . As his image, human beings represent God on earth" (1985, 218-19; italics in original). Hence "likeness to God is both gift and charge": gift and charge to be *stewards* of the earth, which God has lent to humankind as his vice regent (1985, 227). Moltmann's entire book *God in Creation: An Ecological Doctrine of Creation* pursues this theme convincingly.

Wolfhart Pannenberg similarly concludes that the commission to have dominion over the earth "finds its full realization only in the Sonship of Jesus, that is, in the way in which Jesus as Son of the Father perceived his relation to the world. . . . Human beings are to rule over the world in a spirit of responsibility to the Father. It is impossible to argue to a right of limitless exploitation of nature" (1985/1999, 78).

Freedom, Morality, and Creativity

Freedom as applied to God includes the power to make decisions. It is clearly not "autonomy" in the sense of freedom to do anything at all. If God has pledged himself to covenant faithfulness, for example, he "cannot" (i.e., in the logical, not empirical, sense) be untrue to his own nature and retract his promises — or tell lies. This implies a moral and ethical content to "likeness to God." Francisco Ayala has helpfully set out this theme in his chapter in the present volume: "The moral sense emerges as a necessary implication of our high intellectual powers." He also sees moral norms and behavior as a goal that has not yet been reached. This coheres with Paul's utterance: "Just as we have borne the image of the man of dust, we *will* also bear the image of the man from heaven" (1 Cor. 15:49). This verse concerns the image of Jesus Christ in redeemed humans at the future resurrection of the dead. Pannenberg further suggests that just as it is God's nature to create, so those in his likeness may have limited capacities to share in creative work. This may apply, for example, to creative progress in medicine or in the sciences.

Love and Relationality Presuppose Communication

All of these five qualities are to be seen in the context of relationality, representation, and vocation. Those who consider a series of qualities in the image of God do not exclude the notion of representation. G. C. Berkower, a Reformed theologian, writes: "The idea of representation refers to man in the concreteness and visibility of his earthly life; to man, who was created in God's image and likeness, and who is called to represent and to portray this image here on earth . . . similar to the image of Christ. Being in the image of God refers to *this* representation" (1962/1978, 114; italics in original). Emil Brunner considers various views of the image of God in historical retrospect, but also declares: "God creates man as one who can hear his call and can answer it. . . . God creates one . . . to whom he wills to impart himself . . . a rational creature, as a being who is able to receive his Word" (1939, 102, 103).

Alan Torrance reminds us in his chapter in the present volume that the qualities we have been discussing constitute more than merely *human* capacities. Lossky's approach is similar. The remaining element, in engaging with other chapters in this volume, is that of Richard Byrne, who repeats the citation: "Language is regarded, at least in most intellectual traditions, as the quintessential human attribute." The relationship between God and humankind is not only representative and relational; relationship is initiated and sustained through language. This equally applies to the corporate or intersubjective relationship to the other. If a human person is not the individualist ego postulated by Descartes, what allows the self to interact with others in personhood is *language,* or other forms of communication, as Richard Byrne argues.

To return to our single perfect example of a representative of God through being his image and likeness, let me again cite some words of Jüngel: "The word of the cross is the self-definition of God in human language, which implies a definition of man" (1983, 152-69, 226-98). The concrete, visible, image of God in the form of Jesus Christ, in Jüngel's words, enables God to be "thinkable," and even "speakable" (1983, 229). The speech of God "addresses" us, and he addresses us in love (1983, 290, 298).

REFERENCES

Aquinas, Thomas. *Summa theologiae.* London: Eyre and Spottiswoode; New York: McGraw-Hill. 60 vols., Latin and English.

Athanasius. *Letter to Serapion.* In *The letter of Athanasius concerning the Holy Spirit,* ed. C. R. B. Shapland. London: Epworth Press.

Attridge, Harold W. 1989. *The epistle to the Hebrews: A commentary.* Philadelphia: Fortress Press.

Augustine. *City of God* 413-26.

Berkhower, G. C. 1962/1978. *Studies in dogmatics: Man, the image of God.* Grand Rapids: Eerdmans.

Brunner, Emil. 1939. *Man in revolt: A Christian anthropology.* London: Lutterworth Press.

Cairns, David. 1973. *The image of God in man.* London: SCM, 1953; rev. ed. London: Collins.

Calvin, John. 1957. *The institutes of the Christian religion.* 2 vols. Ed. H. Beveridge. London: James Clark.

Campbell, C. A. 1957. *On selfhood and Godhood.* London: Allen and Unwin; New York: Macmillan.

Clines, David J. A. 1968. The image of God in man. *Tyndale Bulletin* 19: 53-103.

Dunn, James D. G. 2003. *Jesus remembered.* Grand Rapids: Eerdmans.

Eichrodt, Walter. 1961/1967. *Theology of the Old Testament.* 2 vols. London: SCM Press.

Furnish, Victor P. 1984. *Second Corinthians: A new translation with introduction and commentary.* Anchor Bible series. New York/London: Doubleday.

Gadamer, Hans-Georg. 1989. *Truth and method*. 2nd English ed. London: Sheed and Ward.

Gregory of Nyssa. *On the making of man.*

Grenz, Stanley J. 2001. *The social God and the relational self: A Trinitarian theology of the imago Dei.* Louisville: Westminster John Knox Press.

Humbert, Paul. 1940. *Etudes sur le récit du paradis et de la chute dans la Genèse.* Neuchatel: Secrétariat de l'Universté.

Irenaeus, *Against heresies.* In *Ante-Nicene Fathers,* vol. 1.

Jacob, Edmond. 1958. *Theology of the Old Testament.* London: Hodder and Stoughton.

Jüngel, Eberhard. 1983. *God as the mystery of the world: On the foundation of the theology of the Crucified One in the dispute between theism and atheism.* Edinburgh: T&T Clark.

Kärkkäinen, Veli-Matti. 2004. *One with God: Salvation as deification and justification.* Wilmington, DE: Liturgical Press.

Käsemann, Ernst. 1969. Primitive Christian apocalyptic. In his *New Testament Questions of Today.* London: SCM.

Lévinas, Emmanuel. 1981. *Otherwise than being, or beyond essence.* The Hague: Nijhoff, 1981.

Lossky, Vladimir. 1974. *The image and likeness of God.* London/Oxford: Mowbray.

———. 1991. *The mystical theology of the Eastern Church.* Cambridge: James Clarke.

Migliore, Daniel L. 1991. *Faith seeking understanding: An introduction to Christian theology.* Grand Rapids: Eerdmans.

Moltmann, Jürgen. 1971. *Man: Christian anthropology in the conflicts of the present.* London: SPCK.

———. 1985. *God in creation: An ecological doctrine of creation.* London: SCM.

———. 1992. *The spirit of life: A universal affirmation.* London: SCM.

Montefiore, Hugh W. 1964. *The epistle to the Hebrews.* Black's New Testament Commentaries. London: Black.

Moule, Charles F. D. 1957/1962. *The epistles of Paul the apostle to the Colossians and to Philemon.* Cambridge: Cambridge University Press.

Niebuhr, Reinhold. 1941. *The nature and destiny of man.* 2 vols. London: Nisbet.

Origen. *De principiis.* In *Ante-Nicene Fathers,* vol. 4.

Pannenberg, Wolfhart. 1985/1999. *Anthropology in theological perspective.* London/New York: T&T Clark International.

———. 1991-1998. *Systematic theology.* 3 vols. Grand Rapids: Eerdmans; Edinburgh: T&T Clark.

Pseudo-Dionysius. *The celestial hierarchy.*

Purves, James G. M. 1996. The Spirit and the imago Dei: Reviewing the anthropology of Irenaeus of Lyons. *Evangelical Quarterly* 68: 99-120.

Ricoeur, Paul. 1988. *Time and Narrative,* vol. 3. Chicago: University of Chicago Press.

—. 1992. *Oneself as another.* Chicago: University of Chicago Press.

Rogers, Eugene. 2005. *After the Spirit: A constructive pneumatology from resources outside the modern West.* Grand Rapids: Eerdmans.

Russell, N. 2004. *The doctrine of deification in the Greek patristic tradition.* Oxford: Oxford University Press.

Stamm, J. J. 1956. Die Imago-Lehre von Karl Barth und die alttestamentliche Wissenschaft. In *Antwort. Festschrift K. Barth,* ed. E. Wolf et al., 84-98. Zürich: Evangelischer Verlag.

Stowers, Stanley K. 1990. Paul on the use and abuse of reason. In *Greeks, Romans, and Christians,* ed. David Balch, Everett Fergusson, and Wayne Meeks. Minneapolis: Augsburg.

Thiselton, Anthony C. 2011-2012. Wisdom in the Jewish and Christian scriptures. *Theology* 114: 163-72, 260-68.

van den Brink, Gijsbert. 1993. *Almighty God: A study of the doctrine of divine omnipotence.* Kampen: Kok-Pharos.

von Rad, Gerhard. 1962/1965. *Old Testament theology.* 2 vols. Edinburgh: Livers and Boyd.

Vriezen, Theodore C. 1962. *An outline of Old Testament theology.* Oxford: Blackwell.

Witherington, Ben, III. 1994. *Jesus the sage: The pilgrimage of wisdom.* Edinburgh: T&T Clark.

Wolff, Hans Dieter. 1974. *Anthropology of the Old Testament.* London: SCM.

Zizioulas, John. 1997. *Being as communion: Studies in personhood and the church.* New York: St. Vladimir's Seminary Press.

Retrieving the Person: Theism, Empirical Science, and the Question of Scope

Alan J. Torrance

Remarkable developments in the empirical sciences have opened new vistas on what it is to be human to the point where they are encouraging us to rethink what it is to be a person. Before we allow the empirical sciences to redefine the nature of the person, it is important not to lose sight of the fact that their explanatory power remains limited in scope. In this chapter I shall argue that Christian theism has not only shaped the very concept of the person but serves to underwrite a conceptuality whose grounds Western society has all but forgotten. It should become clear, however, that Christian theism also remains limited in its explanatory scope and cannot — and should not — be expected to provide the kind of explanation that belongs to the remit of the empirical sciences. This raises the question of how we interpret the interface between these two domains and how we relate these disparate modes or levels of interpretation. Clarity is necessary if the contributions of both Christian theism and the empirical sciences are to be taken seriously within an integrated account of the human person.

Two Influential Attempts to Commandeer the Question of Scope

It is a truism that the tools we use to interpret what it is to be a human person are laden with suppositions. Consequently, they are not as neutral as they may appear. When a neuroscientist, evolutionary biologist, social anthropologist, or philosophical theologian chooses to consider some facet of what it is to be a person, it is necessary to recognize that the methods each discipline uses will shed light on certain specific features of the person, but not others. A universal temptation is to bracket out the insights of other disciplines and thereby arrogate to one's particular discipline wider explanatory power than is warranted by the subject matter. A full-orbed understanding of what it is to be a human person requires the integration and, indeed, correlation of the insights of disparate disciplines. Some, for example, throw light on the drives and inclinations that characterize the acquired, epigenetic conditions of human behavior and flourishing, while others study the outworking of these in the development of human society. Neuroscientists shed light on the hardware of our nervous system, while cognitive psychologists engage in what might be described as a reverse engineering of the software integral to our cerebral processing.

Any interdisciplinary engagement with the nature of the person requires one to assess the extent to which any particular discipline or set of disciplines (the empirical sciences, for example) can claim to offer a *foundational* account of the person, namely, an account that establishes the essential nature or defining function of the person. Consequently, the most challenging questions that haunt interdisciplinary analysis concern the "scope" of the respective academic disciplines present at the table. Might it be the case that one discipline is in a position to "trump" another or displace the explanations offered by another?[1] Or, indeed, are "third-person" forms of inquiry in a position to trump "first-" or "second-person" perspectives? Do the latter stand to make a valid contribution and, if so, how is that to be conceived of as correlating with the former? Integral to these questions are further questions about whether it is useful or valid to speak of different *levels* of analysis. Are all the forms of inquiry to be conceived of as operating on the same level, or is one to be conceived of as more fundamental with respect to defining the *essential* nature of the person?

It appears that two highly influential methodological "fideisms" (that is, absolute *metaphysical* suppositions taken on faith that cannot be shown to be warranted by either the nature of the object in question or empirical scientific data) threaten to commandeer this entire debate. This occurs when they arrogate to their own particular domains a universality of scope in ways that, I would suggest, are toxic to a full-orbed account of the nature

---

1. I should add that there were certainly no attempts by the contributors to this volume to "trump" the explanations offered by other contributors during the conversations out of which this volume emerged.

of the person. The effect of both of these "fideisms" is to collapse all levels of explanation into just one.

1. Nomological Monism and Reductionist Accounts of Causal Agency

The first fideism takes the form of a philosophical and scientific reductionism that is based on a particular account of scientific laws. The questions this fideism addresses concern what kinds of objects have causal properties and where precisely causality is located.[2] In 1999, Nancy Cartwright, an eminent philosopher of science, wrote a monograph entitled *The Dappled World,* in which she sought to repudiate the "fundamentalist" assumption that "all facts must belong to one grand scheme," such that we interpret the world exclusively in terms of one single kind of causal law (1999, 25). She referred to this position as "nomological monism" (1999, 32-33). For nomological monists, all events — including mental events, rational deliberations, processes of logical reasoning, as also market trends and the like — require that they be conceived of as epiphenomena of physical processes that are strictly governed by causal laws that operate exclusively between basic particles. Although these causal interactions are so complex that events at the macro level will be unpredictable in practice (as implied by Chaos Theory), all events at the macro level can be assumed to be determined by causal processes that are operative exclusively at the micro level.

Following such an approach, a grand, unified theory of the events defining the lives of the whole spectrum of complex living creatures, from nanobes to the higher primates, could (theoretically) be provided in terms of the causal interactions between the particles that physically constitute them. This is the position that one would assume to result from the scientific materialism associated variously with Stephen Hawking and Richard Dawkins, for example. What this means is that a complete account of the whole dynamics of human existence, as articulated by social psychologists, evolutionary biologists, cognitive psychologists, social anthropologists, ethicists, theologians, and the like, could be provided simply by analyzing the law-governed, material, or physical relationships between the particles (and

2. The following discussion uses material from my paper "Developments in Neuroscience and Human Freedom: Some Theological and Philosophical Questions," *Science and Christian Belief* 16 (2003): 123-37; and also from my chapter in Malcolm Jeeves, ed., *From Cells to Souls* (Grand Rapids: Eerdmans, 2003).

physical forces) constitutive of these (purely material) entities. There is thus no relevant theoretical difference between the explanation of the events that define a volcanic eruption, the nervous system of an arthropod, the sociopolitical history of the British Labour Party, or the mental operations of Albert Einstein (see Honderich 2004, 36-38).

It is precisely this kind of approach that gave rise to the use of the phrase "nomological monism" (NM) to describe a particular way of interpreting thought processes. This description is first used in Donald Davidson's 1970 article "Mental Events," where NM referred to the view that mental entities were identical with physical entities and subject to strict correlating laws (Davidson 1970). This contrasts with the opposition to which he refers as "anomalous dualism." The latter "combines ontological dualism with the general failure of laws correlating the mental and the physical (Cartesianism)," and thus holds that there are no laws correlating mental and physical reality and that the relevant substances are ontologically discrete (1970, 111).

Nancy Cartwright challenges the "nomological monism" that drives reductionist, materialist accounts. Accordingly, she argues for a *pluralist* account of laws: that we should think in terms of a whole "patchwork" of laws and emergent interactive processes. Consequently, she repudiates the (counterintuitive) reductionist assumption that all the apparent forms of causal relationship that are assumed to apply in the context of abstract philosophical reasoning or in the economics of the marketplace or in the composition of a piano concerto must be reduced to one level of causal explanation, namely, that which applies to basic particles. By contrast, the "dappled world" of our experience is characterized by diverse forms of causal agency and causal interaction between causal agents at a host of different levels. In an article that applies these insights to human identity, Teed Rockwell points out that some of these agents "would be able to control the particles they were made of, rather than exclusively the other way around . . . ." He adds: "Mental processes could be one kind of emergent phenomenon" (Rockwell n.d.). Our mental processes, therefore, would be regarded as simply one of many different kinds of emergent properties that possess *causal power.*

Whether or not one accepts the degree of plurality of causal laws and agencies for which Rockwell argues, if persons possess causal agency of a kind that is not reducible to the "impersonal" particles that constitute them physically, then this has immense significance for how we conceive of the person. Or, to put it the other way around, if mental processes (deductions, inductions, hypothetical speculations, moral reasoning, and the like) have no causal power, that is, if reasons are not causes qua *reasons,* clearly this has extremely significant implications for what it is to be a person. Consequently, the most fundamental question relating to how we conceive of the emergence of personhood concerns where precisely *causal properties* are located. If they belong exclusively to physical objects and occur exclusively at the level of quarks, then this will inevitably have a leveling effect. Personhood, despite all appearances, becomes an epiphenomenal expression of the noncognitive, nonintentional, causal dynamic that takes place at the level of quarks. In short, if we adopt a reductive physicalist approach, then mental phenomena are ultimately identical to physical-chemical states, and the only relevant causality is what operates between basic particles.

Elsewhere I have discussed the question of whether it is possible to make sense of a nonreductive physicalist account or whether, as Jaegwon Kim thinks, physicalism is inherently reductionist and that nonreductive physicalism is an oxymoron (Kim 1993, 351-52). Nancey Murphy and Warren Brown challenge Kim's critique by rejecting the kind of atomistic account of physicalism that is believed by Kim to define physicalism (Murphy and Brown 2007, 233-36). Like Cartwright, Murphy and Brown reject reductionist interpretations of matter ("atomistic reductionism") and argue that one's account of the nature of matter is intrinsically related to one's accounts of causation. A coherent account of both, they suggest, is of fundamental significance for the interpretation of the person. Interestingly, their use of the language of "levels" and "top-down" causation appears to correlate with the "pluralist" account of reality endorsed by Cartwright.

The implication of our discussion should be clear. To adopt a physicalism or materialism that fails to offer a robust, nonreductive account of causal laws must inevitably commandeer the question of scope in a manner that is odious to accounts of the person that see persons as rational, deliberative, moral agents concerned with the question of truth. It is difficult to see how interpretations of the person that make exclusive and foundational recourse to atomistic physicalism will not ultimately see personhood as a mere "epiphenomenon" with the implication that the "person" per se can make no intentional contribution to the dynamics of history or, indeed, the natural order. Nomological monism, therefore, can only mean that the term "person" no longer denotes a particular agent with causal powers but, instead, an arbitrary construct that is, ultimately, little more — indeed, no more — than a conceptual phantom.

2. *Metaphysical Naturalism (MPN)*

The second methodological fideism that is ultimately toxic to the conceptuality of personhood is metaphysical naturalism (MPN). Before we discuss MPN, it is important to distinguish between *metaphysically naturalist* appropriations of science, which we shall reject, and methodologies that bracket out divine action as an explanatory factor within a particular scientific domain. In order to distinguish the two, we might refer to the latter by the somewhat uncharismatic description "Non-Theoreferential Scientific Methodologies" (NTSM). Unfortunately, the widely used expression "Methodological Naturalism" (as we find it used, e.g., by Philip Johnson [1993]) risks confusing the two. Methodological naturalism *can* denote a methodology that assumes MPN, which is critiqued so impressively by Alvin Plantinga, for example. However, it can also be used simply to denote methods of interpreting the natural order that bracket out theism as an explanatory factor (NTSM).

MPN denotes the unwarranted fideistic conviction that God does not exist and that there is not (and can never be) any divine engagement with the natural order. On such a view, theism has no place within a unified worldview. By contrast, methodological naturalism *can be* — and at times *has been* — used simply to denote a strategy that excludes explicit reference to divine action in scientific explanation, what I am referring to here as NTSM. What is important to appreciate here is that there may be cogent *theological* reasons (or reasons compatible with orthodox theological convictions) for deciding to bracket out explicit references to divine action in scientific research. This may be to avoid any confusion of the divine and contingent orders, for example, or to obviate any lax construction of a "god of the gaps."

To assess the rationality or otherwise of MPN, we must distinguish between the prescriptions of naturalism from those of science. Metaphysical naturalism is a philosophical position: it is the fideistic commitment that, as Alvin Plantinga summarizes it, "there is no God, and we human beings are insignificant parts of a giant cosmic machine that proceeds in majestic indifference to us, our hopes and aspirations, our needs and desires, our sense of fairness, or fittingness" (1989, 9-10). Therefore, it constitutes an ultimate faith commitment at the same level as religious commitment. Science, by contrast, is the attempt to interpret contingent reality in its own light and to allow the object of scientific inquiry to challenge and revise the paradigms that it brings to bear in the relevant research. (Importantly, it is nature — or what we might term "contingent reality" — that the scientist

is interrogating in this process and not God, which is part of the justification for NTSM.) In short, scientific investigation is a dialogical process
whereby the rational structures of the natural order interpret themselves
to the scientific mind. What should be clear from this is that, if you wed
science with naturalism, then scientific questioning is *inevitably* driven by
philosophical commitments that have neither resulted from nor *could* result
from investigation of finite or contingent reality itself. And it should also be
clear that including metaphysical naturalism as one of one's premises will
inevitably produce atheistic conclusions — for the simple reason that atheism has already been presupposed! Indeed, whatever one chooses to wed
with metaphysical naturalism will inevitably produce atheistic conclusions,
be it Darwinian evolutionary theory, the Qur'an, the Bible, or the collected
writings of Mystic Meg![3]

To recap, I have highlighted two influential positions that operate sin-
gly but also in tandem to commandeer the epistemic bases in the light of
which we approach the realm of the personal. Each operates, moreover, by
claiming for itself unqualified, all-embracing *scope.* If these two "totalizing"
philosophical commitments serve to shape our thinking, what can be said
about the nature of the person and the emergence of personhood has already
been determined in advance, and the conclusions are clear. A further element is the a priori repudiation of the theistic commitments without which,
I shall argue, the conceptuality of the person would not have emerged in
Western culture.

---

3. Here I am drawing on a point made by Alvin Plantinga in a response to Frederick
Crews in *New York Review of Books* 48, no. 19 (Nov. 29, 2001):

> According to Crews, Daniel Dennett "has trenchantly shown that the Darwinian out-
> look is potentially a 'universal acid' penetrating 'all the way down' to the origin of
> life on Earth, and 'all the way up' to a satisfyingly materialistic reduction of mind and
> soul." Well, satisfaction is in the eye of the beholder; but in any event there is less here
> than meets the eye. Perhaps a "Darwinian outlook," whatever precisely that is, may be
> thus corrosive; evolutionary science itself is certainly not. It doesn't imply that there
> is no God, or that God has not created human beings in his image, or that the second
> person of the Trinity did not become incarnate, or that there aren't any souls, or that
> if there are, they are in fact material processes or events of some sort, or anything else
> of the kind. It is only evolutionary science *combined with metaphysical naturalism* that
> implies these things. Since metaphysical naturalism all by itself has these implications,
> it is no surprise that when you put it together with science (or as far as that goes, any-
> thing else — ancient Greek history, the Farmer's Almanac, the Apostles' Creed) the
> combination also implies them.

If the Situation Is to Be Different . . . :
Challenging Metaphysical Reductionism

I hope it is clear that reductionism and metaphysical naturalism serve mutually to support each other. The appeal of the former serves to underwrite the appeal of the latter, and it is this combination that drives the appeal of metaphysical reductionism, with all its ramifications for the interpretation of the person. Not only is the emergence of the conceptuality of the person grounded historically in Christian theism; there is strong reason to think that the conceptuality of the personal requires this kind of theistic vision. More pertinent to our purposes here, however, is the recognition that it is not possible to advocate the conceptuality of the person without challenging those exceedingly influential fideisms that serve to undermine it. To this end, let us consider very briefly the explanatory power of theism in comparison with the two methodological fideisms that are so damaging to the conceptuality of the personal.

Theism uniquely satisfies the scientific criterion *simplex sigillum veri* ("simplicity is a sign of truth") while, at the same time, possessing unparalleled explanatory power.[4] It explains the most profoundly counterintuitive fact that we are faced with, namely, why anything contingent exists at all. It also explains the intelligibility of the contingent order, which the entire scientific enterprise presupposes, but which it cannot explain. And it also explains the laws science has to deal with, but whose own existence is, again, beyond the bounds of scientific explanation. But its explanatory power does not stop here; it explains the staggering degree of fine-tuning that constitutes the necessary condition for the emergence of any kind of intelligent engagement with the contingent order. In the light of the explanatory power of theism, not to mention the prescriptions of modal logic (and the insuperable problems posed for the naturalist repudiation of God's existence by the modal form of the ontological argument for the existence of God), it is not surprising that a leading metaphysician, modal logician, and atheist, Quentin Smith, former editor of *Philo: The Journal of the Society of Humanist Philosophers,* should conclude, in an article entitled "The Metaphilosophy of Naturalism," that "the vast majority of naturalist philosophers have come to

---

4. Clearly, this is not to suggest that theologians can explain the physical dynamics of the contingent order. Whereas theologians can offer an explanation as to *why* there is something rather than nothing, they are not in a position to explain the *how*. Theologians are not in a position to establish the existence and role of the Higgs Boson particle on theological grounds!

hold (since the late 1960s) an unjustified belief in naturalism. Their justifications have been defeated by arguments developed by theistic philosophers, and now naturalist philosophers, for the most part, live in darkness about the justification of naturalism. . . . If naturalism is true, then their belief in naturalism is *accidentally true*" (Smith 2001).

In sum, there are categorically no scientific grounds for repudiating theism and the personalist universe to which theism opens the door. Precisely the converse is the case! This is not to suggest that there is any philosophical demonstration of the truth of *Christian* theism. Rather, it is to point out that the probability that the scientistic assumptions of metaphysical naturalism are true is almost inconceivably low.[5] Consequently, it is not clear that those who have commandeered the explanatory power of the empirical sciences in order to repudiate a "personalist" account of reality have any justification whatsoever for their conclusions.

The Concept of the Person and Christian Theism

Christian faith is not grounded in detached ratiocination or philosophical speculation; nor is it grounded in some arbitrary leap of faith. Instead, it is grounded in the perception that the God who explains why there is something rather than nothing, who explains the intelligibility of the contingent order and our participation in a moral universe, has disclosed himself to humanity not in abstract or universally accessible ways but in a concrete and irreducibly *personal* way in human history. As Søren Kierkegaard put it, "There is no immanental underlying kinship between the temporal and the eternal, because the eternal itself has entered into time and wants to establish kinship there" (1992, 573). The kinship that is established is established in an irreducibly personal event. Integral to the Christian tradition, therefore, as

---

5. All assessments of probability are, of course, relative. The probability that one explanation is true is considerably higher if there is no alternative explanation of these same phenomena. If, however, there is an alternative explanation that fits the relevant data, is simpler, and possesses greater explanatory power, then the "probability" of the first is greatly diminished. What should be clear is that metaphysical naturalism possesses credible probability only if it is assumed to be the "only game in town." Given the explanatory power of theism and the profound limits on the explanatory power of metaphysical naturalism, any objective assessment of the comparative probabilities should expose the improbability of metaphysical naturalism being true. One suspects that the fact that this is not more widely recognized is indicative of a subjective suspicion of theism.

also its unquantifiable impact on Western thought, is the perception that the divine self-disclosure at the heart of the Christian faith constitutes a categorical endorsement of the personal nature of reality — both of divine reality and of contingent human reality. Not only is this self-disclosure indicative of some general, divine purpose *(telos),* it seeks to communicate as well as fulfill that *telos* for human creatures.

The fundamental recognition at the heart of Christian theism is that the essential divine perfection is God's love. God *is* love in his innermost being. The triune nature of God means that God does not need the contingent order for purposes of self-realization or self-fulfillment. Rather, the creation of contingent reality is a free expression of God's personal reality and the fullest expression of this is evident in the fact that creatures are given to participate in an irreducibly personal universe — a moral universe, indeed, in which we have the created conditions for communion between the divine person and the contingent reality of creaturely persons as also for communion between human persons.

The suggestion that God should disclose himself to creatures within the context of the concrete particularity of history is, of course, deeply counterintuitive to the human mind — "foolishness" to the philosophical mind, as the apostle Paul suggests — that is, it is counterintuitive to those who fail to understand God in terms of the logic of love. Having said that, I need to note that God's involvement in human history should be no less counterintuitive than the notion that God should create something that exists in contradistinction to God. Recognizing God as Creator of the contingent order suggests that God, in the act of creation, freely ceases to be, in himself, the totality of reality, and it determines that there be something alongside God that is real. That God should engage with humanity is no more counterintuitive, therefore, than that God should create — and, in doing so, cease to be the totality of everything. The explanation of both is that they are expressions of the free grace of God. That is, they are expressions of God's primary attribute, or "perfection," what Karl Barth describes as God's love-in-freedom.

Why is this pertinent to an essay on the emergence of personhood? Because, as the contemporary theologian most closely associated with the concept of the person, John Zizioulas, has argued, "The observation of the world cannot lead to an ontology of the person, because the person as an ontological category cannot be extrapolated from experience" (2006, 103). That is, the detached study of the natural order cannot in and of itself confirm either the nature or the significance of the person any more than it can grasp, for example, the nature or character of *qualia*. For Zizioulas, it was the uniquely *interpersonal* (I-thou) experience of the Christian church that led the Greek fathers to affirm the reality of the personal. And it was in tracing the reality of the contingent order to the *person* of the Creator that they came to construe the interpersonal nature of human existence as having ontological significance — that is, significance for understanding the ultimate nature and character of reality.

Such an approach to the history of the emergence of this conceptuality suggests that we are left with two options vis-à-vis the use of the term "person." The first is simply to predicate the term "human animal" as a means of elevating human beings above the rest of the animal kingdom. This would generate two inclinations. The first inclination would be to use the term "person" to endorse either a particular capacity (such as reason, language, the moral sense, or conscience, altruism, creativity, heuristic problem-solving, the sense of self, or a capacity for "transcendence") — or, indeed, whatever combination of such capacities is deemed to be definitive of the human person. The second inclination would be to seek to safeguard the relevant capacity, capability, or set of capabilities by suggesting that they denote a difference not of degree but of kind, thereby setting human beings apart from the rest of the animal kingdom and constituting warrant for the exclusive attribution of the term "person." Such an approach would simply constitute an invitation to evolutionary psychologists and biologists to show that, at best, the relevant ability denotes a difference of degree rather than of kind from the capacities characteristic of apes, dolphins, or, indeed, border collies and carrion crows.

A second consequence of such an approach is that it would inevitably prompt the question of whether it is appropriate to use the term "person" of human animals with mental disabilities, not to mention the very young or the very old (patients with Alzheimer's and dementia, for example) who may not exhibit the relevant abilities. A third consequence would be the conclusion that, given that the evolutionary process is ongoing within what would be, at least in geological terms, an insignificant period of time, certain nonhuman animal kinds would be likely to evolve to the point where they acquired and, possibly, even overtook the capabilities of *Homo sapiens* as characterized by the present state of play. Consequently, even if there has been a "quantum leap" in the evolution of human animals that is perceived as denoting a difference in kind from the rest of the animal kingdom, there is no reason to discount the possibility that this qualitative difference might be temporary and that others among the higher apes could experience evolutionary "quantum leaps." The leveling effect of the above could only mean that the concept of the person had no ultimate or ontological significance.

The second approach to the person perceives the concept of the person as possessing ontological significance for the simple reason that reality is ultimately "personal" in nature. On this approach, rather than pointing to some capacity that elevates the human, the category of the personal is perceived as pointing to the grounds of and also the ultimate purpose of reality per se. It is this kind of approach that most Christian theology would endorse, as we can witness in the leading theological figures not only in the Orthodox tradition (e.g., Zizioulas and Alexander Schmemann) but also in the Roman Catholic tradition (e.g., Hans Urs von Balthasar, Catherine LaCugna, and Joseph Ratzinger [Pope Benedict XVI]) and the Protestant tradition (e.g., T. F. and J. B. Torrance, Jürgen Moltmann, Colin Gunton, and Christoph Schwoebel).

Continuity and Discontinuity in the Emergence of Personhood

How is the person, therefore, conceived theologically? The consensus of contemporary thinking in Roman Catholic, Orthodox, and Protestant circles is that the key to the Judeo-Christian vision of human existence lies in the perception that the person is created for relationship and then constituted as such in communion with God and the other (see A. C. Thiselton chapter in the present volume). Indeed, the entirety of the Christian interpretation of God's purposes vis-à-vis the contingent order requires it to be conceived in these terms; hence the primacy of the categories of covenant, communion, and participation. This is a vision that, as it is commonplace to point out, stands in radical tension with Western, individualistic categories that conceive of the self as a self-contained, monadic substance whose essential attribute is reason (Boethius) or thought (Descartes) or, indeed, experience (Hume, Kant, and much of both modernity and postmodernity).

In articulating the nature of the church's faith, the early theologians grounded the communion between human beings — which constitutes them as persons — in the communion that is constitutive of the being of God. To be a person is to participate, that is, to share by the Holy Spirit in the communion of the triune life of God, which is the key to God's ultimate purposes in creation. The fulcrum that holds together the being of God and that of the true (new) humanity is the incarnation. In the person of Jesus Christ, God brings humanity to participate "by grace" in personal communion *(koinonia)* with humans' own personal reality. In and through this relationship, human creatures are transformed. Their worldview or apperception is reschematized or metamorphosed, to use Pauline metaphors, via a relationship with, or "altercentric" perception of, God — and simultaneously of other persons. As the thrust of the New Testament implies, by means of God's concrete, personal engagement with humanity in Christ, he creates a *new humanity* to fulfill, exemplify, and disseminate God's relational purposes for the human creature: to be the means of what we might term the *personalization* of human creatures by bringing them into *koinonia* with God and each other.[6] As Thiselton articulates so impressively his chapter, it is in these terms that the concept of our being created to image God needs to be conceived. Human beings fulfill their created *telos* in and through becoming a "new creation" that corresponds to God's personal life by participating in it in such a way that humans not only love their family and friends but also love even their enemies.

But it is important for us to be clear that, theologically speaking, the term "person" should never be assumed to be properly exemplified in the lives of Christians in a dysfunctional and alienated world. Human creatures remain "on the way" to becoming "persons" in truth, to becoming the "new humanity." Therefore, personhood is only fully achieved or realized as and when God's creative, reconciling, and (re)creative purposes are complete, when God's interpersonal "kingdom" is fully actualized. It is then, and only then, that human creatures will be describable as properly functional *persons,* constituted in and through full participation in the "communion" of the divine life. In the meantime, personhood is defined not by introspection nor, indeed, by any kind of generic, empirical investigation of human creaturehood, but in and through the presentation of that unique form of communion with God and with his fellow creatures that is manifest in the person of the incarnate Son, in the one described as "Immanuel" (literally, "God with us") — the one in whom we have the full *personal* reality of God present with humanity. It should be clear that the most summary exploration of the roots of this concept highlights the extent to which the concept has lost its original "relational" significance by being commandeered by the individualistic West. The result of this loss of its meaning is that society has

---

6. The language of the New Testament articulates this in various ways. Human creatures are given to share *(koinonein/metechein)* "in Christ" (Pauline writings), to abide in Christ (John's Gospel), or to share in the ongoing life of the sole priest of our confession (Hebrews).

sought to prop up the conceptuality by determining some subjective, individual "capacity" that defines human beings as creatures. The folly of such a strategy should be clear!

Although I have focused on a Christian theological perspective, the Jewish tradition shares much of this vision of personal life, and its impact on modern continental philosophy has been immense. What I am loosely referring to as the "relational" vision of personhood is reflected famously in the second-person approach that we find in Martin Buber's emphasis on the primacy of the I-thou in contrast to the I-it. Furthermore, in his influential *I and Thou* (1923), he argues that all I-thou relationships lead us ultimately into relationship with God, who is the eternal Thou. It is in the recognition of the eternal Thou that we grasp the significance of the personal. A related concept is reflected in the personalist vision of the equally influential French Jewish thinker, Emmanuel Lévinas, whose philosophy privileges the interpersonal relationship he calls the "face-to-face" (Atterton et al. 2004). In the English-speaking world, Judeo-Christian insights had an immense impact on John Macmurray, author of *Persons in Relation*, though he, like Lévinas, seeks to give them philosophical rather than religious expression. In a discussion of "The Field of the Personal," Macmurray concludes: "Persons, therefore, are constituted by their mutual relation to one another" (Macmurray 1961, 24). This means that "the unity of the personal is . . . to be sought in the community of the 'You and I,' and since persons are agents, this community is not merely matter of fact, but also matter of intention" (1961, 27). This leads Macmurray to an affirmation that is particularly relevant to this volume:

> From this it follows that any objective or impersonal knowledge of the human, any science of man, whether psychological or sociological, involves a negation of the personal relation of the "I" and the "You," and so of the relation which constitutes them as persons. Formally, such knowledge is knowledge of the "You," that is, of the other person; but not of the other person in personal relation to the knower, but as object in the world. I can know another person *as a person* only by entering into personal relation with him. (1961, 28)

In short, for Macmurray, no form of "empirical science" that treats human creatures as objects of study and analysis can capture the "personal." But do they make claims to "capture the personal"? They may make claims that they better understand some of the intrinsic mechanisms whereby personal relationships are formed and function. But that is different. The very nature of the personal is that it is perceived in the context of what contemporary analytic philosophy refers to as the "second-person perspective," that is, where the other is perceived as a particular "thou" and thus as a person to whom one is related in an event of concrete, personal address (Darwell 2006, 3).

What Are the Implications of This for the Question of Emergence?

First, no form of empirical science that treats human animals as "objects" of study is going to come to a definition of what it is to be a "person." Why? Because, as John Macmurray argues so impressively, the "personal" has, by the very nature of the situation, been bracketed out of the inquiry. The perception of the "personal" is a primordial perception that is grounded in the subjective recognition of the "thou." As I have argued earlier in the chapter, unless we are clearheaded here about the question of "scope" and obviate the forms of fideism analyzed at the start, a process of self-deception and double-think in the academy will inevitably serve to radically undermine the very conceptuality of personhood.

Second, it is confused to seek to locate the emergence of the "person" in the evolutionary process, as if some defining objective "quality," "capacity," or "capability" emerged at a distinctive point in history. This is not to deny that the "I-thou" relationship may repose, or even "supervene," on other developments whose historical emergence can indeed be traced to the evolutionary process — such as that of language, "deep social mind," or the like. Nor does it deny that the "I-thou" relationship might supervene on the proper functioning of our mirror neurons, as these can indeed be investigated by neuroscientists. If the conceptuality of personhood constitutes a "quantum leap," I would suggest that the historical key to this is denoted by the fathers of the Christian church and their ontological ratification of the grounds of the "personal." Theologically, this quantum leap stems from the historical perception that God has created, and indeed chosen, human beings for a specific kind of relationship — what the New Testament conceives as of *koinonia*, namely, that unique fellowship or "communion" constituted by God's relationship to humanity to which Søren Kierkegaard referred as that unique "kinship" that the eternal has established in time. This perception is, again, not a "natural" perception but a recognition that takes place in and through the creative presence and activity of God, that is, by the Holy Spirit — where "holy" (Greek: *hagios*) served simply to make it clear that this was no natural phenomenon but denoted the presence of God.

In summary, if we are looking for a quantum leap in the history of the emergence of personhood, the most relevant "nodal point" would be not the acquisition by *Homo sapiens* of some capacity but, instead, God's bringing human animals into a specific kind of I-Thou relationship — with all the ramifications for the human community (love, forgiveness, reconciliation, care for the sick and elderly) that stem from this. It is in the context of this theological history that the term "person" finds its warrant and, indeed, that its use becomes appropriate.

Does this mean that there is no continuity between the process of evolution and God's purpose of choosing and commissioning human beings for this unique role and function? If it does, this "election," to use the biblical concept, of *Homo sapiens* for this very specific nexus of relationships that constitute its *personal* reality, then there is clearly *both* continuity *and* discontinuity.

Third, it should be clear from the above that the term "person" refers to the whole being of the self, not just to its rational or linguistic or creative capacities. Just as the concept *imago Dei* refers to the whole human being, so is it true that one's personal reality denotes all that constitutes one as an "I" and a "thou." This refers, moreover, to all those who can be addressed as a "thou": babies, those with mental "disabilities," Alzheimer's sufferers, and so on.

The above may raise the question of how we should conceive of God's creative involvement in the evolutionary process. Is it simply "by chance" that human beings arrive at the point where God determines to establish personal and interpersonal relationships with them? Clearly, people may argue for various kinds of scenarios. They may, for example, press for a distinction between *random* genetic mutations and *chance* mutations.[7] It may be that God surveys the outcomes of all possible worlds and chooses to actualize

---

7. It may be the case that one can adopt a Molinist approach to evolution, where God, foreknowing all the possible counterfactual scenarios, determines to actualize that particular possible world in which *Homo sapiens* will evolve through a process of undetermined mutations. Those mutations would remain "random," but the outcome would not be a "chance" outcome. There are various discussions of these issues and the scope of a Molinist interpretation of reality by such eminent analytic philosophers as Tom Flint, Alexander Pruss, and Michael Almeida.

By contrast, some "open theists" argue that God does indeed play dice and that God determines whether or not to "elect" a certain species on a certain planet depending on what happens to emerge as the result of processes left to their own devices. This would mean that the event of "creation" denotes the creation of mere initial conditions.

a possible world in which he foreknows that the evolutionary process will result in the emergence of creatures with whom he will choose to interact in certain specific ways.[8] For the purposes of what I wish to say in this chapter, however, it is not necessary to determine the kind of scenario that should be endorsed. Suffice it to say, whatever we might wish to argue about the details of the nature and character of God's involvement in the "internal workings" of the contingent order, it is not a reading of these internal workings that leads us to define the nature of the person.

Conclusion

I have argued that (1) not only did the concept of the person emerge historically out of the tradition of Christian theism, (2) but it finds its ultimate grounding within a theistic perspective, most fully a Trinitarian Christian perspective. What this suggests is that (3) human personhood does not emerge by means of a natural evolutionary process even if personal reality may be seen as supervening upon "natural" processes of evolution. The roots of the concept of the "personal" lie within the Judeo-Christian tradition, for which personal existence needs to be understood in the light of God's establishing a relationship with the human animal. For the fathers of the Christian church, this found its focus in God's transformative engagement with humanity and the creation of a "new humanity" through the kinship that the Eternal established with humanity in time — in the person of Jesus Christ. It is (4) this reconstitution of human life in relating it to the personal ground of contingent reality that gives personal existence ontological status and ratifies it as a mode of reality that is not *ultimately* subject to either exclusively evolutionary mechanisms or, indeed, to the contingencies of our biological constitution. Personal existence is both given with — and, ultimately, subject to — the communion that God establishes and sustains through concrete historical, personal communion with human creatures. This is a communion that is transformative and creative of what needs to be conceived in dialogue with evolutionary science, not as an old but as a new humanity. It is no coincidence that a central contrast in the New Testament is between the "old humanity" and the "new humanity," between what is constituted by our natural desires and what is not schematized by the natural and our innate appetites

8. Having said that, I should add that "fine-tuning" might be indicative of precisely this kind of scenario.

but transformed or reschematized for a new mode of existence through the "metamorphosing" presence of the Holy Spirit. That new form of existence is defined in terms of the categories of participation *(koinonein)* and *agape,* the two concepts that "personalism" has used to define human existence to the extent that it can be described as "personal."

REFERENCES

Atterton, Peter, Matthew Calarco, and Maurice Friedman, eds. 2004. *Lévinas and Buber: Dialogue and difference.* Pittsburgh: Duquesne University Press.

Cartwright, Nancy. 1999. *The dappled world: A study of the boundaries of science.* Cambridge: Cambridge University Press.

Darwell, Stephen. 2006. *The second-person standpoint: Morality, respect, and accountability.* Cambridge, MA: Harvard University Press.

Davidson, Donald. 1970. Mental events. In *Actions and events.* Oxford: Clarendon Press, 1980. Republished in *Readings in philosophy of psychology,* vol. 1, ed. Ned Block. Cambridge, MA: Harvard University Press.

Honderich, Ted. 2004. The mental efficacy problem, and identity theories in monograph. In *On consciousness.* Edinburgh: Edinburgh University Press.

Johnson, P. E. 1993. *Darwin on trial.* Downers Grove, IL: InterVarsity.

Kierkegaard, Søren. 1992. *Kierkegaard's writings,* vol. 12, *Concluding unscientific postscript to philosophical fragments,* ed. Howard V. Hong and Edna H. Hong. Princeton: Princeton University Press.

Kim, Jaegwon. 1993. *Supervenience and the mind.* Cambridge: Cambridge University Press.

Macmurray, John. 1961. *Persons in relation.* London: Faber and Faber.

Murphy, Nancey, and Warren Brown. 2007. *Did my neurons make me do it?* Oxford: Oxford University Press.

Plantinga, Alvin. 1989. *The twin pillars of Christian scholarship.* The Stob Lectures, published by Calvin College and Seminary, Grand Rapids, MI.

————. 2001. In Roger Shattuck, Alvin Plantinga, et al. "Saving Us from Darwin": An Exchange. *New York Review of Books* 48, no. 19.

Rockwell, Teed. N.d. Non-reductive physicalism. In the web-based *Dictionary of the philosophy of mind,* ed. Eliasmith. http://www.artsci.wustl.edu/~philos/MindDict/ (accessed Jan. 24, 2004).

Smith, Quentin. 2001. The metaphilosophy of naturalism. *Philo* 4, no. 2: 195-215.

Zizioulas, John D. 2006. *Communion and otherness.* London: T&T Clark.

Afterword: Toward an Emerging Picture of How We Came to Be What We Seem to Be

Malcolm Jeeves

> *If theological anthropology is to avoid theoretical isolation from the wider academic world and maintain its relevance for current and future generations, it must listen to the finer details of a broad range of secular accounts of personhood.*
>
> LEON TURNER (2011, 135)

Any meaningful attempt to provide well-informed answers to questions of who we are and how we came to be the way we are must call on the knowledge and specialist skills of a wide range of disciplines. In this respect, we have followed Turner's advice and listened to the "finer details of a broad range of secular accounts of personhood." And we have listened not only to the obvious scientific ones, but also to the more traditional contributions of philosophers and theologians. In so doing we recognize that some of the greatest thinkers of the past wrote about these issues long before scientists appeared on the scene.

We are strange and complicated creatures. We share many traits, including cognitive skills and emotions, with other animals, and increasingly learn that the borders between them and us are murky and permeable. The contributors to this discussion are leaders in fields of knowledge who can, potentially, bring new insights and afford a better understanding of who we are. They include evolutionary biologists, evolutionary psychologists, social psychologists, cognitive neuroscientists, neurologists, geneticists, archaeologists, anthropologists, philosophers, and theologians.

An understanding of how the human mind achieved its present state and complexity remains a mystery. Nevertheless, after several decades of groundbreaking research into human behavior and the behavior of nonhuman primates, we can begin to detect important clues about how some of our key capacities — for example, reflection, rationality, and deliberation — may have emerged.

We still look for answers to such questions as: How did consciousness arise? How did language develop? How did the potential for ethical decision-making and moral behavior emerge? And as we begin to find answers to some of those questions, we must further ask about what the relationship is between understandings of human nature consisting of response adaptations to recurring problems in our ancestral environment and understandings of human nature based on the theological concept of man being made in the image of God — that is, humans as creatures reflecting the image of their Creator. Raising these questions leads us to revisit and reexamine long-held assumptions about the content of some religious beliefs about human nature. As we do, we ask whether they are reliable answers, given advances in hermeneutics, biblical scholarship, and today's new insights into understanding the origins of cognitive mechanisms whose side effects may have produced many features associated with religion. Within any one discipline there are different answers to questions about our origins. Debates continue as more data accumulate and theories are refined (or discarded). How much more difficult it is, then, to evaluate answers to common questions that come from different disciplines.

In this afterword, as we are mindful of the diversity of opinions held, my principal aims are, first, to identify shared assumptions and common themes in the diverse disciplinary approaches taken; second, to return to the main questions we set for ourselves in the opening chapter; and third, to look for shared conclusions as well as unresolved differences, always remembering that, at times, the latter may have been built into differing basic presuppositions. This is because, while some contributors to this volume are theists, others are not.

Diversity of opinion can be a good thing. It may result in a more profound awareness of the complexity of the issues we are considering and of the relevant evidence to be considered. In recent years, the important roles of diversity of opinion and conflict in argument have been recognized and documented. It is already clear that no attempt to summarize can assume that a set of "monologic" propositions can do full justice to the highly complex issues considered here. To do justice to such complexity will require a number of "voices." Together, these voices form, not a "unity," but a "concordance." As I mentioned in the introduction to this volume, the great theorist of polyphonic discourse was Mikhail Bakhtin; its unrivaled practitioner was Fyodor Dostoevsky. Theologians are familiar with these concepts; they recognize that the biblical canon has sixty-six voices rather than one. It is a view expounded in detail by our contributor Anthony Thiselton in his *Hermeneutics of Doctrine*. Both Roman Catholics (e.g., Hans Urs von Balthasar) and Protestants (e.g., Kevin Vanhoozer) speak of a "symphony" of differing but harmonic voices. As Kierkegaard emphasized, when we are faced with conflict, what is required is thinking and decision. The message will not be found given on a plate, because it is too complex for an easy set of propositions to convey it adequately.

But there are, in what follows, certain shared assumptions. All of our contributors recognize and accept the well-documented and tested — some would say, tested to destruction — claims of the explanatory powers, in its proper context, of the neo-Darwinian theory of biological evolution. Some of our contributors demonstrate how, starting from this common base, the concept of evolution is, nonetheless, itself at risk of being used at times as a catchall when we attempt to understand and explain how we came to be the way we are today. Like all scientific theories, it rests on currently available (and potentially collectible) empirical data. Like all scientific theories, it has matters it can explain and matters it cannot. Evolution is not designed to explain, for example, the challenges faced by particle physicists. They have their own theories. Neither is it designed to answer metaphysical questions about why there is something rather than nothing.

In what follows I would like to revisit the questions posed by our contributors, to briefly summarize their answers, and to look for places of convergence and divergence. In doing this, we may also detect where we should be looking for the next important developments to occur.

Francisco Ayala raises the questions concerning "whether the moral sense is part of human nature, one more dimension of our biological makeup, and whether ethical values may be a product of biological evolution, rather than being given by religious and other cultural traditions." This leads him to ask whether Neanderthals held moral values — or whether our ancestral species *Homo erectus* and *Homo habilis* had evolved a moral sense. Was it, he asks, directly promoted by natural selection, or did it come about as a byproduct of some other attribute, such as rationality, which was a direct target of selection? And alternatively, he asks: Is the moral sense an outcome of cultural evolution rather than biological evolution?

In answering his questions, Ayala notes that the distinction between a moral sense and moral norms is important and central to his thesis. He emphasizes that we must distinguish between the capacity for ethics and the systems or codes of ethical norms accepted by humans being biologically determined. He says that a similar distinction can be made with respect to language. The capacity for language is determined by biological nature, but this is a different question from whether we speak a *particular* language — and this is not biologically determined.

Ayala also raises the critical question of whether, in evolutionary terms, the moral sense is an adaptation or an exaptation. He points out that "for evolutionary biologists, exaptations are features of organisms that evolved because they serve some function, but are later co-opted to serve an additional or different function, which was not originally the target of natural selection." He gives the example that feathers seem to have evolved first for conserving temperature, but were later co-opted in birds for flying. He also notes that art, literature, religion, and many human cultural activities might also be seen as exaptations that came about as the consequences of the evolution of high intelligence.

Another important concept that Ayala introduces, which will come up later from time to time, is the notion of the crossing of an evolutionary threshold. He says that "thresholds occur in other evolutionary developments — for example, in the origins of life, multicellularity, and sexual reproduction — as well as in the evolution of abstract thinking and self-awareness." He concludes: "Surely, human intellectual capacities came about by gradual evolution."

Evolutionary psychologist Richard Byrne picks up on the potential importance of the evolution of the capacity for language that Ayala identifies as one of the key factors that possibly were required for the development of moral codes when he asks: "Do any substantive differences remain that distinguish us from animals . . . in a way that can properly justify separate treatment in terms of personhood and morality?" He declares: "If a hard and fast cognitive dividing line is ever to be found, my own vote is for human language. . . . As a cognitive psychologist, using the natural behavior of nonhuman animals to discover precursors to human mental abilities, for me the Holy Grail has always been the evolutionary basis of language." He continues: "Nevertheless, human language did not emerge de novo: it was built on cognitive foundations we share with the living apes." The focus of his search is on the natural gestural communication of the bonobo, which he believes deserves special attention because, he says, "that is how my hypothesis of a linguistic dividing line can most easily be tested."

Byrne's conclusion is quite clear:

Many of the obvious differences between man and all other animals are misapprehensions: like us, chimpanzees can make tools to a plan, use a series of different tools toward a single aim, recognize themselves in the mirror, show forethought in planning, hunt mammals, and deliberately kill members of neighbor communities after commando-style raids. Nor do genetic insights help: the chimpanzee is more closely related to us than it is to any other animal. [I argue] that linguistic communication is the only robust dividing line, and even that was undoubtedly built on cognitive foundations we share with other species.

Reflecting on Byrne's proposals, our first reaction is that they come as no surprise. Every time someone has sought to identify a feature of human behavior that they believe clearly distinguishes humans from animals, it has seemed only a matter of time before an ingenious study has demonstrated that, studied in the right way and under the right conditions, these supposedly unique abilities are already there in embryonic form in our nonhuman ancestors. We can speculate further that, for whatever reason, there may have been at some point in evolution a chain of events that led to differences between human achievements and nonhuman achievements. One possible candidate that we shall come across later would be the emergence of what are known as Von Economo neurons in humans.

Another, reported in June 2013 by a genetics research group at Edinburgh University, is the discovery of a gene that "may yield insights into how humans evolved from apes." We are told that "the discovery represents the first time the new gene carried only by humans and not by apes has been identified as having a specific function within the human body." The report goes on to say that "fundamental to the breakthrough was the research contribution of Martin Taylor, who led the study at the Medical Research Council Institute of Genetics and Molecular Medicine." Taylor explains that miR-941 is "a new gene born, which may be important in changing the development of the human brain." He adds that "the really important aspect of this work is that it shows that something that was previously not functional at all in the genome has acquired a function." He continues: "We know genes must have come from somewhere, and we have 20-odd thousand genes in the genome. But pretty much every instance has come from copying another gene or part of a gene. The human genome has invented something entirely new, and found a use for it. That's something which has never been convincingly demonstrated in the human lineage before" (Hai Yang Hu et al. 2012, 16-17). As they say in journalism, "Watch this space."

The relevance of this early report is that because, up until now, there have been no clear clues as to how "a quantum leap" in our human lineage may have occurred, it remains unwise to stake human uniqueness on "something" that, given time, may have a perfectly "natural" explanation. To look ahead, as Anthony Thiselton makes clear, there are no theological issues at stake here. The crux of the *imago Dei* is not "some thing" — but a unique calling.

IF THE FIRST GROUP of questions arose from the implications of evolutionary theory, a second group arose from detailed studies of human brains compared with any others in our biological lineage. These are questions asked by neuropsychologists Warren Brown and Lynn Paul, and by neurologist Adam Zeman.

Acknowledging that the properties of personhood are rooted in physical processes and emergent in our evolutionary trajectory, Warren Brown and Lynn Paul underscore a key feature of who and what we are. We are, above all, "embodied creatures." They note that "comparative neuroanatomy has made it clear that, while humans do not have the largest brains, they have a relatively larger cerebral cortex and, most markedly, a very much larger prefrontal cortex." This enlargement of the prefrontal cortex in humans is primarily the result of increased white matter. Brown and Paul point out that there is a positive linear correlation in the gray-to-white-matter ratio across primate species, and that the human brain falls on this regression line for all nonfrontal neocortical areas. But as they also note, "Due to a disproportionate increase in prefrontal white matter, the human prefrontal cortex is well outside of what would be predicted of other species. Thus the human prefrontal cortex is not simply larger, but more intensely interconnected within itself and with other cortical and subcortical structures of the brain."

These authors believe that some of the core properties of humanness must emerge from complex patterns of physiological interactivity particularly within the brain. This leads them to ask: What happens if, in the course of normal development, or through later damage to the brain, some of these patterns of physiological interactivity are missing or reduced? They explore this hypothetical relationship between connectivity and the emergence of human capacities of personhood by looking at a group of children with abnormalities of cerebral connectivity, specifically children with autism and those with agenesis of the corpus callosum.

Their clearly stated hypothesis is that, "if the properties of humanness and personhood are emergent from complex patterns of physiological interactions, then neuropathology that reduces (or alters) the interactivity of brain regions, particularly within the cerebral cortex, will reduce (or alter) the nature of important human characteristics." Using available data, they make a convincing case for the plausibility of their supposition. There is another concept that permeates the Brown and Paul argument: the notion of the emergence of higher cognitive capacities in humankind. This interpretation of emergence with respect to brain function, referred to in different ways by several of the scientist-contributors, is examined under close scrutiny and analysis later in Timothy O'Connor's chapter.

Brown and Paul's approach to the emergence of personhood resonates closely with that of Adam Zeman, who specifically focuses on the emergence of subjectivity. With disarming honesty, Zeman refers to our "uniqueness and inwardness" and how they can appear as particularly mysterious elements of our being. For Zeman, "subjectivity is at the heart of human selfhood." But while subjectivity may appear mysterious, he makes a strong case for the ways in which several forms of subjectivity emerged over the course of biological evolution and also matured over the life course of individual human development. These, he believes, go a long way toward explaining the natural origins of subjectivity.

Zeman's essay focuses on the relationship of our physicality to the remarkable cognitive and behavioral achievements that humans today exhibit. Although recognizing that many of the features we regard as demonstrating our uniqueness, such as aspects of our inwardness, can appear as mysterious elements of being, Zeman nonetheless has no doubt that the origins of subjectivity, one of these features of our nature, were natural and not magical — "at least no more magical than anything else in our magical universe." As he discusses the emergence of subjectivity — its nature and its functions — he reminds us that the various aspects and varieties of our subjectivity, nested within one another, arise from recursive processes of growth. Moreover, these nested capacities give rise to five distinctive kinds of knowledge that we humans boast about. And these nested capacities develop both during ontology and phylogeny. Zeman maps these developing capacities onto our knowledge of our biological makeup and in particular on specific brain mechanisms, notably those primarily associated with the neocortex of the brain.

Zeman goes on to note that so much of the focus of the problem to which attention has repeatedly been drawn turns out to be essentially another version of the mind-brain problem. "It can easily seem," he observes, "that minds and brains are such very different kinds of things that there is little hope of understanding how one can give rise to the other (if, indeed, it does). It can seem utterly mysterious that the intricate biological processes involving the firing of millions of neurons in our heads giving rise to the varieties of subjective experiences, like the sight of blood or a surge of joy. But we have to ask ourselves, in fairness: How sure are we that we know what the mind is and what experience consists in?" Bluntly, as he puts it, "all the minds we know are vested in matter; all the matter we encounter is represented in our minds."

Zeman identifies what he sees as two key misunderstandings as we reflect on conspicuous qualities that we, as human selves, possess. First, that on our better days we are creative entities; second, that our subjectivity is suffused by human culture. Zeman argues that we need to recognize that "the brain is itself dynamic, autonomous, and creative, and quite at home with human culture." Regarding his second claim, he notes that "the period during which the specifically human features of our brains evolved, the past two million years through successive species of *Homo habilis, Homo erectus,* and *Homo sapiens,* was the period over which human culture first appeared and gained momentum. . . . We are precisely cultural creatures."

Zeman also makes an important point by reminding us that nothing is gained by pretending that we *understand* our mysterious human nature when all we are doing is *describing it* in different terms. One thing, however, is clear: "Mind arises from matter, while matter is conceived by mind. The problem of subjectivity or the mystery of mind tends to be formulated as if we knew everything there was to know about subjectivity and matter." But this, he notes, is far from the case: "We understand the nature of mind and matter roughly equally well — or equally poorly." He notes that "today's dominant computational model of the brain can obscure the fact that the brain is very much alive, intrinsically active, autonomous, creative, and a natural host for the self," and that, indeed, "the human brain was shaped by and for human culture."

For paleoarchaeologist Ian Tattersall, personhood "implies an active sense of self: the ability of each individual not only to view him- or herself as simultaneously engaged with, and entirely distinct from, the surrounding environment, but to acknowledge a similar identity on the part of the other members of the same species . . . and modern human beings who, to all intents and purposes, are unique in the living world in possessing something we can call personhood, as opposed to mere individuality." It is, in

MALCOLM JEEVES

Tattersall's view, our "unique cognitive condition" that "makes human beings qualitatively different as cognitive entities from every other inhabitant of the planet."

While endorsing the general evolutionary story of emergence, Tattersall claims that "the acquisition of our unique cognitive style did not involve a strong process of long-term burnishing" that "a traditionally gradualist view of evolution would suggest." Regarding the neural and cognitive capacities, he comments that "while large brain size may be an essential underpinning for our remarkable way of dealing with information, pure neural mass evidently does not equate directly with symbolic thought, as witness the stark contrast between the archaeological records left behind by the large-brained but evidently nonsymbolic Neanderthals, and the fully symbolic Cro-Magnons (modern *Homo sapiens*) who replace them. . . . Instead, it is becoming increasingly clear that our characteristic cognitive style is the result of an emergent event, in which the addition of some new factor, probably unremarkable in itself, gave rise to a brain with an entirely unprecedented information-processing potential." (Could the miR-941 gene, just discovered, be an example of such a development?)

Having examined the human fossil record carefully, Tattersall observes that "this record is, of course, but a dim mirror of the full behavioral richness of any bygone hominids; but it nonetheless contains very little indeed to support the gradualist picture." In saying this, he notes that Colin Renfrew's description of "regular but incremental augmentation in the complexity of human society since the end of the last Ice Age" is one view. Tattersall adds, however, that "it is significant that Renfrew's account of stepwise lifeway change in our species begins only with the achievement of behavioral modernity." He adds that "a fortuitous combination of elements gives rise to a whole new order of complexity." (Is this reminiscent of the phase change that occurs in studies of superconductivity, where there are changes in properties exhibited by the same basic materials?)

Commenting on Renfrew's views, Tattersall says: "If I am correct in believing that personhood — at least in the sense in which we human beings individually experience it today — is necessarily based on the capacity for self-reflection, then human beings have possessed this quality only as long as their cognitive mode has allowed it." He notes, however, that "Renfrew is generously disinclined to exclude the big-brained *Homo neanderthalensis* from personhood, based on the large brains and complex lifeways of members of this recently extinct species; and there is certainly an argument to be made for the inclusivity he advocates." Tattersall concludes that "human beings really are different in a profound sense — and not just from their closest living relatives, but from their closest extinct ones as well." These are strong claims, and they call for examination in light of Renfrew's contribution.

Renfrew makes clear that the essence of his argument in the title he gives to his chapter: "Personhood: Toward a Gradualist Approach." According to his view, just as we observe "the emergence of personhood in the ontogenetic sense in the birth and development of every human baby, so we might look for the emergence or multiple emergences of personhood in a succession of ancestral species." Starting from the perspective of an archaeologist of prehistory who seeks, in his own words, to "understand the human story on the basis of the material remains that have come down to us from the human past," Renfrew finds "a story that is today becoming clear in outline."

At the outset of his chapter, Renfrew very helpfully asks the question, How, in the perspective of time, did the emergence of human personhood come about? It is worth quoting his opening statement because it summarizes some very important evidence that we must all consider:

> Ten million years ago there were no humans on earth. There were no people. There were multitudinous living species, including the great apes from which our hominin ancestors evolved. Over those ten million years, as paleontological research has established, a succession of ancestral species, including *Australopithecus* and *Homo erectus,* developed, culminating (from our perspective) in the emergence of our own species, *Homo sapiens,* apparently in Africa, more than 100,000 years ago. The out-of-Africa diaspora of *Homo sapiens* seems to have started about 60,000 years ago. These early people were hunter-gatherers, already equipped with quite an elaborate material culture. Some ten thousand years ago, transitions toward a new agricultural economy can be seen in the communities living in different parts of the world, accompanied by a move toward sedentarism. Out of these sedentary communities the first literate societies and the first cities emerged some five or six thousand years ago. This is a phylogenetic story of our species, concisely summarized.

With this overview before us, Renfrew asks the key questions: "Where, along this narrative line, does one situate the emergence — or, no doubt in reality, the multiple emergences — of personhood? Where and how did those qualities emerge that we recognize as those of sentient persons, of people imbued with the qualities that we recognize as inherently human?"

For Renfrew, "the criteria for personhood seem difficult to separate from those of being human. The emergence of personhood in the phyloge-netic sense initially considered might then well be equated with the emer-gence of humankind." And in tracing out the emergence of humankind, Renfrew reminds us that "it was the development of DNA analysis, applied to a wide range of living humans, using first mitochondrial DNA and then Y-chromosome analysis, that led to the firm conclusion that the key aspects of human speciation took place in Africa, in the 200,000 years or so prior to around 60,000 BP."

The picture that Renfrew sets out from what he calls the speciation phase (200,000 to 60,000 BP) and the dispersal phase (60,000 to 12,000 BP) raises the question that he describes as the "sapient paradox." He writes: "If our species was established perhaps by 100,000 BP in Africa and certainly by 60,000 BP, why did the new behaviors that we associate with the tectonic phase and that led within a few thousand years to the rise of civilization and of literacy, take so long to emerge?" That, he says, "is a problem that has not yet been clearly answered and is overlooked by most existing accounts of the 'human revolution.'"

During what Renfrew describes as the tectonic phase (from about 12,000 BP), he notes that there is evidence of the development and con-struction of the first places of congregation. Some of these were places of assembly and possibly of pilgrimage. However, in his view, though there are "indications of what one might term ritual practices, there is little evidence for religion if religion is defined as the worship or veneration of specific tran-scendent and immortal deities." They, Renfrew says, "make their appearance in a subsequent phase."

This is the phase that he labels "later social processes" (i.e., those occur-ring after 5000 BP), during which he notes that it is often with the emergence of state societies that "the first evidence is found for institutionalized reli-gion, where, by that term, is intended the worship of transcendent deities."

Reflecting on the trajectory of developments he has outlined of the three phases into which the human revolution can be divided, he asks about where we can place the emergence of personhood. For him it is not easy to identify any kind of a "quantum leap," and this might thus lead us to adopt a grad-ualist approach. He goes further, adding that if we were looking for some kind of an evolutionary leap, then possibly "the ability to talk, to understand and be understood" (echoes here of Byrne's views), which "is an important component of personhood," may have evolved gradually over several million years, as some have argued, or it may have developed more rapidly as an evolutionary leap, as others argue. It remains an open question. Again, one wonders whether discoveries such as the miR-941 gene could contribute to understanding such a leap.

Social psychologist Roy Baumeister writes that "the challenge and purpose of [his] chapter are thus to understand the emergence of selfhood and identity, as guides to illuminate the emergence of human personhood." And in that context he believes that "culture" is a key concept. Culture, for him, is "defined as a novel form of social life based on accumulating shared information (knowledge), systems of corporation that use division of labor, and systems of economic trade, which is the human species' strategy for solving the problems of survival and reproduction." Therefore, in his view, "human selfhood and identity, and indeed human personhood per se, can be understood as adaptations (or side effects of adaptations) that make culture possible."

In his wide-ranging analysis, Baumeister emphasizes that the human person is unique; culture is a biological strategy; human personhood emerges from our collective and individually competing efforts to participate in culture; the human person is a blend of physical structures and cultural meaning; and the emergence of personhood was the appreciation and utilization of meaning to improve their collective lives.

Thus far our contributors have offered their diverse and distinctive contributions from a wide range of scientific disciplines, all having a bearing on central questions about the emergence of personhood. Only very briefly has religion been mentioned, as when Colin Renfrew, toward the end of his chapter, notes how big questions remain about how, in the course of evolution and human development, practices of religion and religious beliefs developed that for many of the population became an important and intricate part of what they regarded as their full personhood.

At this point in the book it may have come as a surprise to some readers that we are taken back once again to evolutionary theory combined with developments in cognitive science to discover the origins of religion.

Justin Barrett and Matthew Jarvinen, drawing heavily on cognitive science, evolutionary theory, and evolutionary psychology, ask how religion may have emerged as a key part of human personhood. They ask what cognitive mechanisms humans must have to conceptualize a god and to generate actions for interacting with that god. Their answer is that higher-order theory of mind appears as a central player in any satisfactory answer. Barrett and Jarvinen identify "a few features of the CSR [cognitive science of religion] account of religion that merit highlighting." Briefly, in their own words:

First, these cognitive accounts typically presume strong biological and cognitive continuity with ancestral species and, by extension, with nonhuman primates thought to approximate human ancestors. Second, though conceding the possibility of later exaptation, cognitive accounts are at their core evolutionary byproduct accounts of religion. That is, the cognitive equipment that gives rise to religious expression is presumed to have evolved under selection pressures unrelated to religion or religious entities. Third, many different cognitive subsystems or "mental tools" cooperate to encourage religious beliefs and practices, and hence belief in gods (or souls, the afterlife, etc.) are byproducts of multiple cognitive adaptations and not just one. Nevertheless, one "mental tool" takes center stage in these accounts: ToM [Theory of Mind].

We are all aware from the history of science how advances are made when widely accepted theories are challenged and their adequacy called into question. Over the past two decades, many fresh new insights into an understanding of the evolution of religion have undoubtedly been contributed as a result of a variety of cognitive science of religion approaches to the study of religion. Perhaps now, as in other areas of science, the time has come to ask whether we may have become too satisfied with the adequacy of the most widely accepted CSR approaches to the understanding of religion and whether they can, in fact, adequately answer the many questions about the emergence of religion and do justice to religion in all its historical diversity and complexity. A recent book has addressed just this question, in the concluding chapter of which I attempted to reflect on the diverse opinions expressed and to speculate on where research might go next. After reviewing the contributions of eleven scientists representing a diverse set of approaches under the overall umbrella title of "Evolution, Cognitive Science, and Religion," I wrote: "Finally, these particular contributions to the understanding of mechanisms that are supposed to account for the emergence and development of religion will undoubtedly be revisited as the twenty-first century evolves. After one or two decades have passed, it will be possible to see how firmly some of the views expressed here have become established, how others have been significantly modified, and how others, in the light of accumulating empirical evidence, no longer seem tenable" (2014, 246).

The spirit of that conclusion applies equally to the fields of knowledge covered in this present volume. We and our successors will find out how, in the light of accumulating empirical evidence, some of these views will need to be discarded or significantly modified. All of this is work in progress, but there is no doubt that an emerging picture enables us to give a multifaceted account of the evolution of human personhood. In the views of some of the contributors, this is essentially a gradual process, and there is no need to make any reference to a quantum leap. In the views of others, there is a certain uniqueness about human personhood that they find it impossible, at least at this stage, to fully explain and understand by taking a purely gradualist approach. Hence they consider it possible that a sudden change occurred at some point in the evolutionary process. Either way, whether it turns out to be an entirely gradualist process or one that involves what looks like a quantum leap at some point, it remains the case that the accounts offered will be purely natural accounts. After all, the well-known and well-documented changes of state in studies of superconductivity with cooling, referred to as "phase changes," make it clear that there may be changes in the properties exhibited by the same basic materials, and that there is no need to declare that something mysterious is happening.

THE CHAPTER BY Justin Barrett and Matthew Jarvinen, with its reference to religious claims that humans are made "in the image of God," forms a natural bridge to the contributions of the biblical scholars and theologians in Section Three. Barrett and Jarvinen say that they begin with two assumptions: "(1) all humans are *imago Dei* — we did not earn it and we cannot lose it; and (2) only humans among the animals are *imago Dei*," which are affirmations of their personal beliefs and not anything derivable from their science. Given these assumptions, they say they want to ask: "What distinguishes humans as imagers?" Taking seriously Anthony Thiselton's views, which we shall consider in a moment, they accept the latter's warning "against isolating distinct capacities as essential to *imago Dei*." They agree with Thiselton (who draws on the writings of Vladimir Lossky) that "the biblical narrative points to no specific human capacities as characteristic of the image of God; instead, representing God occurs in our unified wholeness."

I do not think it unfair to say that, in Barrett and Jarvinen's own chapter, there is perhaps not a phase change but a move from a plausible account from within the cognitive science of religion for the emergence of religion to a series of what must be called their personal "faith affirmations." These faith affirmations are relevant to their argument because, taking them as possible starting points, they are then able to ask: What evolved ability makes possible the important capacity for reciprocal relationships (a pervasive theme in their list of faith affirmations)? How, they inquire, did this ability evolve?

Once the question is posed in that way, Barrett is back again into his work as a cognitive scientist of religion, and he and Jarvinen put forward a case that draws heavily on what they refer to as "higher-order Theory of Mind."

The argument of Barrett and Jarvinen makes very good sense in the light of today's evidence. However, we must underscore yet again the phrase "in the light of today's evidence," because intensive research in many quarters into Theory of Mind and higher-order Theory of Mind are likely to shed new understanding on these concepts, and, if the history of science is anything to go by, we shall in due course expect major revisions in this field. For the time being, though, it is the best story in town.

By this time readers will have noticed that the concept of *emergence* has been frequently invoked. This is no surprise, given that the title of the book poses the question: *The Emergence of Human Personhood: A Quantum Leap?* Most of the contributors to this book have invoked the concept of "emergence" as they seek to understand how aspects of religious thinking and religious behavior emerged in evolutionary context. But do all these contributors mean the same thing by this? Or are there different forms of emergence? In order to avoid confusion, we need to apply some semantic hygiene here. Who better to provide it than philosopher Timothy O'Connor, who in some of his writings has specialized in examining the different ways in which the concept of emergence has been used in the past and is being used today?

One of the key themes of O'Connor's contribution is to draw attention to, as he puts it, "two importantly distinct ways *(weak and strong)* in which organized macroscopic phenomena might emerge from underlying microphysical processes." He says: "While degree of complexity is not a bridge between *weak and strong emergence,* it is a theoretically significant feature for the study of complex systems and of interest in its own right" (italics added). He acknowledges that there are those (citing Brian McLaughlin) who seem to think — and he believes wrongly — that *strong emergence,* while possible, is inherently improbable given the methods of science and especially the advances of physical and biological science since the beginning of the twentieth century. This, O'Connor believes, keeps such writers from giving proper weight to the powerful evidence that "we have for strong emergence in the form of our own conscious mental lives." In his discussion of consciousness, he writes: "Taking consciousness seriously means abandoning the ontological reductionist dream in favor of a strong emergentist understanding in which the appearance of new basic properties within certain neurally complex physical systems must . . . be accepted with [quoting Samuel Alexander] the 'natural piety of the investigator.'"

O'Connor says that his views on emergence differ from those of Brown/
Paul and Zeman because those authors "give appropriate analysis to the
complexity of interactive processes in human brain activity. But, seeing no
alternative to mind-body dualism and a thoroughgoing physicalism/mate-
rialism, they embrace the second alternative and opt for a weak emergentist
account of human conscious states." He acknowledges that that remains his
view of their position, despite their own suggestion that they have used approximate strong emergence in O'Connor's sense.

O'Connor also applies his concept of strong emergence to the discussion of free will. He notes that in the past few decades the most widely
discussed empirical basis for skepticism about free will stems from the work
of neuroscientist Benjamin Libet. Perhaps surprisingly, O'Connor, apart
from a reference to a paper by Peter Clarke (2013), does not refer to the
many further studies by neuroscientists following up on Libet's work, the
sum total of which demonstrate that Libet's original experiment did not
demonstrate what he claimed he was demonstrating. We know how it is all
too easy to have knee-jerk reactions to reported scientific findings if they
seem to threaten some of our most deeply held religious convictions. As the
further work by other scientists has demonstrated, much time and energy
could have been saved had philosophers and others followed the practice
of scientists and waited for necessary replications and careful analyses of
Libet's experimental conclusions so as to ensure that there were no uniden-
tified artifacts in the experimental design and/or the data analyses, which
may call into question some of the inferences made from his experimental
results.

A further helpful link made by Timothy O'Connor is to the chapters
by Roy Baumeister and Adam Zeman, pointing to the evidence for strong
emergence from social processes. He notes perceptively that this begins to
tie in with the suggestion of a possible social dimension to *emergence* that
connects well the writings of the theologians Anthony Thiselton and Alan
Torrance, who urge a *corporate* eschatological understanding of the Christian theological doctrine that human persons are divine image-bearers.

In his very important conclusion, O'Connor returns to the question he
raised at the beginning of his chapter as to "whether the distinctive abilities and tendencies of mature human beings indicate a *discontinuity* in the
evolutionary processes that gave rise to us." His answer is that "capacities
associated with human and other animal conscious awareness, and with the
enhanced conscious feature of subjectivity, or having a point of view as a self,
are not only weakly but also strongly emergent." He continues:

If this is correct, then the historical and comparative psychological discontinuities that prove to be the case entail fundamental discontinuities: deeply novel characteristics on the world stage. To be human is to be made of the same substrate as everything else in the physical world and to be a product of a very long process of incremental biological change. Yet it is also to be a part of the world that transcends its constituting material by becoming aware of oneself as a self, separate from the rest of reality and acting in intentional ways that reflect that awareness. It is also to be rooted in a community of fellow beings, whose purposes and fortunes are deeply interwoven. What is the relationship of "we" to "I" and "you": is it always merely a conjunction, or are there respects in which we — in temporary, interacting communities or in its widest scope, encompassing all of humanity — constitute an ontological whole, making a fundamental difference as a whole to the way our corner of the world unfolds?

Reflecting on O'Connor's conclusions, one is especially struck by this observation: "To be human is to be made of the same substrate as everything else in the physical world and to be a product of a very long process of incremental biological change. Yet it is also to be a part of the world that transcends its constituting material by becoming aware of oneself as a self, separate from the rest of reality and acting in intentional ways that reflect that awareness." In identifying an essential feature of humanness as "to be a part of the world that transcends its constituting material by becoming aware of oneself as a self, separate from the rest of reality and acting in intentional ways that reflect that awareness," he appears to be setting the agenda for the next set of studies to be carried out by evolutionary psychologists. Presumably, if it is found that nonhuman primates can pass a suitably experimentally embodied test of "becoming aware of oneself as a self, separate from the rest of reality and acting in intentional ways that reflect that awareness," then these capacities no longer constitute either "fundamental discontinuities: deeply novel characteristics on the world stage" or a "unique quantum leap."

With these thoughts in mind, I find it interesting that Anthony Thiselton represents the most sustained and careful attempt in the whole book to do justice to the contributions of the scientists while applying the main brushstrokes of the picture of humankind offered from a theological approach. In his chapter, Thiselton repeatedly and very helpfully cross-references the contributions of the scientists already reviewed. After his very detailed exposition of what is meant by claims that have been made that humans are made in the image and likeness of God, an exposition that covers reflections over the past two millennia and before, as well as more recent trends, Thiselton looks again at the three key aspects of what it means to be made in the image of God — relationality, representation, and vocation, or attainment — in the light of some of the contributions from the scientists in earlier chapters. He writes:

> Justin Barrett's account of continuity within a relational framework also coheres well with Paul Ricoeur's sense of self against Hume. . . . His appeals to a theory of mind remain entirely relevant. C. A. Campbell has pointed out that on the basis of Hume's theory of the self as near successive perceptions, we might perceive the striking of a clock ten times as the tenfold repetition of its striking one o'clock; where continuity of a stable mind would interpret this as striking ten o'clock! Barrett's emphasis on potential qualities rather than actual ones also coheres with our emphasis on location and attainment. . . . Francisco Ayala's account of the moral and ethical also offers close resonance with my references to Ricoeur. Roy Baumeister and Warren Brown have indicated, with Barrett and this chapter, that the self does not denote an isolated individual. The importance of relationality in communion is not limited to theology alone. Baumeister devotes a section of his chapter to the question: "Solitary Selves?" He asserts: "The selfhood of a thoroughly solitary being would be quite limited." He adds: "Identity is thus not inside the person but in the social matrix."

In closing his chapter, Thiselton makes meaningful links with Richard Byrne's account of the possible ways in which language may have emerged. He notes that Byrne repeats the citation "Language is regarded, at least in most intellectual traditions, as the quintessential human attribute." And Thiselton comments: "If a human person is not the individualist ego postulated by Descartes, what allows the self to interact with others in personhood is *language,* or other forms of communication, as Richard Byrne argues."

Theologian Alan Torrance acknowledges that we have witnessed in all that has gone before "remarkable developments in the empirical sciences that have opened new vistas on what it is to be human to the point where they encourage us to the rethink what it is to be a person." He believes — and sets out the grounds for his belief — that "Christian theism has not only shaped the very concept of the person but serves to underwrite a conceptuality whose grounds Western society has all but forgotten." This leads him to ask how we are to relate what we have learned from the scientists to what we may learn from Christian theism. For him, "clarity is necessary if the contributions of both Christian theism and the empirical sciences are to be taken seriously within an integrated account of the human person."

Torrance briefly reminds us that where you start from in your research for an answer to the question posed in the title of the book will significantly affect what kind of an answer you produce. In other words, presuppositions and methods of study matter enormously and should be exposed as clearly as possible at the outset to avoid unnecessary conflicts and misunderstandings. They should not be smuggled in as assumptions that need both clarifying and, at times, challenging. Hence he says: "It is a truism that the tools we use to interpret what it is to be the human person are laden with suppositions."

For Torrance, we need to examine carefully two highly influential methodological approaches to what he calls "fideisms," which, he believes, threaten to commandeer the entire debate. The effects of both of these fideisms are, in his view, "to collapse all levels of explanation to just one." The first of these is nomological monism, which, he says, is essentially a reductive physicalist approach. About this approach Torrance writes: "It is hard to see how interpretations of the person that make exclusive and foundational recourse to atomistic physicalism will not ultimately see personhood as a mere 'epiphenomenon,' with the implication that the person per se can make no intentional contribution to the dynamics of history or, indeed, the natural order."

The second methodological fideism Torrance identifies is *metaphysical naturalism,* which, he emphasizes, is a philosophical position. "It constitutes an ultimate faith commitment at the same level as religious commitment. Science, by contrast, is the attempt to interpret contingent reality in its own light and to allow the object of scientific inquiry to challenge and revise the paradigms that he or she brings to bear in a relevant research."

Underscoring the need to recognize these fundamental starting points, Torrance says: "If these two totalizing philosophical commitments serve to shape our thinking, what can be said about the nature of the person and the emergence of personhood has already been determined in advance, and the conclusion is clear." He argues that, beginning from an approach of Christian theism, we may come to a more open-minded understanding of personhood: "Not only is the emergence of a conceptuality of the person grounded historically in Christian theism, there is strong reason to think that the conceptuality of the personal requires this kind of theistic vision."

He sums up this section of his argument this way: "In sum, there are categorically no scientific grounds for repudiating theism and the personalist universe to which theism opens the door. Precisely the converse is the case! This is not to suggest that there is any philosophical demonstration of the truth of *Christian* theism."

This leads him to his account of the concept of the person from the standpoint of a Christian theism. He specifically raises this question: "Why is this pertinent for a book on the emergence of personhood?" And his answer is that "because, as the contemporary theologian most closely associated with the concept of the person, John Zizioulas, has argued, 'The observation of the world cannot lead to an ontology of the person, because the person as an ontological category cannot be extrapolated from experience.'"

Keeping to the title of this book, he says further: "[E]ven if there has been a 'quantum leap' in the evolution of human animals that is perceived as denoting a difference in kind from the rest of the animal kingdom, there is no reason to discount the possibility that this qualitative difference might be temporary and that others among the higher apes could experience evolutionary 'quantum leaps.' The leveling effect of the above could only mean that the concept of the person had no ultimate or ontological significance."

He further writes:

The second approach to the person perceives the concept of the person as possessing ontological significance for the simple reason that reality is ultimately "personal" in nature. According to this approach, rather than pointing to some capacity that elevates the human, the category of the personal is perceived as pointing to the grounds of, and also the ultimate purpose of, reality per se. It is this kind of approach that most Christian theology would endorse, as witnessed in the leading theological figures not only in the Orthodox tradition but also in the Roman Catholic and Protestant traditions.

At this point Torrance takes us back to the questions raised by Thiselton and to the answers that he has already given us. He directly addresses the question of how the person is conceived theologically: "As Anthony Thiselton articulates so impressively in his chapter, it is in these terms that the concept of being created to image God needs to be conceived."

Recognizing the importance of the implications of what he has portrayed on a wider canvas, Torrance asks what the implications of this are for the question of emergence.

If the conceptuality of personhood constitutes a "quantum leap," I would suggest that the historical key to this is denoted by the fathers of the Christian church and their ontological ratification of the grounds of the "personal." Theologically, this quantum leap stems from the historical perception that God has created — and, indeed, chosen — human beings for a specific kind of relationship, what the New Testament conceives of as *koinonia,* namely, that unique fellowship or "communion" constituted by God's relationship to humanity to which Søren Kierkegaard referred as that unique "kinship" that the eternal has established in time.

Torrance concludes his chapter with a personal "faith affirmation" that follows from his presuppositions:

> Personal existence is both given with and, ultimately, subject to the communion that God establishes and sustains in and through concrete, historical, personal communion with human creatures. This is a communion that is transformative and, indeed, creative of what needs to be conceived in dialogue with evolutionary science — not as an old, but as a new humanity. It is no coincidence that a central contrast in the New Testament is between the "old humanity" and the "new humanity," between what is constituted by our natural desires and what is not schematized by the natural and our innate appetites but transformed or reschematized (to use Paul's metaphor) for a new mode of existence through the "metamorphosing" presence of the Holy Spirit. That new form of existence is defined in terms of the categories of participation *(koinonein)* and *agape* — the two concepts that "personalism" has used to define human existence to the extent that it can be described as "personal."

AS WE REFLECT ON all the diverse contributions making a sustained effort to answer the question posed by the title of this book, *The Emergence of Personhood: A Quantum Leap?* a pervasive theme has emerged. As our contributors have sought to trace out the emergence of personhood over millions of years, there were occasions when it looked as though there might have been a leap, a discontinuity, if not a quantum leap. However, as Ian Tattersall has emphasized and exemplified many times in his book *Palaeontology,* on such occasions these apparent discontinuities turn out to have a perfectly natural explanation in terms of events that have also occurred in the earth's history. In one form or another, the gradualist approach advocated by Colin Renfrew in his chapter has been endorsed by many of those seeking an answer to our question. This is important because, in the contexts of wider debates about the relationship between science and religious beliefs, there has been a constant temptation to look for gaps in the scientific evidence and to fit God into those gaps as an additional explanatory concept. There is no place in well-grounded Christian belief for a "god of the gaps."

All this resonates well with Alan Torrance's efforts to point us away from any kind of desperate search for a quantum leap in the scientific emergence of human personhood:

> In summary, if we are looking for a quantum leap in the history of the emergence of personhood, the most relevant "nodal point" would be not the acquisition by *Homo sapiens* of some capacity, but God's bringing human beings into a specific kind of I-Thou relationship, with all the ramifications for the human community (love, forgiveness, reconciliation, care for the sick and elderly) that stem from this. It is in the context of this theological history that the term "person" finds its warrant and indeed that its use becomes appropriate.

REFERENCES

Hu, Hai Yang, Lin He, Ksensya Fominykh, et al. 2012. Evolution of the human-specific micro RNA miR-941. *Nature COMMUNICATIONS* 3:1145: http://www.nature.com/ncomms/journal/v3/n10/full/ncomms2146.html. Quoted in Kerr, Shona. Genetically determined. 2013. *The University of Edinburgh: The Alumni Magazine* Summer: 16-17.

Jeeves, Malcolm. 2014. Concluding reflections. In *Evolution, religion, and cognitive science,* ed. Fraser Watts and Leon Turner. Oxford: Oxford University Press.

———. 2013. *Minds, brains, souls, gods: A conversation on faith, psychology, and neuroscience.* Downers Grove, IL: InterVarsity.

Turner, Leon. 2011. Disunity and disorder: The problem of self-fragmentation. In *In search of self: Interdisciplinary perspectives on personhood,* ed. J. Wentzel van Huyssteen and Erik P. Wiebe. Grand Rapids: Eerdmans.

Contributors

FRANCISCO J. AYALA, a pioneering geneticist and evolutionary biologist, is University Professor and Donald Bren Professor of Biological Sciences at the University of California, Irvine, where he also holds appointments as professor of philosophy and professor of logic and the philosophy of science. The winner of the 2010 Templeton Prize and the 2001 U.S. National Medal of Science, he is a member of the National Academy of Sciences (NAS) and was the principal author of *Science, Evolution, and Creationism* (1984), a study commissioned by NAS and the Institute of Medicine. Prof. Ayala is the editor or co-editor of seventeen volumes, including (with Theodosius Dobzhansky) *Studies in the Philosophy of Biology* (1974), a foundational volume in the then new discipline, and the author or co-author of twenty-six other books, including *Darwin and Intelligent Design* (2006), *Darwin's Gift to Science and Religion* (2007), *Am I a Monkey? Six Big Questions about Evolution* (2010), and *The Big Questions: Evolution* (2012).

JUSTIN L. BARRETT, the Thrive Professor for Developmental Science at Fuller Theological Seminary, directs the Thrive Center for Human Development, which is concerned with positive youth development. Much of his scholarship is focused on cognitive approaches to the study of religion. Prof. Barrett is the editor of the four-volume *Psychology of Religion* (2010). His books include *Why Would Anyone Believe in God?* (2004), *Cognitive Science, Religion, and Theology* (2011), and *Born Believers: The Science of Childhood Religion* (2012).

ROY F. BAUMEISTER is Eppes Eminent Scholar and professor of psychology at Florida State University. He is internationally known for his research in social psychology that spans topics ranging from the human need to belong and the effects of rejection to how people seek to make their lives meaningful, the interpersonal consequences of forgiveness, and the psychology of willpower. Prof. Baumeister is the author or editor of more than thirty books. His recent books include *The Cultural Animal: Human Nature, Meaning, and Social Life* (2005), *Is There Anything Good about Men?* (2010), and the *New York Times* bestseller (with John Tierney) *Willpower: Rediscovering the Greatest Human Strength* (2011). In 2013 he received the William James Fellow Award, which is given by the Association for Psychological Science to recognize lifetime achievement in scientific psychology.

WARREN S. BROWN, a professor of psychology at the Graduate School of Psychology at Fuller Theological Seminary, is also director of Fuller's Travis Research Institute and a member of the UCLA Brain Research Institute. He was the principal editor (with Nancey Murphy and H. Newton Maloney) of *Whatever Happened to the Soul? Scientific and Theological Portraits of Human Nature* (1998), which was awarded a prize for Outstanding Books in Theology and the Natural Sciences by the Center for Theology and the Natural Sciences; he was also the editor of *Understanding Wisdom: Sources, Science, and Society* (2000). Professor Brown is the author (with Nancey Murphy) of *Did My Neurons Make Me Do It? Philosophical and Neurobiological Perspectives on Moral Responsibility and Free Will* (2007), (with Malcolm Jeeves) *Neuroscience, Psychology, and Religion: Illusions, Delusions, and Realities about Human Nature* (2009), and (with Brad Strawn) *The Physical Nature of Christian Life: Neuroscience, Psychology, and the Church* (2012).

RICHARD W. BYRNE, a professor of psychology at the University of St. Andrews, studies the evolution of cognition, particularly the origins of distinctively human characteristics, via comparative study of great apes, elephants, and other species. He is the editor (with Andrew Whiten) of *Machiavellian Intelligence: Social Expertise and the Evolution of Intellect in Monkeys, Apes, and Humans* (1988) and *Machiavellian Intelligence II: Extensions and Evaluation* (1997). His book *The Thinking Ape: Evolutionary Origins of Intelligence* (1995) won the 1997 British Psychological Society Award.

MATTHEW J. JARVINEN is a doctoral student in clinical psychology at the Fuller Graduate School of Psychology at Fuller Theological Seminary. He has been a teaching associate at San Diego State University and serves as an adjunct professor of psychology at Azusa Pacific University.

MALCOLM JEEVES, a past president of the Royal Society of Edinburgh, Scotland's National Academy, and former editor-in-chief of *Neuropsychologia*, is professor emeritus of psychology at the University of St. Andrews. He was Foundation Professor of Psychology there for twenty-four years and established the university's acclaimed psychology department. His own research has focused on brain mechanisms and neuroplasticity. The author of sixteen books, including nine related to science and faith, his most recent studies are *Human Nature at the Millennium* (1997), (with R. J. Berry) *Science, Life, and Christian Belief* (1998), (with Warren Brown) *Neuroscience, Psychology, and Religion: Illusions, Delusions, and Realities about Human Nature* (2009), and *Minds, Brains, Souls, and Gods: A Conversation on Faith, Psychology, and Neuroscience* (2013), along with two edited volume of essays, *From Cells to Souls — and Beyond: Changing Portraits of Human Nature* (2004) and *Rethinking Human Nature* (2011), both published by Eerdmans.

TIMOTHY O'CONNOR, a philosopher of mind and of religion, is professor of philosophy and a member of the Cognitive Sciences Program at Indiana University. Much of his writing centers on the nature of human action and on concepts of emergence that may have application to complex systems and to the conscious mind in particular. He is the editor of six books, most recently two volumes published in 2010: (with Constantine Sandis) *A Companion to the Philosophy of Action* and (with Antonella Corradini) *Emergence in Science and Philosophy*. He is also the author of *Persons and Causes: The Metaphysics of Free Will* (2000) and *Theism and Ultimate Explanation: The Necessary Shape of Contingency* (2008).

LYNN K. PAUL is a senior staff scientist and lecturer at the California Institute of Technology. Her primary research focuses on the role of the corpus callosum in emotions and social cognition. She serves as director of Caltech's Brain Imaging Center Psychological Assessment Laboratory, as well as heading the university's Corpus Callosum Research Program. She recently co-founded the International Consortium on Corpus Callosum and Cerebral Connectivity. The recipient of a NARSAD Young Investigator Award given by the Brain and Behavior Research Foundation, Dr. Paul was the founding president of the National Organization of Disorders of the Corpus Callosum.

COLIN RENFREW, Disney Professor of Archaeology Emeritus at Cambridge University and senior fellow at the university's McDonald Institute for Archaeological Research, is internationally renowned for his contributions to archaeological theory and science as well as to the understanding of European prehistory and linguistic archaeology. A fellow of the British Academy, he is an honorary fellow of the Royal Society of Edinburgh and a foreign associate of the National Academy of Sciences. In 1991, he was created a life peer by Queen Elizabeth II, and, among many honors, he is the recipient of the Rivers Memorial Medal and the Huxley Medal of the Royal Anthropological Institute, the Prix International Fyssen of the Fondation Fyssen in Paris, the Lucy Wharton Drexel Medal of the University of Pennsylvania Museum of Archaeology and Anthropology, the European Science Foundation Latsis Prize, and the Balzan Prize. His own archaeological excavations in Greece have led to numerous publications, and he is the editor of twenty books. Prof. Renfrew is also the author of another thirteen volumes, including *The Emergence of Civilization: The Cyclades and the Aegean in the Third Millennium BC* (1972), *Before Civilization: The Radiocarbon Revolution and Prehistoric Europe* (1973), *Archaeology and Language: The Puzzle of the Indo-European Origins* (1987), and, most recently, *Prehistory: The Making of the Human Mind* (2007).

IAN TATTERSALL, curator emeritus and senior scientist in residence in the division of anthropology at the American Museum of Natural History (AMNH), is widely acclaimed for his studies of speciation and diversity in the human fossil record. His current research involves a continuing investigation of the emergence of *Homo sapiens* and of modern human cognition. He has been responsible for a number of AMNH's major exhibits throughout the past three decades. Dr. Tattersall is the author or co-author of more than twenty books, including (with Jeffrey Schwartz) three volumes of *The Human Fossil Record* (2002, 2003, and 2005), as well as, most recently, *Paleontology: A Brief History of Life* (2010), (with Rob DeSalle) *Race? Debunking a Scientific Myth* (2011), *Masters of the Planet: The Search for Our Human Origins* (2012), and *The Strange Case of the Rickety Cossack and Other Cautionary Tales from Human Evolution* (2015).

ANTHONY C. THISELTON, professor of Christian theology emeritus at the University of Nottingham, is widely respected for his work in biblical and philosophical hermeneutics. A fellow of the British Academy and King's College London, he is canon theologian emeritus both of Leicester Cathedral and of the diocese of Southwell and Nottingham. He has written twenty books, including *The First Epistle to the Corinthians: A Commentary on the Greek Text*, which Eerdmans published in 2000, and most recently, *The Living Paul: An Introduction to the Apostle and His Thought* (2009), *1 and 2 Thessalonians: Through the Centuries* (2011), and three new volumes published by Eerdmans, *Life after Death: A New Approach to the Last Things* (2011), *The Holy Spirit — In Biblical Teaching, through the Centuries, and Today* (2013), and *The Thiselton Companion to Christian Theology* (2015).

ALAN J. TORRANCE, a philosophical theologian, holds the chair in systematic theology at the University of St. Andrews. He has worked extensively in the field of Christian doctrine and is also engaged in research and writing about issues of personhood, faith and rationality, and political reconciliation. The editor of four books, including, most recently, (with Marcus Bockmuehl) *Scripture's Doctrine and Theology's Bible: How the New Testament Shapes Christian Dogmatics* (2008), he is also the author of two other books, *Persons in Communion: An Essay on Trinitarian Description and Human Participation* (1996) and *The Theological Grounds for Advocating Forgiveness and Reconciliation in the Sociopolitical Realm* (2006). Prof. Torrance is completing a new book based on his Didsbury Lectures (Nazarene Theological College, Manchester) and his Hensley Henson Lectures (University of Oxford). The work in progress will challenge the critics of the Christian faith by exploring both Christianity's "unrivalled" explanatory power and its constructive implications for social and political relations.

ADAM ZEMAN is professor of cognitive and behavioral neurology at the University of Exeter Medical School. His clinical work and research focus on the neurology of cognition, including neurological disorders of sleep. He has also written on the science and philosophy of consciousness. His books include *Consciousness: A User's Guide* (2002), *A Portrait of the Brain* (2008), and (edited with Narinder Kapur and Marilyn Jones-Gotman) *Epilepsy and Memory* (2012).